WORSHIP

ITS THEOLOGY AND PRACTICE

WORSHIP
ITS THEOLOGY
AND PRACTICE

by

J.-J. von ALLMEN

NEW YORK
OXFORD UNIVERSITY PRESS
1965

© 1965 LUTTERWORTH PRESS

Library of Congress Catalogue Card Number: 65-23571

Printed in Great Britain

Contents

5

CHAPTER IV: *The approach to forms*

CHAPTER VII: *The participants in the cult*

CHAPTER VIII: *The time of the cult*

Introduction

THE theme of "worship" has never been treated as a major one in the thinking of the Reformed Churches. It even arouses in us a certain suspicion—a suspicion which is probably one of the outstanding features of Protestantism. Yet, as Karl Barth so rightly says, "Christian worship is the most momentous, the most urgent, the most glorious action that can take place in human life".

Liturgiology—the theology of Christian worship—has for its special work, not to create, but to examine, test and direct formal worship, so that it may approximate as closely as possible to what it should be. "Christian worship is, in essence, not a theological blue-print drawn up by specialists, but an event, an encounter between the Lord, Who through the Holy Spirit acts in Word and Sacrament, and His people; its liturgical form is the fruit of faith and obedience. The theology of worship provides the critical canon for a testing and appraisement of the Christian cult in the forms which it has historically assumed . . . It shows that course in practical liturgy, i.e. in the proper ordering and holding of services, which the Church may follow in worship" (J. Beckmann, quoted by W. Hahn). Thus, liturgiology presupposes the existence of Christian worship, even the existence of a given cult (for the purpose of this study, that of the Reformed Church), and involves the specialized knowledge necessary for the critical examination and expert direction of public worship. So our concern here is first to establish the broad outlines of a doctrine of worship, and then to see how to work it out in practice.

My approach to the subject in this study has no theological pretensions; it is primarily that of a teacher. The plan followed is only one of many possible ones. It has two main divisions: problems of the principles of worship, and problems of its actual celebration. The plan in full (set out in the Table of Contents) might appear to cover the whole field of liturgical study: this is not so. It excludes, for instance, from chapters to which they might seem relevant, the history of worship, comparative liturgics, ancillary acts of worship such as the baptismal liturgy or the divine service, the sociology or psychology (and even the psycho-analysis) of worship; or ascetical theology, which would be involved in the study of the relationship between parish worship and personal spiritual life. It is concerned with the regular Sunday worship. Apropos of the Scottish Confession, Karl Barth remarked that all worship is bounded by baptism, which attests that God wills that His Church should come into being, and by the Eucharist, which attests that He wills its continuance. Our concern here, then, is that form of worship by which God, in His mercy, grants to the Church its continuance as the Church.

A Note on Terminology

This problem is complicated by the fact that it has varied so much over the centuries, and also because we must determine whether these variations in terminology have brought about, or have merely reflected, changes which have taken place in the doctrine of worship itself. I shall not attempt to assess this here. Two things, however, should be noted:

(1) With a few significant exceptions, and without there being the slightest hint that worship is unimportant, *the NT has no specific liturgical terminology*. It uses apparently neutral terms, such as "to gather together in the name of Jesus" (SYNAGESTHAI EIS TO EMON ONOMA, Matt. 18: 20) or "to meet for the breaking of bread" (SYNA-GESTHAI KLASAI ARTON, Acts 20: 7; cf. SYNER-CHESTHAI EIS TO PHAGEIN, 1 Cor. 11: 33), in which it shortens such circumlocutions.

(2) The very word "Church", however, has evident liturgical overtones, since the Church is essentially the assembly of those who live by the salvation which Christ has wrought, invoke His presence and await His return. Hence the most specific NT terms for the Christian cult are the "assembly", the "breaking of bread" or quite simply "church".

None of these terms however became authoritative, though "assembly" was the accepted designation of the cult up to the fourth century. But from the peace of Constantine—perhaps because the discipline of the *arcana* was becoming superfluous—specifically liturgical terms did arise, and spread, and that in competition with one distinctively Christian term, that of "mass". At the Reformation the word "mass" was suppressed, partially in Lutheranism and completely in the Reformed Churches and in Anglicanism,

15

reappearing in the latter in the nineteenth century. By what was it to be replaced? An attempt was made to restore the use of the term "assembly" (coetus), but without lasting success. John a Lasco used the word current in the Eastern Churches and entitled the book of common prayer of the refugees at Frankfurt *Liturgia sacra* (1554). The word became established in western terminology, without, however, displacing more usual expressions such as "divine service", "cult", "worship", "mass" and so on (the term "Church" becoming universal).

The word "liturgy" itself is a NT term denoting not only (as in the Septuagint) the priestly office under the old covenant (translating *aboda*), (cf. Luke 1: 23; Heb. 9: 21; 10: 11), but the worship of Christ (Heb. 8: 6) and the worship of the Church (Acts 13: 2). Taken over from the Septuagint, it has no justification as a term in secular literature. Its secular use, however, does provide two interesting points of information: etymologically it means an action of the people (LEITOURGIA—LEITOS and ERGON) and not of priests, and suggests therefore the need to declericalize the cult. In non-religious usage in antiquity it denotes a political or civil action in which the wealthy take the place of the poor who are unable to pay. Hence the suggestion is that in its liturgy the Church acts on behalf of the world, which is totally incapable of adoring and glorifying the true God, and that the Church in its cult represents the world before God and protects it. Like the word "mass", the word "liturgy" bears witness to the necessary involvement of the Church in the world. These points, however, are only curiosities, and Christian worship is not built on any interpretation of the word "liturgy". To try to make basic theological choices coincide with the acceptance or rejection of words is a useless logomachy.

N.B. The French original contains hundreds of footnotes, in which the author refers to the very rich modern continental literature on liturgics, and in which he explains why he approves of or disapproves of diverse liturgical or historical hypotheses held by Reformed, Lutheran or Roman scholars of the Continent. As most of these books do not exist in an English version, the author agreed to leave them out, and to make this mainly a book of plain teaching. Editor and author hope that a possible loss of scholarship will be balanced by the undeniable gain that in its English edition this book will be helpful not only to clergy but also to lay readers who, Sunday after Sunday, joyfully celebrate the resurrection of the Lord and the outpouring of the Holy Ghost: the presence, real though sacramental, of the world to come.

Nevertheless, as some extracts are often quoted *verbatim*, evident honesty demands that the authors should at least be named. Therefore the following indications are given as to the most important sources:

H. ASMUSSEN: *Die Lehre vom Gottesdienst*, München, 1937.

K. BARTH: *Gottes Erkenntnis und Gottesdienst nach reformatorischer Lehre*, Zollikon-Zürich, 1938.

K. BARTH: Dogmatics: *Die kirchliche Dogmatik*, several volumes, EVZ-Zürich, 1933ff.

P. BRUNNER: "Zur Lehre und zur Feier der in Namen Jesu versammelten Gemeinde" (*Leiturgia vom Gottesdienst*, vol. I), Kassel, 1954.

F. BUCHHOLZ: *Vom Wesen der Gregorianik*, München, 1948.

O. HAENDLER: *Grundriss der praktischen Theologie*, Berlin, 1957.

W. HAHN: *Die Mitte der Gemeinde* (Handbücherei für Gemeindearbeit No 1), Gütersloh, 1959. Eng. trans. *Worship and Congregation* (Ecumenical Studies in Worship, No 12), Lutterworth Press, London, 1963.

W. D. MAXWELL: *An Outline of Christian Worship*, London, 1958.

A. D. MÜLLER: *Grundriss der praktischen Theologie*, Gütersloh, 1950.

PART ONE

PROBLEMS OF PRINCIPLE

CHAPTER ONE

CHRISTIAN WORSHIP CONSIDERED AS THE RECAPITULATION OF THE HISTORY OF SALVATION

IN this first chapter, we have three problems to take into consideration. We must begin by affirming the Christological basis of the Church's worship; we shall speak next of the presence of Christ in church worship and of the epiklesis, and finally we propose to expound, in greater detail, the profound meaning of the liturgical event, which is to sum up the history of salvation.

1. The Christological basis of church worship

(a) A superficial reading of the New Testament is sufficient to teach us that *the very life of Jesus of Nazareth is a life which is, in some sense, "liturgical"*, or, if the expression is preferred, *priestly*. One may even go so far as to say that the true glorification of God on earth, which is the perfect worship, has been fulfilled by Jesus Christ in His ministry. If the title of sovereign high priest (after the order of Melchisedek) is clearly supremely appropriate after His ascension,[1] it still remains true that His whole life also must be seen in this liturgical perspective. Moreover, it is probable that Jesus Himself understood His ministry in this way; since He came to destroy the works of the devil (1 John 3: 8) and to reconcile men with God through His death (Rom. 5: 10 etc.). His whole life has meaning only in terms of this liberation and reconciliation. We have only to think of the way in which He saw in Ps. 110 an allusion to His own

---

[1] "The Lord says to my Lord: Sit at my right hand . . . You are a priest for ever after the order of Melchisedek" (Ps. 110: 1 and 4; and Heb. 5: 10; 6: 20 and again Acts 2: 34; Heb. 1: 3 and 13; Rom. 8: 34, etc.).

passion (Mark 12: 35ff. par.; 14: 62 par.), of the high-priestly prayer (John 17: 1–26), or of the deep meaning of the cleansing of the temple (John 2: 13ff.),[1] or above all of the way in which He willed, embraced and interpreted His own death. When the Letter to the Hebrews says that *He offered up Himself* (7: 27; cf. 9: 11), it does but confirm what all the evangelists attest, namely that Jesus did not seek to avoid death, that He was not caught unawares by it, but that He foresaw it and willed to undergo it as the culminating point of His ministry. To such an extent was this the case, in fact, that it has been possible to say, with reason, that the Gospels are "Passion narratives with a detailed introduction" (M. Kähler). It is indeed in this priestly sense that the New Testament understands the death of Christ, even though this is not always deliberately proclaimed—except in the Letter to the Hebrews and perhaps in the Johannine writings: otherwise what would be the meaning of the allusion to the rending of the temple veil at the moment of Jesus' death? (Mark 15: 38 par.)[2]

Moreover, it is interesting, in this connexion, to note two further points: firstly, the regular allusions to the worship of the early Church made by the evangelists in the course of the witness which they bear to the life of Jesus. O. Cullmann has studied these allusions in the Fourth Gospel. A similar study could be made, in particular, in St. Luke's writings. His two accounts of the appearances of the Risen Christ— to cite only these—seem to describe the very structure of worship in the infant church (Luke 24: 13–35; 36–53),[3] and thus deliberately to refer the Christian cult to the life of Jesus, in which it finds both its basis and justification. Above all, it must be pointed out that the very plan of the synoptic Gospels corresponds to the order of worship which doubtless goes back to apostolic times and has become

[1] If, as the Fathers thought doubtless with good reason, the Good Samaritan represents Jesus, one may wonder whether, in narrating this parable, Jesus did not wish to affirm that the ministry of the true cult consists neither of priest nor Levite, but of Himself, Jesus.

[2] We may think also of the priestly seamless robe which He wore, according to John 19: 23.

[3] Cf. also the eucharistic reverberation of the stories of the feeding of the multitudes.

traditional. Once the presence of Christ is assured, a first part—the Galilean ministry—is centred on the preaching of Jesus, on the appeal addressed to men, on the choice with which they are confronted. (This is what will later be described as the mass of the catechumens.) Then follows a second part which explains, justifies and elicits the true content of the first; it deals with the ministry in Jerusalem and is centred on the death of Christ, and the irruption of the eschatological resurrection, taking events up to the point when Jesus leaves His own, blessing them and sending them forth into the world to bear witness to Himself. (This is what will be later described as the mass of the faithful.)

There is no need for us to enter here into greater detail. It is sufficient to affirm that the New Testament shows us the historical ministry of Jesus and hence His whole life, as a liturgical process and in fact as *the* liturgy, *the* life of worship, accepted by God. In this sense, the Christian cult has its basis in the "messianic" cult celebrated by Jesus between His incarnation and ascension.

(b) This cult offered by Christ, which culminates in the EPHAPAX of the "single offering by which He has perfected for all time those who are sanctified" (Heb. 10: 14) has nevertheless a far wider temporal dimension. If this is the ground and justification of all Christian worship, if it inaugurates the latter in the strongest sense of the word, it is not, for Christ Himself, accidental. It brings to concrete embodiment His whole work, which was prepared before the incarnation, has borne fruit since the ascension, and will be manifested in glory in the day of His appearing.

St. Peter speaks of the Christ as "the Lamb without spot and blemish, predestined before the creation of the world, and manifested at the end of the times" for the sake of the elect (I Pet. 1: 19ff.).[1] This is equivalent to saying that "With the fall and original sin there begins before God and in God the mystery of the bloody sacrificial death of Jesus

[1] May we find a similar idea in Rev. 13: 8? E. Lohmeyer (*Hdb. z. N.T., ad loc.*) thinks that, according to position, APO KATABOLES KOSMOU should be connected with TOU ARNIOU ESPHAG-MENOU. But it should rather be connected with OU GEGRAPTAI TO ONOMA EN TO BIBLIO TES ZOES, as in Rev. 17: 8.

Christ" (P. Brunner). This heavenly cult, this predestination of the faultless and spotless Lamb provided as it were a screen, behind which and in whose shelter the world could continue to live without undergoing the threat of destruction which God had decreed against the sin of Adam (Gen. 2: 17) because already, by anticipation, its historical manifestation "at the end of the times" was efficacious with God.

This perfect act of worship which culminated in the sacrifice of the cross and the Ascension is—if one may dare to say so—exploited by Jesus Christ since His entering into glory: He is the ARCHIEREUS MEGAS (Heb. 4: 14) who has passed into the Holy of Holies, He is the LEITOURGOS TON HAGION KAI TES SKENES ALETHINES (Heb. 8: 2): He is the One who now appears on our behalf in the presence of God (Heb. 9. 24; cf. 7: 25; Rom. 8: 34): He is the sovereign high priest "for ever" (Heb. 7: 3), until the manifestation of the world to come (Heb. 6: 20).[1] "Inasmuch as He is the great high priest, Jesus fulfils then a double ministry: on the one hand, that of the expiatory act accomplished once for all; on the other hand, the ministry of extending and exploiting the full benefits of this saving work which lasts unto eternity" (O. Cullmann).

We might ask ourselves whether the "liturgy" of Jesus of Nazareth, the unique work of His expiatory action, which already protected the world before the incarnation, and which bears fruit in the present reign of Christ, considered too as a priestly work will not reach its supreme glory and plenitude at the time of the *parousia.* We might indeed think so when we read in Heb. 9: 28 of the promise that Christ "having been offered once to bear the sins of many, will appear a second time, not to deal with sin but to save those who are eagerly waiting for Him". However, it must be pointed out that at the time of this second coming the sacerdotal ministry of Jesus will cease to be expiatory, will be merely hallowing and sanctifying; it will no longer concern the whole world but only those who have accepted the

[1] Ought we to translate EIS TON AIONA by "until the final advent of the world to come" or by "for ever and ever"? Seeing that Heb. is familiar with the expressions EIS TOUS AIONAS TON AIONON (13: 21), EIS TOUS AIONAS (13: 8), EIS TON AIONA TOU AIONOS (1: 8) the first translation seems justifiable.

salvation which He secured by His death at Golgotha. This idea of a ministry of Christ which is sanctifying rather than expiatory appears again elsewhere in the Letter to the Hebrews (2: 10ff.; 10: 14). It seems related to the ministry which Jesus ascribes to Himself in the high-priestly prayer of John 17. Cautiously, we might perhaps see here an allusion to the sacerdotal ministry which the eternal Son of God would have exercised even if the Fall had not occasioned a radical disturbance of God's created order: then Christ would have come not to reconcile God and man but to enable men to dwell for ever where the Son abides that they may behold His glory (John 17: 24).

(c) The *Christological basis of the Church's worship* consists of the ministry of Jesus, the act of perfect worship which He made of His life. It is of this messianic cult that the Church is both a memorial and an effective echo. But it is not enough to link the Church's worship with the incarnation, to see it rooted in its historical institution through the words, life, death and resurrection of Jesus of Nazareth. We have seen, in fact, in the Letter to the Hebrews and the Johannine literature in particular, that this earthly worship of Christ has repercussions in heaven, where its full value is elicited. The Ascension is not only a royal procession, as we are too easily inclined to believe. It is also a liturgical procession: in ascending to heaven, Jesus enters into the heavenly sanctuary. Hence when we affirm the Christological basis of the Church's worship, we must not—unless we are to set aside an important part of the New Testament witness on liturgy—restrict the cult of the Christian Church solely to Jesus' command: "Do this in remembrance of me". We must go further, in view of the heavenly repercussions of the one sacrifice, and see in the Church's worship a reflection of the perpetual heavenly offering of which Jesus Christ is the eternal and sovereign high priest.[1]

[1] In Revelation, the heavenly cult is not merely offered *by* Christ, but is supremely offered *to* Christ as the Lamb that was slain, and "is worthy to receive power and wealth and wisdom and might and honour and glory and blessing" (5: 12), following that adoration which was never refused by Christ and which already glorified His earthly ministry from His birth (Matt. 2: 11) to His ascension (Luke 24: 52).

There is thus a twofold Christological basis to the worship of the Church: there is the earthly cult celebrated by the life, the death and the glorification of the incarnate Christ; and the heavenly cult which, in glory, He celebrates until the time of the world to come. Or rather: the earthly worship which Jesus Christ offered from His birth to His death, and which the synoptic Gospels present in a structure that is to be commemorated by the cult of the Church, becomes, while Christians await the eternal liturgy of the Kingdom, the basis of a double cult: namely, the heavenly offering of Christ which is a prolongation and a harvesting of the Jerusalem ministry of Jesus—and secondly, the worship of the Church on earth, which is a recapitulation of both the Galilean and the Jerusalemite ministry of Jesus. Between these two recapitulatory cults there is not only a theological but also a chronological link, although the heavenly cult is without the interruptions of the earthly cult which are due to its weekly rhythm.[1] That is what emerges from Revelation: even in heaven, there is a temple (7: 15; 11: 19; 14: 17; 15: 5, 8) and an altar (6: 9; 8: 3, 5; 9: 13; 14: 18; 16: 7) before the new Jerusalem comes, in which there will be no longer a temple (21: 22).

(The problem, posed by Barth and Paquier and not admitted by Hahn, of whether there is a Christological basis for the cult in the fact that the Church's cult illustrates and attests the two natures, can be considered when we come to examine the theological approach to the structure of worship. It still remains true that the problem of Christ, who is the foundation of the cult because He is the point at which God and man meet in union, as the cult is the point at which God and His people meet in union, is a problem that must be faced, and what an interesting one it is!)

2. *The presence of Christ in Christian worship and the epiklesis*

(a) Jesus Christ inaugurated the worship of the Church when He instituted the celebration of the Lord's Supper. Breaking bread, He said: "This is my body", and of the cup of the

[1] Cf. the EIS TO DIENEKES of Heb. 7: 3 and the HOSAKIS EAN PINETE of 1 Cor. 11: 25.

26

new covenant He declared that it was His blood. Further, He promised to be with His own (Matt. 28: 20) even unto the end of the world, and to be in the midst of them (Matt. 18: 20) when two or three were gathered in His name. The presence of Christ in Christian worship is the subject which we must now, briefly, consider.

This presence was promised by Christ Himself. Hence the Church is not living on illusions when it assembles in the name of Christ. It is not remembering a beautiful hope that has faded—as were the disciples on that first Easter Day before the Risen Lord appeared in their midst. On the contrary, in every act of worship it experiences afresh the miracle of the coming of the Risen Christ to be with His followers; and if, as we have previously noted, the Lucan accounts of the appearances of the Risen Lord on the evening of Easter Day seem like a mirror reflecting the worship of the nascent Church, their essential feature is not the alternation between a part in which there is speech and a part in which a meal is shared: the essential feature is rather the coming, the presence and the action of the Risen Christ. Because of this presence, Christian worship is neither the outcome of an illusion, nor an exercise of magic, but a grace that is offered.

A grace, because the presence of Christ is the presence of salvation. He gives Himself to us, He who is the Bread of Life which imparts life eternal (John 6: 51–58), and He draws us and binds us to Himself by arousing and strengthening our faith. And the means by which He supremely attests His presence are the proclamation of the Gospel and the eucharistic communion: "He who hears you, hears me . . ." (Luke 10: 16); "This is my body, this is my blood". Hence Christian worship comprises the fact of salvation. We shall return to this point in the next paragraph when we see in the cult a recapitulation of the history of salvation.

Two things however must further be made clear: if the Christian cult is—to use the expression of A. D. Müller—"the most vivid, the most palpable, the most central and the plainest form of the actualization of Christ's presence", such presence is not directly apparent. To be sure, the Church may, by its conduct and discipline, effectually convince an unbeliever of the presence of its Lord (1 Cor. 14: 23ff.), but such a conviction is engendered by faith, as it is for believers also. It is a question of "sacramental" presence. No more than one could without faith recognize in Jesus of Nazareth the Christ, the Son of the living God, can one, in Christian worship, be assured of His presence and behold His living reality. We have here a spiritual process analogous to the recognition of the Word of God in Holy Scripture, or to the recognition of the sacrificed body of Christ in the eucharistic elements. This means in effect—and we shall return to the point—that the Church has not this divine presence at its disposal, and cannot conjure it up by an automatic process which it might use as it pleases.

The second point is that this presence is imperfect, that it awaits its completion and fruition with the advent of the parousia. The worship of the Church, while effectively fore-shadowing the Kingdom, is not yet the Kingdom itself. As compared with the presence of Christ at the Messianic banquet, His presence in Christian worship is, as it were, partial and broken. We are saying the same thing when we declare that this presence is perceptible only by faith.

(b) While the presence of Christ in worship is a real presence, on which the believer can count, as he can count on all the promises of his Lord, the Church, nevertheless, is not the dispenser of this presence. It springs out of the free action of Christ. Such freedom certainly does not mean that the Lord might weary of visiting His Church, or that He might grow indifferent to His promise, or that His presence in divine worship is subject to some dialectical fluctuation. If one thought this, the faith, hope and love of the Church would be jeopardized. Their place would be taken by anxiety, illusion and solitude. In celebrating its cult, the Church is not "waiting for Godot"! "Here is no room for dialectical doubt, here an inviolable certitude prevails" (P. Brunner). But it is not the Church which is the dispenser of this presence; it cannot be induced, it can only be besought. *Maranatha!* And here we are at the heart of one of the problems which, in a liturgical study, must be eluci-dated at the outset: *the problem of the epiklesis.*

Let us begin by considering it in a quite general way. What is its essential meaning?[1] It is a question here—and this is already suggested by the etymology of the word—of an invocation (EPIKALEISTHAI) addressed to the Lord as free and sovereign. In other words, if the cult is epikletic, it means that those who celebrate it recognize that the Lord whom they serve is not at their disposal, that they are indeed His ministers and not technicians. This certainly does not mean that they have to distrust their Lord, as though He might fail to keep His appointments or might forget His promises; it means that they do not control the actualization of His presence, that they therefore recognize Him as their Lord. And this is so basic, not only for the liturgy, but for Christian life as a whole, that the New Testament calls Christians "those of the epiklesis" (Acts 9: 14; cf. 9: 21; I Cor. 1: 2, etc.). By its invocatory character, Christian worship is open to the free and sovereign action of its Lord: it does not seek to manipulate it. In this sense, it is the antithesis of magic. Because of its invocatory character, the cult gathers together the Church in an attitude of hope and expectation which is quite the contrary of the unseemly gluttonous haste which St. Paul accused the Corinthians of showing when they celebrated, or rather falsified, the Lord's Supper (I Cor. 11: 17–34).

The liturgical epiklesis, perhaps first manifested in the invocation *Maranatha*, has a long history on which I shall not dwell. This epiklesis was, from the second century, more and more addressed to the Holy Spirit that He might descend to make of the cult the promised and expected act of salvation and secure to the faithful the real presence and communion of Christ. Increasingly the epiklesis found its normal place at a particular time in the Church's worship: at the celebration of the Lord's Supper. Although this "sacramental localization" of the epiklesis raises questions which do not necessarily honour ancient tradition, it does not imply that Christ, before such invocation, was not present in the cult: in apostolic times also, the *Maranatha* was probably not uttered at the beginning of worship, but

[1] It will be noted that the noun EPIKLESIS is not used either in the NT or by the early church fathers.

at the moment of the eucharistic celebration,[1] while Christ was known to be present from the first.

We cannot here enter into details which would involve a minute discussion of the history of the epiklesis in Christian worship. Let us observe that the eastern liturgical tradition, fixed in the great liturgies of the fourth century, includes a prayer of epiklesis *after* the words of institution, whereas the western tradition, whether Roman or Protestant, either excludes this prayer or places it sometimes *before* the words of institution.[2] This difference might appear slight, and we might at first be tempted to say that the problem of the epiklesis is not of primary importance. It may be, however, that the Orthodox Church is right in thinking that essentially the whole difference between the Christian East and West concerning the doctrine of the Holy Spirit becomes apparent in the situation of the epiklesis. If, with the Christian East, it is placed after the words of consecration, then it is implied that the latter have not in themselves the power of bringing into effect the real presence of Christ; that this presence, consequently, depends not on the celebrant but on the action of the free grace of God. Hence any suggestion of sacramental automatism is removed, and the idea repudiated of an unconditional coincidence between the liturgy of the Church and the act of salvation. God remains free.

If, with the Christian West, this prayer is avoided, or if it is placed before the words of institution, then there arises the threat of an implication that it is the words of institution themselves, correctly spoken by the celebrant, that are efficacious to bring into operation the real presence of Christ and enable Him to prove to the faithful that His flesh is

[1] St. Paul (I Cor. 16: 22) does not place it at the beginning of a letter which he knew was to be read at an assembly for worship, but at the end; and if the Didache (10: 6) seems to place it after the meal, it is however immediately preceded by what appears to be an invitation to communion: "if any one is holy, let him approach; if not, let him repent"—implying that this text describes a cult which included a meal taken in common before the Eucharist itself.

[2] According to the Gallican rite of the seventh century, a collect *post mysteria* was said after the words of institution. Note that the oldest Egyptian tradition placed the epiklesis before the words of institution. This tradition was renewed by Thomas Cranmer in the Book of Common Prayer of 1549; it had also been proposed in the order of Pfalz. Neuburg, 1543.

meat indeed and His blood drink indeed (John 6: 55). And it cannot be denied that no matter how prudently one tries to choose words theologically justifiable, however careful one is to stress that it is the words of Christ's own institution that are repeated, there arises the evident danger of an attempted compulsion of the presence of Christ by the celebrant, of an automatic evocation of His body and blood through the correct utterance of the formula of institution.

The Orthodox custom of using an epiklesis after the words of institution, and even of seeing in that epiklesis the culminating moment of the eucharistic liturgy, may arouse a certain uneasiness in those who consider that the presence of Christ in the Church's worship overflows His real presence in the eucharistic elements and is not necessarily manifested in the highest degree by the consecration of the eucharistic elements. However, the placing of an epiklesis at the moment when the dangers of deviation into magic or idolatry are at their greatest shows an absolutely exemplary soundness of liturgical judgment; to emphasize at that moment of the rite that the presence of the Lord flows from His favourable hearing of prayer rather than from the exercise of priestly power, is to impress on the cult as a whole its true character. The presence of Christ there is real; but it is not the result, on the worst hypothesis of a mechanical action. Christ's presence springs from His grace.

Obviously, this affirmation of Christ's free action, implicit in the startling position which Orthodoxy assigns to the epiklesis, distorts somewhat the structure of the cult. It introduces into it an element of contradiction, a note of reserve. The protest of P. Brunner is understandable enough: "For the churches of the West—those which confess the *filioque*—it is no longer possible to have a prayer of consecration *after* the words of institution. Because the work of the Spirit in the process of consecration does not complete but only co-operates with the work of Christ, an epiklesis, invoking consecration, must in the western tradition stand *before* the words of institution, if it is to be used in any way at all." But one might ask whether the illogicality of the Orthodox Church which refuses to see things going according to a pattern, which introduces incoherences—one might think for example of the refusal of the Orthodox Church to give a precise and simple juridical structure to the Church as a unit—does not constitute a sort of providential reflex against a system, a doctrine, a structure which run the risk of injuring the work of divine grace and of reversing the roles of God and His servants. To place the epiklesis at a point where it seems most embarrassing is not only, as we might think, to recall, according to a trinitarian scheme, the work of the Spirit after recalling the work of the Father in the preface and the work of the Son in the words of institution; it is to stress the fact that we have not the Lord, nor even His promise, at our disposal, and that as long as this world endures, the worship of the Church runs the risk of dangers which must be avoided at all costs. Thus the epiklesis, placed where it is in Orthodox tradition, shows that in spite of all the glory of the cult (and on this point they are quite agreed) the latter is not yet the equivalent of the Kingdom.

3. The cult as recapitulation of the history of salvation

We have seen that the worship of the Church is possible only because Jesus Christ in His earthly ministry lived a sufficient and perfect life of worship. We have also seen that the worship of the Church is true and real because Jesus Christ is freely present therein as Lord, abiding with those who are gathered together in His name. We must now consider what takes place in Christian worship.

Lancelot Andrewes (1555–1626), who was successively Bishop of Chichester, Ely and Winchester, put forward in a Christmas sermon the bold idea that "for as there is a recapitulation of all in heaven and earth in Christ, so there is a recapitulation of all in Christ in the holy sacrament". The worship of the Church would be thus a recapitulation of the major event in the history of salvation and so, implicitly, of the whole history of salvation.

This idea, as we shall try to demonstrate, is true. However, one might question whether the term "recapitulation" is well chosen. Does not the word necessarily mean—like the ANAKEPHALAIOUSTHAI of Eph. 1: 10—" to give or to restore a head to what was without one or had the wrong one", and thus, in short, to give to what is "recapitulated" a justification, a *raison d'être*, an orientation, a fulfilment. In this meaning it is not Christian worship but Jesus Christ who recapitulates, i.e. who fulfils and justifies the process of saving history, imparting to it its true purpose. Now nothing could be worse than to reverse the order of Christ and worship, to cephalize Christ by worship, whereas in fact it is worship which is cephalized by Christ. However, *recapitulare* normally means more simply to "sum up" or "confirm" or "repeat", and in this sense the term is perfectly appropriate: the cult sums up and confirms ever afresh the process of saving history which has reached its culminating point in the intervention of Christ in human history, and through this summing-up and ever-repeated confirmation Christ pursues His saving work by the operation of the Holy Spirit. This recapitulation concerns the history of salvation both from a chronological and theological point of view.

(a) Let us begin by speaking of the cult as a recapitulation of the history of salvation in the chronological sense. But, first of all, what is the chronological structure of this saving history? It is known that it is entirely governed by the work of the incarnate Christ, by His death and resurrection. "The centre of God's economy of salvation is the incarnation of the eternal Son of God in Jesus of Nazareth, His cross and His resurrection" (P. Brunner). This is its obligatory point of reference, its justification. The whole history of the world is here in principle brought to its conclusion and completed. Like a watershed it dominates on the one side the OT period, all history preceding the Nativity back to pre-history and the mystery of the creation; and on the other side the NT period, all history following the Ascension, to beyond all present knowledge, even to the mystery of the end of the world. This history *post Christum natum* brings nothing new, moreover; it is simply a perpetual struggle against the Evil One, who is unwilling to surrender; it is a dramatic exploitation of Christ's victory up to the day when it will shine forth triumphantly before the whole world, on the day of the parousia of the Lord.

To say that the Christian cult recapitulates the process of salvation in a chronological sense is then to say that it sums it up and confirms it in so far as this process itself is recapitulatory; in other words, inasmuch as it is essentially a summing up of the work of Christ.)

The cult is firstly an anamnesis of the past work of Christ. In instituting the Eucharist, i.e. Christian worship, Jesus said: TOUTO POIEITE EIS TEN EMEN ANAMNESIN (1 Cor. 11: 24ff.). This anamnesis or memorial (ANAMNESIS, words belonging to the family ZKR) is something quite different from a mere exercise of memory. It is a restoration of the past so that it becomes present and a promise. In the world of Biblical culture "to remember" is to make present and operative. As a result of this type of "memory", time is not unfolded along a straight line adding irrevocably to each other the successive periods which compose it. Past and present are merged. A real actualization of the past in the present becomes possible. It is on this doctrine also that is based the paschal rite, of which Exod. 12: 14 says that it was instituted *le-Zikaron*, i.e. for a memorial. This implies that every one, as he calls to mind the deliverance from Egypt, must realize that he is himself the object of the redemptive act, to whatever generation he belongs. When it is a question of the history of redemption, the past is re-enacted and becomes present. Thus, similarly, at each Christian act of worship and so—within the perspective of the NT—at every Eucharist, those who participate learn that they are themselves the objects of the redemptive action of the cross.

But the cult, while being an anamnesis, is not merely "a re-enactment of the past", it is, further, an engagement in His service and a confession of faith on the part of those who thus remember the death of Christ. "To Him who is remembered, the worshipper pays homage and confesses allegiance."[1] Consequently, Christian worship, and supremely the Eucharist, is what the OT would describe as an *oth*, a sign which, by the power of God, brings to life what it represents, if it is anamnetic; or brings it to pass if it is prefigurative.

But the Christian cult does not merely recapitulate the life, death and resurrection of Christ by making them operative

[1] Michel, art. MNEMONEUO, *ThWbNT*, IV, p. 686.

in the present. The history of salvation, in fact, is not only something past: it is also what is to come. Not that the future can add to the focus of the whole process of saving history, the incarnation of the Son of God, and especially His death and resurrection. But the future will bring its confirmation, manifestation, and ultimate and eternal fruition. In summing up the process of salvation, the cult is also directed towards the future. It is not merely a re-presentation of the death and victory of Christ, it is also an anticipation of His return and foreshadowing of the Kingdom which He will then establish. It does not merely com-memorate Jesus' last meal with His disciples; it also pre-figures the Messianic feast at which, with His disciples, Christ will drink the new wine in the Kingdom of His Father (Matt. 26: 29). Thus in sharing in the Eucharist the faithful are invited to receive the sign of their belonging to the Kingdom that is to come. And the prefiguration of the future is no more of an exercise of imagination than the re-presenta-tion of the past is an exercise of memory: in the cult—and we shall see that this is the work of the Holy Spirit—past and future, the chief event of the saving process and its glorious manifestation become effectually present.

In our survey of the chronological recapitulation of the saving process, effected by the Holy Spirit in the Christian cult, there remains a third dimension. It is not merely the past which becomes again present; nor is it merely the future which is already dawning. There is also the present itself which is affirmed, and the present of the history of salvation is the heavenly offering which Jesus Christ renders to His Father in the glory of the Ascension. Here, however, we leave the temporal for the spatial framework. Just as in Christian worship past and future meet in an effective present, so also heaven touches earth or earth is lifted towards heaven: "The worship of God in the Church . . . is a participation in the one world-saving and uninterrupted offering of the crucified and ascended Lord before the throne of God" (P. Brunner).

Because it recapitulates the drama of salvation in the sense that it makes the past effectively present, foreshadows the future and glorifies the Messianic present, the cult may be called an eschatological phenomenon. And this is why, despite the ambiguity in which it is still celebrated, it is a joyful phenomenon, for the Christ who gave Himself for the world did not remain enslaved by death, and it is as the Risen Lord, as at the time of His Easter appearances, that He is present among His followers. How then can they repress the AGALLIASIS, the exultation of worship (Acts 2: 46; 16: 34; 1 Pet. 1: 8; cf. 1 Pet. 4: 13; Jude 24)? Here we have an absolutely basic element in Christian liturgy; the cult, because it recapitulates the process of salvation, is an act of joy. Certainly it also proclaims the death of Christ (1 Cor. 11: 26), but, because of the victory which crowned that death, it becomes, for those who share its benefits, less an occasion of sorrow than an inexhaustible source of joyful thanksgiving. This should have a clear impact on liturgical formulation in general, and in this respect our Protestant liturgical tradition has much to learn.

One further question: We have seen that the cult makes present and operative the perfect and sufficient act of worship offered once for all by Christ on the cross, that it foreshadows the joy of the undisputed worship in eternity, and that it enables the Church to share in the heavenly offering which accompanies the drama of salvation. We might go on to ask whether the worship of the Church restores the primordial, paradisial life of worship which God had willed, not only in making man the liturgical representative of creation, with the task of leading the whole world in thanksgiving, adoration and praise, but also in fixing—in a supralapsarian manner—a day of worship, and perhaps even —if we are to follow Luther here—a place of worship (the tree which was the limit of good and evil) and a form of worship (Ps. 148).

I think that we must give a positive reply to this question, since Christ, the new Adam, has, by His coming, restored and fulfilled the plan of the Creator and has rehabilitated those who find in Him the true purpose of their manhood, and of the basic liturgical orientation which God willed in creating man in His image. In summing up the process of salvation which culminates in the incarnate intervention of Christ, the Christian cult thus regains and restores to its place that supralapsarian cult which had no sacrifice, and it regains it not simply by way of anamnesis but also by way of prolepsis: I am thinking of what has been said earlier about the cult which is no longer expiatory but purely sanctifying, and over which Christ will preside so that God may be all in all.

But just as the worship of the Church is but a prolepsis of the Messianic feast and the joys of the Kingdom—so ambiguous as to be perceptible only to faith—so also is it with regard to the anamnesis of worship before the Fall. While it is true that in the cult of the Church man rediscovers the purpose for which he was created—to be a royal priest, and his right to summon the whole creation to join with him in adoration and praise of the Lord (this is a problem of liturgical art to which we shall return) yet this rediscovery is constantly compromised by sin, so that it is not possible to say more than this: the Christian cult, because it is based on the reconciliation of all things in Christ, is the advance-guard of that cosmic quest of which St. Paul speaks, that cosmic longing for a restitution of what God, in His love, had established at the first (Rom. 8: 18ff.). It does not in any evident way restore paradise any more than it brings about the Kingdom; it justifies the hope and furnishes the pledge of these; it offers the day and the place in which the past before the Fall, and the future after the Judgment, still survives or already breaks forth. And because of that, we may not say that this present reality is too ambiguous to be expressed. On the contrary, to refuse it the possibility of expression shows that we do not love it. If we love the Kingdom which will both restore and complete the mystery of the first creation, we cannot refuse it—where its self-expression is most appropriate, i.e. in the cult of the Church—some means of expression, even if that means is ambiguous and unsatisfactory. The Church's worship—and we shall often return to this point—is the most splendid proof of love for the world. Those who do not love the cult do not know how to love the world.

(b) We have, all too briefly, reminded ourselves that the cult sums up the drama of salvation from a chronological point of view; in it the Messianic past, present and future

37

meet and are joined. But the cult also sums up this drama from a theological standpoint. What does this mean? In answer, we must remember of what elements the history of salvation is constituted. If we adopt the traditional scheme we can group these under three heads and say that the history of salvation is composed of a revelation of the divine will for salvation, a reconciliation which makes possible the fulfilment of this will, and a protection which safeguards the efficacious operation of this will. Thus it has a prophetic, a priestly and a royal aspect.

Here again, examining the drama of salvation not chronologically but theologically, we must recognize that its culmination, which wholly justifies it, explains it and sums it up, is the work of Christ. Christ is the supreme prophet, because He is both the bearer and the contents of the revelation of God. He is the supreme priest, because He is both the great high priest and the Lamb that was slain. He is the supreme king, because He is both the Lord and the Servant, He who commands and He who carries out the command.

Thus the cult will be a recapitulation of the history of salvation by being—in relation to Christ who is and was and is to come—at once prophetic, priestly and royal. The cult, in which the Word of God is proclaimed, sums up all that God has taught us of His will for the world. The cult in which the Eucharist is celebrated sums up all that God has done to reconcile the world to Himself. The cult, where the people of God come together in freedom and joy before Him whom they worship, sums up all that God has made of those who accept reconciliation with Himself; men delivered from the fear of death, freed from bondage and thus capable, like Moses and Miriam at the Red Sea, of rejoicing in the defeat of the Evil One and the victory of the Lord (Exod. 15).

I merely mention this problem at this point. We shall return to it in the first two chapters of the second part where we speak of the elements and participants in the cult.

(c) Among all the systematic problems which should be examined, I take only one, but one which is important: that of the relation between the cult of the Church and the

38

continuance of the history of salvation, after the latter has, in Jesus Christ, reached both its culminating point and fulfilment. There is no question of going deeply into this matter. We shall confine ourselves to suggesting the direction in which the solution appears to lie. This is of capital importance for what follows.

The history of salvation is completed in Jesus Christ. God has nothing further to say or to do than what He has already said and done in Jesus Christ. Why then does the history of salvation continue and how does it continue?

One thing strikes us constantly: it is clear that, as far as the witness of the NT is concerned, the death of Christ has accomplished all things and that His ascension has crowned for ever this final fulfilment. And yet at the very moment when He ascends into heaven, angels proclaim that He will return (Acts 1: 11). Thus it is implied that the history of salvation is not ended. It will continue for centuries or millennia, which will still not bring to it any new feature, for all is accomplished. If the history of salvation continues— as is proved both by the fact that history itself continues and above all by the fact that Jesus Christ has promised to return—it is because the central event of this saving process, the cross and the resurrection of Christ which had as it were absorbed, concentrated into itself, the whole history of salvation from the expulsion from paradise up to the morning of Good Friday, must in some way pour itself out, bring into operation its full efficacy,[1] a process which will however be interrupted before its term by God's plan to put an end to the world. What was once concentrated in Jesus alone, in that "baptism" (Luke 12: 50) by which He substituted Himself for the whole world, must now shed itself abroad, bear its fruit, be exploited. "The virtual inclusion of all human existence in the crucified body of Jesus must be realized and actualized in the concrete historical existence of every single man until it becomes an ontically real and

[1] That which is a central event will never happen. In itself it would suffice for an unending history of this world, hence the end of this world will not come when the central event of the saving process has exhausted its efficacy—like an electric battery that is exhausted—but when God has determined "to shorten the days" (Mark 13: 20).

personally apprehended inclusion, until it culminates in its ultimate form" (P. Brunner). In this sense, according to the normal mode of Biblical revelation, the EPHAPAX brings into being an OEKONOMIA. Christian worship pre-eminently forms part of this OEKONOMIA. That is why the saving process continues even after finding its fulfilment in Jesus Christ.

But how does it continue? It seems to me that the correct answer is that it continues as a result of the anamnesis which springs from it. But in saying this we must give to the term anamnesis its fullest significance. It is not merely a question of informing men of past events but rather of launching them on the full flood tide of salvation. If I may dare to use such expressions, it is a question of the act by which a man (or an event) is grafted on to the cardinal event of Good Friday and Easter and of the act by which this cardinal event of the saving process is grafted, in the course of the following centuries, on to such a man (or such an event). By anamnesis the Christian is brought to share in the benefits of that event which is remembered, and by the same action, the recalled event is made effectively present and operative. "What God does, He always does once only *for* all the other times and *in view of* all the other times when His intervention will continue to show itself in a saving way. On the level of the life of faith, nothing is more actual and operative than what God has done once for all" (Fr. J. Leenhardt).

What we are here describing is the work of the Holy Spirit, which, since Easter Day, does not consist in producing a new EPHAPAX, or in repeating the former one as though it were not eternally sufficient. It consists, on the one hand, in efficaciously applying what God has done *illic et tunc* in Jesus Christ to the *hic et nunc* of such and such a man or community (or event)—the Holy Spirit thus mediates Christ to us—and, on the other hand, in efficaciously referring the *hic et nunc* of such and such a man or community (or event) to the *illic et hunc* of what God has done in Jesus Christ at Golgotha and in the garden of Joseph of Arimathea—the Holy Spirit brings us into communion with Christ.

We need not here enter into details of liturgical or

40

eucharistic history. Suffice it to say that if we do not deprive the idea of anamnesis of its true nature; if we refuse to make of it a simple memorial; then there is no need, in order to emphasize the efficacious character of this anamnesis and its eschatological bearing, to have recourse to a doctrine which would threaten the oneness of the EPHAPAX and multiply the sacrifice of Christ by the number of its celebrations. But let us say especially that the remedy for any weakening of the character of the anamnesis lies in a reverent doctrine of the Holy Spirit. We deny the power of the Spirit if we deny the efficacious virtue and the eschatological bearing of the anamnesis. But we do so no less, if we call in question the uniqueness of the death (and the resurrection) of Christ by allowing it to be supposed that that event must be repeated to retain its efficacity, that its uniqueness is not sufficient for the salvation of the whole world. And it is perhaps because the Eastern Orthodox Church has quite another doctrine of the Spirit, far more powerful than that which characterizes the West, that it has escaped the Western dilemma with regard to the interpretation of the Eucharist.

The history of salvation thus continues, efficaciously operative, in the form of an anamnesis of its central event. What then took place in a substitutionary way on behalf of the whole world is shed abroad by the power and work of the Holy Spirit, to become the ontological reality of those who rejoice in it and live by it. And because the worship of the Church—its baptismal and eucharistic sacraments both of which are acquainted with the power of the proclaimed Word—is the privileged sphere where this application, this actualization takes place, it may be said that Christian worship is one of the most conspicuous agents in the process of saving history. Through the Christian cult— not exclusively, but as one agent and in a very special way— the history of salvation continues. That is one of the reasons for its necessity; it is an instrument which the Holy Spirit uses to carry on His work, to render efficacious today the past work of Christ, and also to bring into saving contact with this work of the past the men and the events of today, that they may enter into its benefits.

CHAPTER TWO

THE CULT AS THE EPIPHANY OF
THE CHURCH

1. The Church as a liturgical assembly

We have spoken of the cult as a recapitulation of the process of saving history, and so of the mystery of what happens in the liturgy. In this chapter, on the basis of what we have already seen, we are to show a second fundamental aspect of the doctrine of Christian worship: namely, that by its worship the Church becomes itself, becomes conscious of itself, and confesses itself as a distinctive entity. Worship thus allows the Church to emerge in its true nature. In this sense—and this is the point at which we begin—the cult of the Church must be understood within the perspective of the *qâhâl* of Israel.

The importance of this OT term for Christian ecclesiology is well known: it seems probable in fact that if the NT calls the Church EKKLESIA it is not so much for etymological reasons as because the LXX usually translates by this word the Hebrew term *qâhâl*. Now the *qâhâl Yahwé* is the assembly of the people saved from Egypt, and confirmed as a holy people at the foot of mount Sinai (Deut. 4: 10), so that this solemn meeting between God and His people came to be called, by a quasi-technical term, "the day of the assembly" (*iôm haqâhâl*, Deut. 9: 10; 18: 16). This solemn assembly is met with at several of the great moments and crises in the history of Israel: after the capture of Ai (Josh. 8: 30ff.), at the dedication of Solomon's temple (1 Kings 8 = 2 Chron. 6–7), at the time when Moab and Ammon overshadowed Israel with a terrible threat (2 Chron. 20: 5ff.), on the occasion of great reforms (2 Chron. 29–30; 2 Kings 23; Neh. 8–9), etc.; and almost every time, this assembly, in which

42

the people of God meet, become aware of themselves and appear in their true character, includes the same elements of divine initiative, divine presence, proclamation of the divine Word, and the sealing of the encounter between God and His people by sacrifices.

We must remember all this when in the NT we meet the word "Church". This word, even where it may appear to be somewhat trite, has a clear liturgical coefficient: the Church is the people whom God has assembled, beyond death (even if this is still very threatening), to meet their Lord and to become themselves, to become conscious of themselves and confess themselves as a distinctive entity in this en-counter. The term "Church"—EKKLESIA—is thus not in the first place, or merely, a sociological or juridical term, but very definitely a liturgical term. This appears conspicuously to be the case in the "liturgical" chapters of the First Letter to the Corinthians (cf. 11: 18–22; 12: 28; 14: 4ff., 12, 19, 23, 28, 33ff.) but it is quite normal elsewhere too. The reading of the NT would often be much clearer if this were borne in mind, if it were remembered that the Church is essentially the eschatological people assembled to meet its Lord and to become itself in and through this encounter. As P. Brunner observes so justly: "Church worship, as an assembly in the name of Jesus, of the Christian community, is what might be described as the true manifestation of the Church on earth. The occurrence of such a meeting is the epiphany of the Church".

2. *The implications of the cult considered as the epiphany of the Church*

The Christian cult, because it sums up the history of salvation, enables the Church to become itself, to become conscious of itself and to confess what it essentially is. In other words, to learn to know the Church and to understand its life, it is indispensable to go to church and to take part in its worship. The study of dogmatic texts, of confessions of faith, of ecclesiastical disciplines, of the history of Christianity, of personal piety, important and essential as this is if one is to know the Church, is something that comes later: it is in the sphere of worship, the sphere *par excellence* where the life of the Church comes into being, that the fact of the Church first emerges. It is there that it gives proof of itself, there where it is focused, and where we are led when we truly seek it, and it is from that point that it goes out into the world to exercise its mission.

Thus it is readily understandable that the cult is not a marginal or discretionary element in the life of the Church, and that the care which the Church takes over the order of its worship is not misplaced. On the contrary, liturgical questions are for the Church vital questions, because it is by its cult and in its cult that it shows the degree of its faithfulness and soundness. This is seen in particular in the fact that the great reforms of Israel are liturgical reforms (cf. 2 Chron. 29–30; 2 Kings 23), and further in the fact that the transition from the old covenant to the new is a liturgical transition: the "sacraments" change, the day and also the place of the cult change because perfect worship has been offered by the preaching, the sacrifice and the glorification of Christ.[1] And that is why the almost total absence of any allusion to the cult, for example, in the *Constitution of the Evangelical Reformed Church of Neuchâtel* shows much less a carelessness which might be excusable on grounds of confessional atavism, than wilful theological blindness: it is rather as if, in a course of lectures on human anatomy, there was no mention of the heart.

Now if the cult is the major moment in the epiphany of the Church, it should provide the key to the meaning of the Church. For this "liturgical" description of the Church, one may have recourse to several formulae. One may say—with K. Barth—that by its cult and in its cult, the Church is manifest as a community of faith, of baptism, of eucharistic communion, and of prayer; one may also say that the Church appears as a community which expresses the election, vocation, unity and salvation of its members; again, one may say—and this is the plan which we shall adopt—that by its cult the Church becomes aware that it is a baptismal,

[1] It would be worth while to examine, in this respect too, the theology of the Temple, elaborated by Jesus Christ and the NT witness to it.

44

nuptial, catholic, diaconal and apostolic community. Let us look at this more closely.

(a) By its cult and in its cult, the Church becomes manifest and aware of itself, first of all, as a baptismal community.

This amounts to saying in the first place that the cult differentiates the Church from the world. In worship, "the Church emerges, without pretentiousness but firmly, out of the profanity of the environment in which it is normally immersed" (K. Barth, *Dogmatics*). It shows that it is not of the world, and that, in consequence, the only justification for its temporal existence is to offer worship. The cult brings about a rupture between the Church and the world, and this is why—contrary to the situation in missionary preaching—the worship of the Church is not public: those who take part in it are those who have passed through baptism, who have renounced the devil and his works, the world and its pomps, the flesh and its desires. It was after the passage of the Red Sea that Israel was consolidated as the *qâhâl Yahwé*, or EKKLESIA TOU THEOU. The Christian cult shows that the Church is not a human society, but the result of the election which God promotes and fulfils by causing to die and rise again with Christ those who respond to the appeal of the Gospel. This is something which centuries of Christianity have made us forget, and which it is urgent for us to relearn: it is through God's forgiveness that Christian worship takes place. In this sense, it must also be said that the *Christian* cult is not one among other liturgical practices natural to men. We must "go outside the camp" (Heb. 13: 13) in order to be able to offer to God the worship which He approves.

But this is not enough. To say that worship demonstrates the Church as a baptismal community does not imply only that by its worship the Church is marked off from the world and so proclaims the end of the world (we shall return to this point in more detail in the next chapter); it implies further, on the one hand, that the cult transfigures the world, and, on the other, that it remains threatened by the world.

Firstly, the cult transfigures the world. We shall have to return several times to this affirmation, which is basic for liturgical study. At this point I shall consider only one aspect

45

and state, paradoxically, that if the cult shows the Church as a baptismal community, this also means that the world is present in the cult but—because of what we have seen just now—it is present there only after dying to itself. Baptism, in fact, if it causes the baptized to die also raises them to life again, and what it brings to life again is what it has caused to die. Baptism does not produce a dissolution of identity: the Risen One of Easter morning is the One who had been buried on the evening of Good Friday. This is what is implicitly brought out by all the accounts of Christ's burial: they are there, in their wonderful unanimity, to bear witness to the reality of the resurrection. The community of the baptized which the Church creates is indeed a community of men and women and children who have renounced the world and have "died unto sin" (Rom. 6: 11). But such a death did not annihilate them or make them untrue to themselves. They rediscover themselves in the cult, with their language and culture, their emotions and their characteristics, which have also died and also been quickened to new life. That is why the sphere of Christian worship is the very place where a nation and even a whole epoch can, more deeply than anywhere else, express themselves, and appear for what they are in the light of Easter Day.

But this world from which the Church has not been able entirely to free itself even in the waters of baptism, this world which it has condemned and which, pardoned, has been restored to it, can become a threat to Christian worship. Let us ponder on the use which Israel made of the Egyptian jewels which they had been bidden to take with them through the Red Sea (cf. Ex. 11: 2; 12: 35ff. and 32: 1ff.). Seeing that baptism is not yet the last judgment, but only a "sacrament" of it, it does not yet lead into the promised land, but into the wilderness, the sphere of temptation where salvation may yet be lost (cf. 1 Cor. 10: 1–13). Certainly Egypt has been left behind, and the hymn of Moses has been triumphantly sung; certainly, too, God is here with His people, and also His law and His representative, and the miraculous means of food and drink. But all this takes place in the expectation of the final fulfilment; and in the time of waiting the baptismal metamorphosis might still be reversed by a lapse into conformity with this world (Rom. 12:2). Thus, in showing forth the Church as the community of the baptized, the cult shows not only that the Church is in a state of rupture with the world, but also that the Church enables the Christian to rediscover a world that has been exorcized and reconciled, and finally intimates that the Church is never free from the danger of lapses.

(b) We may hesitate about the precise adjective which should designate the second characteristic of the Church revealed by the cult. Must we say that the cult is an epiphany of the Church inasmuch as the latter is an eucharistic community? But the term Eucharist is far too comprehensive of the total life of the Church and hence of the totality of its worship, to denote exactly what we must now emphasize. I will say therefore that the cult reveals the Church as a *nuptial community*. What is implied by taking up this Biblical and patristic image? We imply that by its cult the Church emerges as the Bride of Christ.

The Bride of Christ: that is to say, first, she who has given a positive answer to His word, His appeal. She who promises herself because Christ has promised Himself, who gives herself because Christ has given Himself. In showing forth the Church as a nuptial community, the cult then first discloses her as a community of faith.

The Bride of Christ next means she who is eagerly expectant of His coming, who waits for Him and calls Him, who relies on His promise, and lives in the strength of that promise, who would be utterly lost, destroyed and disproved if the Bridegroom failed to come to her or delayed His return. In showing forth the Church as a nuptial community, the cult discloses her as a community of hope.

The Bride of Christ means, in sum, she who loves her Liberator and Husband, she who dedicates to Him her beauty and all beauty, her joy and all joy; again, she who knows that in seeing her it is He whom men should recognize, and who, because of that, devotes herself wholly to doing Him honour and to celebrating in a splendid and glorious way what He has done for her. In showing forth the Church as a nuptial community, the cult reveals her as a community of love.

47

The Bride of Christ means—polemically—one who is not an adulteress, who does not deceive her Liberator and Husband, who is able to discriminate wisely between the word of the Bridegroom who loves her and that of those who would seduce her, and so refuses to give herself to others, to believe in others. The Bride of Christ, again, is she who does not rejoice to see her Lord delay His coming, who does not justify, by this delay, any complaisance in herself or any committal to other hopes than the sole hope which justifies her own being. The Bride of Christ—she who refuses to live for herself, to be beautiful and glorious for herself, to conceal, by the parade of her own righteousness, Him whose body she is and whom she is commanded to reveal to the world.

(c) Thirdly, the cult shows forth the Church as a catholic community. The term "catholic" is one of the finest and richest in Christian ecclesiology. I will not make an exegesis of it here, but merely the following points:

To say that the cult shows forth the Church as a catholic community is to recognize that the Church is poised beyond sociological barriers, that it refuses to sanction the sociological patterns of this world.[1] There is room within the Church for all those whom Jesus Christ calls. Like the inn where the good Samaritan lodged the wounded man, she is a PAN-DOCHEION, a place of welcome for all (Luke 10: 34). Women have their place in it as well as men, children as well as adults, young and old, wise and foolish, rich and poor, powerful and weak, Jews and Gentiles, the black man and the white. There is no room for pride, covetousness, exploitation and envy. Where the world separates or confuses, the Church distinguishes and unites.

To say that the cult shows forth the Church as a catholic community is to recognize that she enables the baptized who have become members of her body to live out their membership in the fulness of their humanity. In the Church, they can be themselves, for they are restored to the humanity which salvation has placed again within their reach, and which, by way of paradigm, is proclaimed through the

[1] There recurs here the aspect of the Church as a baptismal community.

healing miracles reported in the Gospels. They are not transformed into monsters, they are not all ears or all eyes; but they are there to hear the word and to reply in their turn; they are there to look and to move. We must never forget that Jesus did not cure only the deaf, and that the breadth of His healing miracles has evident liturgical implications.

But the catholicity of the Church as revealed by the cult has not merely sociological and anthropological aspects. If the Church bears witness to its catholicity by challenging whatever divides men, calling them on the contrary both to fellowship and to fulness of life in Jesus Christ, it does so too by challenging whatever divides men in space: it gathers together what is scattered, it repudiates the indifferent or bellicose juxtaposition of cities and nations. It brings all men together in bonds of solidarity, again without confusion, but insisting that others should not be forgotten or despised. To see what this means in practice, we may recall the injunctions and examples reported in the NT of intercessions and thanksgiving by distant churches, or again of the system of communication between the churches, which is immediately apparent as a feature basic to NT church life.[1] And this undoubtedly goes further: the catholicity of the Church as disclosed by the cult has not only a horizontal spatial dimension, it has also a vertical dimension: heaven and the abode of the dead must also have access, as we shall have occasion to explain when we come to consider the question of the ministers of the cult.

The cult which makes manifest the catholicity of the Church reveals further a fourth dimension of this catholicity: namely, catholicity in time. In its worship the Church bears witness that it unites the centuries, refusing to allow what is past to fall into oblivion, or what is promised to fade into illusion. It is, as St. Bernard used to say, *ante et retrooculata*, it sees before and behind, and embraces the totality of the process of salvation. When in worship the Church emerges as what it is, the whole history of salvation is secretly present from Abel to the parousia.

[1] One of the most striking examples is afforded by the account of St. Paul's career: the church of Damascus had been warned of the sinister intentions behind the journey of Saul of Tarsus (Acts 9: 13ff).

A final dimension of the catholicity of the Church, as disclosed in and through its worship, is that the Church is catholic rather in the way in which Noah's ark was. I mean that the Church is catholic in the sense that it was constituted by God as the guarantor of the world, as the bearer of the world's future, for in it—as already seen in the baptismal aspect of the Church apparent in its cult—the world has found a welcome; because the Church even now intercepts and gathers into its own worship the sighs and longings of creation and sacramentally restores to the latter the liturgical function for which it was created.

The cult thus discloses the Church as an essentially catholic community in the sense that on the sociological, anthropological, spatial, temporal, and liturgical planes, the Church opposes whatever divides and separates—once the separation marked by baptism has taken place—and welcomes and gathers into its bosom all for whom Jesus Christ died, all who in Him are destined for salvation. Thus it becomes clear that the adjective antithetic to "catholic" is not "protestant" but "diabolic". The cult, which is thus an epiphany of the catholic Church, offered on behalf of the whole world, constitutes a veritable exorcism.

(d) By its worship, the Church becomes conscious of itself, fourthly, as a diaconal community. This seems to me to imply two things:

The church learns through its cult, and manifests thereby, that it does not exist for itself, and has no justification in itself. It exists—as did the incarnate Christ—for God and for men. Thus it has a twofold orientation.

The Church becomes aware of itself as a diaconal community through the cult because the cult enables it to emerge, not as a block, but as a living body whose members are diversified in their functions and importance. The cult invites the members of the Church to co-operate in the work of salvation, to bring to bear special vocations intended to serve the edification of the whole body: "As each has received a gift, employ it for one another, as good stewards of God's varied grace" (1 Pet. 4: 10: cf. 1 Cor. 12, etc.).

(e) The Church by its cult shows what it really is: it appears as a baptismal, nuptial, catholic, diaconal, and finally as an apostolic or missionary community.

First of all, why does the Church, in and through its cult, emerge as an apostolic community? Because by its worship—to quote the words of K. Barth—"it issues, without pretension, but firmly, from the profanity of the milieu in which it is normally immersed", i.e., by its worship it is differentiated from the world. And this in two ways. Firstly, it does not yet embrace all men, but only the baptized. From this fact there emerges a special attitude towards those who are not yet members of the Church. Her very existence is, for those who do not belong to her, at once a challenge and a promise. Secondly, it does not include all men, but also it is not always gathered together but has a day of its own, a day of worship, Sunday. The fact that one day is singled out for divine worship teaches the Church that it is still in the world, that the hour of the great Sabbath has not yet struck. If the comparison were not too bold, I would say that the Church emerges, week by week, rather as a cetaceous animal, at regular times, comes up for air. But this very intermission, the fact that the cult is not continuous but sporadic, emphasizes the Church's otherness in relation to the world, and thus confronts the Church with the question of its justification for existing in the world and for the world.

And how does the Church, in and through its worship, become aware of itself as an apostolic community? Without prejudicing here what we shall consider in the following chapter, which will be entirely devoted to this matter, we can say at once that it does so precisely through the realization that it is only as yet APARCHE TON KTISMATON, only the first fruits of the creatures (Jas. 1: 18), and not the totality, and that as yet it is gathered together only on the first day of the week (cf. Acts 20: 7, etc.) and not every day of the week. In other words, the cult is an epiphany of the Church as a missionary community in the sense that it obliges the Church to send forth, into the world throughout the rest of the week, those whom it has assembled out of the world on the first day.

This gives us an opportunity of introducing a brief aside

on the term "Mass" which, from the fourth century, gradually supplanted in the West all other terms denoting the cult and which, among the Lutherans, even survived the Reformation. The origin of the word has given rise to some doubt. It now seems established, in spite of some risky hypotheses, that the term "Mass" comes from the Low Latin *Missa—missio*—i.e. *dismissal*: in other words it is the last note of the cult, the solemn act of dismissal which sends the faithful forth into the world (cf. Luke 24: 46–53), which has been used to denote the cult as a whole as though to emphasize the justification of the Christian cult in a world which is not yet the Kingdom. "The cult," affirms A. D. Müller who insists on the term, "must be understood as the Mass, *missio*, dismissal. In it is kindled the light which is to illuminate the world."

(f) "The cult is the most concrete answer to the question as to where the Church is to be found" (A. D. Müller). We cannot here consider all the implications of this obvious theological fact. In particular, to avoid having to introduce into this treatise on liturgy a whole treatise on ecclesiology, we must pass over the problem of the relations between the local Church (i.e. the liturgical assembly) and the universal Church, and that of the catholic authorization of the normal ministry of the local Church, of the liturgical PROISTAMENOS (Rom. 12: 8; 1 Thess. 5: 12). Three points only can be considered:

First of all, we must lay stress on the truth of the affirmations of the sixteenth-century confessions of faith, which see the Christian Church wherever the Word of God is preached in purity, and where the sacraments are legitimately administered; in order to describe the true Church, they refer to its cult.[1] If they do so, it is because they know perfectly well that it is in the preaching of the Word and in sacramental life that the Church both manifests and stakes its fidelity. If the reformed confessions of faith usually add—often explicitly—a third mark, namely (to use the words of the

[1] Est autem ecclesia congregatio sanctorum, in qua evangelium pure docetur, et recte administrantur sacramenta" (Confession of Augsburg VII, cf. *Die Bekenntnisschriften der evangelisch-lutherischen Kirche*, Göttingen, 1930, pp. 59ff.; cf. *ibid.*, p. 297).

Scottish confession of faith of 1560) the rigorous observation
of ecclesiastical discipline as it is drawn from the Word of
God,[1] they do not thereby remove the Church from its
liturgical position, but on the contrary they suggest that the
Church does not accord to all and sundry the right to
celebrate the Christian cult. We have already made it
sufficiently clear that by its cult, which always localizes it,
the Church is manifested as a catholic community, so we
need not be afraid of stating definitely in this context that
the cult "congregationalizes" the Church. In doing so, we
are insisting on one of the many points in which the Reformation showed itself to be faithful to patristic tradition, which
has been maintained and illustrated by the Churches of the
Orthodox East also.

If it is pre-eminently in the cult that the Church reveals
its true being, this implies that it does not do so primarily
by its catechesis, its structure or its diaconate. Not of course
that the latter are negligible or optional. They too are
spheres where the Church stakes its fidelity, and it would be
quite wrong to wish to make light of them to the advantage
of worship; but in relation to the latter, they are secondary.
I mean, that it is not the cult which must be shaped in
accordance with them, but vice versa. A catechesis which
does not seek to remind men of their basic vocation to
worship, ministers who have no care for a constant spiritual
renewal through acts of worship, a diaconate which has lost
sight of its primary intention to show how committing a
thing is intercession for the sick, the poor, the afflicted and
the captive, are in a way uprooted and risk degenerating
into mere intellectualism, legalism or socialism.

A third remark to be made here may seem either dangerous
or facile. None the less here it is: it is clear that if the true
character of the Church is revealed in and through its
worship, then it is in the sphere of worship that the Church
proves its fidelity or otherwise and it is therefore—if unfaith-

[1] ". . . disciplinae severa et ex verbi divini praescripta observatio"
(cf. W. Niesel, *Bekenntnisschriften und Kirchenordnungen der nach
Gottes Wort Reformierten Kirche* (Munich, 1958, p. 103; cf. *ibid.*,
p. 72, 131, 251. In the text of the Augsburg confession quoted above,
discipline also is presupposed since there is reference to a *congregatio
sanctorum*.

fulness breaks out—the cult that must be reformed when there is need to reform the Church.

Among ourselves there is great suspicion of Church reform which aims primarily at a reform of worship, of movements which believe that they are reforming the Church by reforming its worship. It is feared that in such cases the reform may be merely formal, not striking to the heart of the Church, as though the Church could have any other heart but its worship. Evidently we must avoid misunderstanding here: it is not by the cult that the Church is reformed. The cult—especially if it shows that the Church is unfaithful—could not become the lever of a reform. It is the Word of God which reforms the Church: we may think of the Reformation of Josiah which was initiated by the rediscovery of the book of the Word of God (2 Kings 22ff.). But if this Word is to reform the Church, it must basically reform the cult. Under Josiah, the rediscovery of God's word did not merely arouse an awestruck repentance, this repentance led to the performance of a task: to the radical abolition of idolatry so as to restore to the people, in an unparalleled Passover, the grace, the joy and the beauty of its cult.

A Church reformation which would stop short of a liturgical reformation, and miss the means of concrete expression which this affords, would sterilize the Word of God instead of allowing it to bear its fruit. And for this reason I do not think it an exaggeration to say that if the Biblical renascence which our time has witnessed is reluctant and afraid to engage in the immense task of a liturgical reform, it will turn to our condemnation. It is not a better catechesis, nor a reorganization of the Church, nor a new awareness of the appeal sounded in our ears by the weary and the heavy-laden —it is not these things which will justify the Church of our time: it is a liturgical reform because it is this which will justify in its repercussions this catechesis, this reorganization, this diaconate inasmuch as it will prevent them from degenerating into a Biblicist intellectualism, an Erastian legalism or a socialistic activism.

3. *The cult as the heart of the local Christian community*

A reading of contemporary Protestant theologians suggests

54

that a consensus of opinion has been established: they consider that the cult is the centre of Christian community life and that this is axiomatic. In practice this means two things:

(a) First of all the cult is in some sense the criterion of parochial life: whatever is entitled to its place in worship, whatever stands the test of being orientated by worship, whatever provides conditions for the ready fruition of worship, is healthy; whatever does not stand up to these tests is unhealthy. A catechesis which had not the intention of supporting "worshippers whom the Father seeks" (John 4: 23) would be faulty. A parochial organization which was indifferent to rooting itself first of all in the cult would be parasitic. A diaconate which did not clearly emerge as an answer to the Church's intercession would be profane. When we see the agitation which overtakes some parishes and which causes them to confuse insomnia with vigilance, we sometimes feel that we would like to impose on them a sabbatical year during which they would abstain from all activity except that of the Church's worship, in order that they should learn once again to measure by that standard what they must do and what they can leave aside. And probably they could leave undone many more things than they in their feverish activity imagine.

(b) But to say that the cult is the heart of the Christian community is not merely to remind them that the cult is the criterion of the real life to which they are called, it is also to remind them that if the cult ceases the community dies. It is by its worship that the Church lives, it is there that its heart beats. And in fact the life of the Church pulsates like the heart by systole and diastole. As the heart is for the animal body, so the cult is for church life a pump which sends into circulation and draws in again, it claims and it sanctifies. It is from the life of worship—from the Mass— that the Church spreads itself abroad into the world to mingle with it like leaven in the dough, to give it savour like salt, to irradiate it like light, and it is towards the cult— towards the Eucharist—that the Church returns from the

55

world, like a fisherman gathering up his nets or a farmer harvesting his grain. The only parochial activities which have any real justification are those which spring from worship and in their turn nourish it.

People are often afraid of the systole movement, as if the Church were thus going to fold itself up or shrink into self-absorption, forgetting its mission in the world. This fear seems to me an idle one for two reasons. Firstly, for the psychological reason that the Church would die of a cult that was not a "Mass" (in the sense we have attached to the term) just as certainly as a living body would die from a heart which ceased to dilate as well as contract. In other words, evangelization is the necessary complement to worship just as worship is the necessary complement to evangelization. But above all it is for a theological reason, that it seems to me needless to fear the systole movement which is part of worship: when the Church assembles for worship, becoming a liturgical society, it is not that it turns inwards to itself but that it turns towards God, to offer to Him in thanksgiving and the Eucharist what it is and what it has. To distrust liturgical life is to doubt the presence of God in the cult, just as to distrust missionary activity is to doubt the victory of Christ over the world. The Church cannot have either the one or the other; it must have both.

CHAPTER THREE

THE CULT, THE END AND FUTURE
OF THE WORLD

WE HAVE seen that what takes place in the Church's worship is the summarizing of the process of salvation. We have seen the importance of worship for the Church: it is in and through worship that it becomes itself, becomes self-aware, confesses its true being, that is to say that worship is for the Church the sphere of its epiphany. But worship, just because of this, is not yet the exultation of the Kingdom which will be without end: the cult is celebrated in this world. What we have to consider in this chapter is whether the fact that Christian worship takes place in it has any sort of importance for the world, whether the worship of the Church concerns the world.

To this question we must reply with calm certainty and say, despite all the world's denials, that it is of paramount importance for the world that Christian worship should be celebrated therein. The mere fact that worship is being offered underlines the impermanence of the life of the world, while at the same time offering to men, if they are willing to enter into the New Covenant, a real future for the world in the transformation which worship brings about.

In this chapter we have therefore to discuss the cult as both a threat and a promise to the world, after which we shall try to show, very briefly, the connexion between the cult and evangelization.

1. Two preliminary remarks

(a) In order to estimate the place of the cult in the life of the world, we must be able to distinguish between the Church and the world, between the sacred and the profane.

Often we shrink from such a distinction: it is thought that while valid under the old covenant, and while of real significance in pagan religions, it is a distinction which has been ended and rendered basically anachronistic by the incarnation of the Son of God in Jesus of Nazareth and the reconciliation between God and the world sealed in His sacrifice on the cross. The proof of this, it is urged, is seen in the rending of the temple veil at the moment when Jesus gave up the ghost (Mark 15: 38 and par.) and the destruction of this temple a few years later.

The distinction between the sacred and the profane must nevertheless be maintained, and on its maintenance depends a just appreciation of the mission of the Church in the world, as a prophetic, priestly, and royal people. Of course the desire to maintain the distinction in the Jewish manner is out of date and anachronistic: circumcision is superseded, the temple worship at Jerusalem is superseded, the observance of the Sabbath is superseded. But circumcision, the temple and the Sabbath have not been eliminated by the new covenant: they have been replaced. Henceforth it is baptism which is the mark of initiation into the people of the promise, it is the body of Christ which is the sacrament of God's presence among men, it is Sunday which brings the faithful together for worship. The very fact that there is baptism, a Church and a Sunday shows that it is still necessary to distinguish the sacred from the profane; to give up the distinction is to doubt the need for baptism, the distinctive nature of the Church, the legitimacy of Sunday observance; much more, it implies that we are setting up a *theologia gloriae* or rejecting the doctrine of the incarnation.

This means taking one's stand in a *theologia gloriae*, in the life of the world to come, because it is when the Eternal Kingdom is set up that everything will then become sacred or secular (the two terms then being interchangeable). In this sense the refusal to distinguish between sacred and secular is symptomatic of thinking on the human and temporal level. Or else it means to question the very principle of incarnation; to imply that the world to come is too unreal or too remote to arouse here anything but wistful desire, or to bring into being any signs of its actual presence here below.

One is faced with equating the world with the Kingdom or of denying the possibility of their ever coming together. It is to succumb to Christ's third temptation (Matt. 4: 8ff.) or to deny that this temptation can have an existential bearing. In other words, it means refusing to place oneself where God has placed the Church: namely, before the parousia but after Pentecost. It is to deny the simultaneity of the two aeons, either by affirming that this world is not only terminated but superseded; or by affirming that the world to come is radically incommunicable in earthly life, here and now and that it cannot even establish bridgeheads on this earthly territory. To put the matter positively, if we must make a distinction, or a new distinction, between the sacred and the profane, it is because of the overlapping of the two aeons.

What is the reason for being suspicious of such a distinction? Doubtless, in the first place, it reflects the spirit of this world, which seeks to assimilate all that has to do with the world to come, and consequently all that challenges the existence of this world. Since it does not wish to have in its midst a people of prophets, priests and kings, a people which judges it, a people which claims to supersede it in vital matters, to be its rightful representative in the recognition of its true destiny, a people who are determined to remain free, the present world tries as far as possible to naturalize grace and make light of it, to make people think that it has no supernatural source.

This distrust springs in the first instance from a profanation of the Church and from the Church's consent to this profanation. Such consent is shown in a particularly painful way in the degradation of the miracle of baptism to the status of a generalized folklore ceremony which may be taken for granted, or in the Church's admission of the claim of the state to integrate religion and gear it to normal state machinery. It is when people feel no uneasiness about mass movements that they most distrust the distinction between the sacred and the profane. But this distrust is also caused by the Church's impatience: knowing itself to be catholic, it forgets that from now to the parousia its catholicity must pass through the narrow gate of holiness. Entrusted with the mission of making known to the whole world the love which God has for it and the salvation which He has won for it, the Church forgets that there are still swine and dogs in the world (Matt. 7: 6), and it lavishes grace upon the world without any longer checking the way in which such grace is received. So blinded is it by its certainty of the victory of Christ, that it ceases to reflect that until His return, its Lord will be for the world a SEMEION ANTILEGOMENON (Luke 2: 34): The Church looks upon the world as being so thoroughly defeated that it has lost all powers of revolt, all its claws (cf. Deut. 21: 12); it seems to have become an ally that need no longer be mistrusted. Instead of contradicting the world, it feels it can now be satisfied to sanctify it. And it is not a matter of chance that the recommendations of the Fathers in favour of paedo-baptism all date in effect from after the conversion of Constantine, and reflect the Church's hope that all persecution would henceforth cease.

In other words, the distrust of this distinction between the sacred and the profane—where it does not stem from a docetism which refuses to believe that the sacred can truly disclose its presence in earthly life—springs from a lowering of eschatological tension. I mention this to remind the reader that impatience with this distinction is not merely a theological fault, but shows an evident lack of capacity to read the signs of the times.

Thus everything inclines one to believe that contemporary history, in quite a new way, will serve to recall the Church to an awareness of its otherness in relation to the world, of its sacred character. And this is a matter for rejoicing. For we must not exaggerate the danger that the Church might take advantage of this rediscovered distinction by complacently shutting itself up in the realm of the sacred. To be too fearful of this danger, which certainly exists, is to show a lack of trust in the Spirit which indwells the Church. If the Church did not die as a result of the close agreement between the sacred and profane which characterized the period of historic Christianity (when the sacred was illustrated and defended by ordination to the sacred ministry rather than by baptism, by the eucharistic species rather than by worship as a whole), we need not fear its dying from its re-emergence, face to face with the world, as a prophetic, priestly and royal people. It was in the days of historic Christianity that pietism was suspect. In a pre-Christian or post-Christian political situation, "pietism" is for the Church the very condition of its mission to the world; and it is not accidental that the Church of our time should show its new self-awareness as a minority group both by a liturgical and missionary renascence.

(b) The second preliminary remark concerns the public character of the cult. The Later Helvetic Confession here again strikes the true note. In chapter 22, treating of "sacred and ecclesiastic assemblies", it stipulates :"Now it is required that Church assemblies should be public and much frequented, and not clandestine or held in secret: provided that persecution by the enemies of Jesus Christ and His Church presents no obstacle. For we know that formerly assemblies in the primitive Church were held in secret places, under the tyranny of the Roman emperors."[1] There are different points to be noted here:

First of all, it is not its public nature, but its celebration, which makes the cult foreshadow the end and the future of the world. Public celebration is desirable, but it is not that which qualifies or disqualifies it as valid. Besides, the cult as such cannot be public in the full sense of the word without perversion. I mean, on the one hand, that the celebration of the cult is by right a community celebration, to which only the baptized are admitted. In this sense it can be public only if the "public" of a locality are all baptized, and if none of the baptized is excommunicate. Now this is a situation which will become ever more exceptional, the more so because undoubtedly confessional divisions will for many years yet impede all the baptized of any one locality celebrating Christian worship together. On the other hand, for it to become public and so open to all, it would have to be—in our circumstances—not necessarily a communal celebra-

[1] cf. W. Niesel, *op. cit.*, p. 21, 175, etc.

tion, but rather a spectacle which could be attended without direct participation.

Next, we must distinguish between the preaching of the Gospel and the celebration of worship. It is preaching which must seek publicity (Matt. 10: 27), which must become mpatient when political circumstances constrain it to secrecy or veiled language. It is preaching which must enter into an encounter with the world so as to place the world in a position to make a response. The celebration of worship, on the contrary, takes place among those who have professed their belief in the Gospel: communion is confined to the baptized. Traditionally, the part of the cult which is open and public is its homilectic phase, although that was really intended for the baptized and catechumens rather than for believers and unbelievers alike. This seems already to have been the case in apostolic times, since "the outsiders or unbelievers" whom St. Paul mentions as guests of the homilectic phase are so somewhat hypothetically (1 Cor. 14: 23ff.). Hence missionary work is done much more by public preaching than by the celebration of the cult itself.[1]

In short, we wished to recall here the fact that the cult does not need to be public and open to all in order to be a phenomenon which concerns the world. Even when celebrated in secret by two or three, Jesus Christ is present there, and it is this presence in Church worship which imparts to the latter a dimension that makes it of direct concern to the world, for whom it then becomes a threat, but also a promise. It is this point which we must now examine.

2. The cult considered as a threat to the world

(a) *The cult—a challenge to human righteousness.* The Christian cult is a memorial of the body of Christ broken and the blood of Christ shed for the salvation of the world. It is the memorial of the complete fulfilling of what God willed, of the consummation of history. "With the death of Jesus on the cross, all is fulfilled. In this body of Jesus bleeding

[1] When Irenaes insists, to counter the secret traditions of the Gnostics, on the publicity of the traditional teaching in orthodox episcopal seats, he doubtless means not a "worldly" publicity but a publicity within the Church.

and broken, God has attained His end. Basically the course of world history has here reached its goal. This death on the cross with its mighty explosive power shakes the deepest foundations of the history of our world, and the highest summits of supraterrestrial thrones and dominations. By its virtue the whole of history becomes penetrable, so that the judgment day can already break into it" (P. Brunner). Every time the Church assembles to celebrate the cult, to "proclaim the death of Christ" (1 Cor. 11: 26), it proclaims also the end of the world and the failure of the world. It contradicts the world's claim to provide men with a valid justification for their existence, it renounces the world: it affirms, since it is made up of the baptized, that it is only on the other side of death to this world that life can assume its meaning: on the other side of death to this world, that is, in resurrection with Christ. Christian worship is the strongest denial that can be hurled in face of the world's claim to provide men with an effective and sufficient justification of their life. There is no more emphatic protest against the pride and the despair of the world than that implied in Church worship.

By way of example we might refer to the doxologies which resound throughout the cult. They have an eminently polemic implication. When the Church, in its responses, confesses the dominical prayer as its own and says: "for Thine is the kingdom, the power and the glory, for ever and ever . . .", when it proclaims "to the only wise God be glory for evermore through Jesus Christ, Amen" (Rom. 16: 27), when it exclaims: "Worthy art Thou, our Lord and our God, to receive glory and honour and power, for Thou didst create all things, and by Thy will they existed and were created" (Rev. 4: 11), or "Salvation belongs to our God who sits upon the throne and to the Lamb" (Rev. 7: 10),[1] when from very ancient times it ends the singing of the psalms by the antiphonal *Gloria Patri*, as also at the moment of the *credo*, what it does is in some way to repeat the vows of baptism: it is renouncing the devil and his works, the world

---

[1] Cf. also 1 Tim. 1: 17; 6: 16; Jude 25; Rev. 1: 5; 4: 8; 5: 9–10; 5: 12, 13b; 7: 12; 11: 15, 17–18; Luke 2: 10–12; 15: 3b–4; 16: 7; 19: 1–2, etc.

and its pomp, the flesh and its lusts, it is dedicating its life—at whatever cost—to the Father, Son and Holy Ghost, in opposition to the powers that rule this world. To say "glory be to God" is to protest against the powers and the powerful who imagine that they can fulfil the longings of humanity; it is to deny their claim, and to remind them, at the risk of suffering vengeance at their hands, that the days of their pride are ended, that Jesus has stripped them and publicly made of them an example, triumphing over them in the cross (Col. 2: 15).

In this sense, by the mere fact of its celebration, the Christian cult is a basically political action: it reminds the state of the limited and provisional character of its power, and when the state claims for itself an absolute trust and obedience, the Christian cult protests against this pretension to claim a kingdom, a power and a glory which belong of right to God alone. That is why, in gathering together for Christian worship, men compromise themselves politically.

(b) *The cult as a prelude to the Last Judgment.* The cult is in a twofold sense a prelude to the Last Judgment.

It is so first in regard to the world, because, with reference to the world, it is situated as the Kingdom will be situated with reference to the great assize when the eschatological discrimination is made. In this life the cult is the sphere where are gathered together those who have been "transferred into the Kingdom of the Son" (Col. 1: 13), those who have been taken out of the world and gathered into the fold of the Church. In fact, the Christian cult unites those who, by anticipation, have sacramentally undergone the process of the Last Judgment by the very fact of their baptism, by becoming associated with that determinative foreshadowing of the Last Judgment which was the death and resurrection of Christ. The very presence of the Church assembled in the joy of its Lord is thus, for the world, a prelude to the Last Judgment.

But the cult is also such a prelude for those who take part in it, for baptism effected no more than a sacramental transference. Not that it lacks efficacy and reality, but it can still be compromised or even annulled by the indolence

64

of those who are its beneficiaries, their failure to demonstrate its effectiveness in their lives (cf. I Cor. 10: 1–13). For Christians too, man-made righteousness remains a real threat; because if they are holy, they have yet to "become what they are", and the struggle is not made up of victories only. Again, the Christian is still a man of this world and consequently one who is challenged by the celebration of Christian worship. He knows within himself the antagonism and tension which exist between the Church and the world, although it is clear to him that it is the new man in Christ who will win the day. For those who take part in it, the cult forms a prelude to the Last Judgment in two ways; firstly, by its component elements, and, secondly, by its structure.

Of the elements of the cult, I will for the sake of brevity enumerate only preaching, the Lord's Supper, and the prayers.[1] Preaching—and also parochial preaching—is an eschatological event by which God intervenes to challenge men point-blank, to call them to renounce themselves (or to confirm their self-renunciation) and to entrust their life to the One alone who can deliver them from perdition, to Jesus Christ. It is in truth—as is observed by J. Bengel in commenting on I Pet. 3: 19—a *praeludium iudicii universalis*. "In the midst of the community assembled to hear the apostolic word of the Gospel, questions of eternal life or eternal death are in the balance" (P. Brunner). Contrary to what, alas! is often thought, something really takes place for men in the act of preaching. Something happens to them. Preaching is an event, which in fact can be compared to the event in exorcism: demons are cast out, what belongs to God is restored to Him, as at the last judgment He will take back to Himself for ever those who finally escape the snares of the devil.

The Eucharist also is an eschatological event, a prefiguration of the future. In this connexion we should bear in mind the parables of the great feast, or the wedding parables, which show that it is through judgment that man gains access to the table of the Lord. This means that the invitation

---

[1] We have just been speaking of doxology and of the *credo*. I leave out of account baptism, because it is not a regular element in parish worship.

to the Lord's Supper makes a fundamental challenge to man's being. And, further, the approach to communion in itself is not a guarantee of salvation as is shown by the participation of Judas Iscariot in the ceremony of the institution of the Supper, or, in the parable, by the expulsion of the guest who was without the wedding garment (Matt. 22: 11ff.). That is why, on the threshold of the Supper, the communicants are warned: "If any one has no love for the Lord, let him be accursed" (1 Cor. 16: 22; Didache 10: 6; cf. 1 Cor. 11: 28ff.). If it is indisputable that the eucharistic feast is that PHARMAKON ATHANASIAS of which Ignatius of Antioch spoke (Eph. 20: 2), this remedy functions in no automatic or magical manner: it is a promise on which the communicant can count in faith, but to one who does not see it as an act of trust it becomes an eating and drinking to condemnation: in the Lord's Supper too the eternal destiny of men is at issue.

Finally let us mention the prayer which makes the cult a prelude to the Last Judgment. The liturgical prayer is deeply eschatological: it invokes the end of the world and hence it threatens the present order and not only, directly, Christians who are still living in it (as do parochial preaching and the Lord's Supper), but the world as a whole. "Hallowed be Thy name, Thy kingdom come, Thy will be done, on earth as in heaven"! Or again: ELTHETO CHARIS KAI PAREL-THETO HO KOSMOS HOUTOS.[1] In praying thus, Christians certainly express their hope, but they also invoke the Judge and ask to be judged: each time that the Lord's prayer is recited, we run the risk that the answering of the prayer will strike us in a very mortifying way.

But the cult looks towards the Last Judgment not only in its main elements but also in its traditional structure, because it includes—as does what is known of the end of the world—two moments: one in which the Word calls for a decision and effects a discrimination, and a moment when, on the further side of that discrimination, the faithful are welcomed to the joy of the Messianic feast. This division will

---

[1] Didache 10: 6. The eucharistic prayers of the Didache are very typical of this prefigurative character, foreshadowing judgment, intrinsic to the Christian cult.

later be described as the mass of the catechumens and the mass of the faithful.

Even though, in the course of centuries, the formula of dismissal at the end of the first part has been attenuated from an anathema to a benediction, the very fact that there has been maintained (in the East, up to the present day) an exclusion of the non-baptized and the excommunicate at the moment when the eucharistic celebration was about to begin, is the sign that the cult forms a prelude to the Last Judgment, that it suggests the latter and foreshadows its unfolding, that it indicates that salvation is intimated by permission to remain for the second part of the cult, although it must not be taken for granted that such permission is an automatic fact.

Thus, by its very structure and presentation, the cult is a threat to those who refuse to die and rise again with Christ, or to those who refuse to confirm by their life the grace of their baptism. It shows that salvation is not a matter of course but is to be reached only after conversion.

(c) *The Christian cult as a protest against non-Christian cults.* Finally, the Christian cult is a threat to the world because it unmasks the vanity and the perversion of those things in which the world seeks its most inward justification; the vanity and the perversion of the cults invented by the world. We shall see that Christian worship suggests not only a judgment on, but also a forgiveness of non-Christian forms of worship; we must, however, begin by saying that it constitutes their judgment. There is no transition, no ladder reaching from the one to the other. There is a gulf, and it is precisely this gulf which requires the maintenance of a distinction between the sacred and the profane: "Do not be mismated with unbelievers. For what partnership have righteousness and iniquity? Or what fellowship has light with darkness? What accord has Christ with Belial? Or what has a believer in common with an unbeliever? What agreement has the temple of God with idols? For we are the temple of the living God; as God said: "I will live in them and move among them, and I will be their God, and they shall be my people. Therefore come out from them, and be separate from them, says the Lord, and touch nothing unclean; then I will welcome you, and I will be a father to you, and you shall be my sons and daughters, says the Lord Almighty" (2 Cor. 6: 14–18).

Thus it is not possible to have access to the Christian cult except by conversion, which is not a quickening of the natural manner of life, but a rupture, a death, a renunciation. This does not mean to say that the Christian cult has no relation with pagan cults. But the relation is one which separates truth from falsehood. "The lie exists only in relation to the truth. The lie is the murdered reality of the truth . . ." (P. Brunner), but the lie must be unmasked and swept away. It is not a preliminary, provisional, preparatory truth; it is the contrary of the truth. And that is why the Christian cult by its celebration protests against what, in the world, is deeper, more mysterious and determinative, namely, the pagan cult.[1] The celebration of the Christian cult in this world is a provocation to all non-Christian cults, and implies consequently a proclamation of the Lordship of Christ and of the overthrow of Satan. We must not imagine that it is only the missionary preaching of the Gospel which repulses the pretensions of Satan. The celebration of the cult has the same effect in the world of dominions and authorities. As Ignatius of Antioch wrote to the Ephesians: "and when you often assemble together, the powers of Satan are overthrown and his ruinous work undone by the harmony of your faith. Nothing is better than the peace wherein all the warring of celestial and terrestrial powers (against us) is brought to nought" (Eph. 13: 1ff.).

3. The cult as a promise for the world

Jesus Christ is not only the end of our world: He is also the One in whom the world, if it consents to renounce itself, its own self-righteousness and self-justification, regains its true destiny: "Jesus Christ is our hope", said St. Paul (1 Tim. 1: 1; cf. Col. 1: 27). He is not only the One who condemns and causes to die, He is also the One who forgives

---

[1] Conversely, we see the importance of the cult as a milieu determinative of the whole of human life when we recollect the totalitarian repercussions of a perverted cult: see Rom. 1: 24–32.

and makes alive. If in the preceding section it was necessary to evoke Good Friday, here it is the paschal mystery which we must recall. Systematically and briefly, we wish to do so by showing that the Church in its worship is doing what the world can no longer, or cannot yet, do; that the Christian cult constitutes for the world a promise; and that it becomes, by this fact, the pardon and the fulfilling of non-Christian cults.

(a) *The vicarious character of the cult.* Let us begin by a deep and true affirmation made by Otto Haendler: "the cult, celebrated *hic et nunc* in a specific way by the Christian Church, is the concrete and vicarious (or substitutionary) expression of the deep meaning and the essential attitude of the whole cosmos, which is, the expression of uninterrupted adoration of the living God by the whole of creation". The divine purpose in creation was that man should lead the entire universe in offering to the Creator a worship in which all creation would find its true fulfilment and know real peace (Gen. 1: 1 to 2: 4). God's intention was basically a liturgical intention. But man by his sin has led the world astray, deflecting it from its true destiny, and reducing to sighs of anguish the adoration which ought to be its life. This confusion of the world has been refuted and contested by God and what He has done in history by pursuing within it a saving process: beginning with that prefiguration of the end of the world suggested by the Flood or the destruction of the Egyptian armies at the Red Sea, ending with the victory of Easter and the outpouring of the Holy Spirit, and passing through all the stages, progressive or regressive, of the elect people up to that culminating and determinative point, the incarnation of God the Son in Jesus of Nazareth. And in this regard it is suggestive that Jesus not only restores peace to men, but also to things: the wild beasts grow tame (Mark 1: 13), the birds of heaven are brought within the scope of God's providence (Matt. 10: 29), the lilies of the field in their natural doxology far surpass that which Solomon could only feebly stammer (Matt. 6: 28), the storm is stilled (Matt. 8: 23f.) and the waters become a pathway for those on foot (Matt. 14: 22ff.), the bread and the wine are for ever sufficient (Matt. 14: 13ff.; 15: 29ff.; John 2: 1ff.), while the treasures of the nations are lavished at His feet (Matt. 2: 11). All these facts attest that "if Jesus Christ is our hope" (1 Tim. 1: 1) He is also the hope of the whole creation.

But this re-orientation of men and things by Jesus Christ is as yet only very partial; it is not yet manifest since it is hidden in the Christian cult. But there it is to be found. Thus the cult is the moment and the place where on this earth men and the world rediscover their original and their ultimate destiny, which is to glorify God. The cult is thus the sphere where men and the world can become once more and actually be what they are intended to be. Only—and this especially must be underlined here—the cult is not that moment and that place for its own sake, it is so for the sake of the world, it is so by substitution for the world: it renders what all humanity and all creation ought to render, and it is what all humanity and all creation ought to be. This is what is meant by speaking of the vicarious character of the cult: it substitutes itself for the world because in Jesus Christ it can accomplish a work which the world can no longer or cannot yet accomplish. That is why the Church owes its cult not only to God but also to the world, to show the latter the past which it ought never to have lost and the future which is promised to it. The absence of the cult would decisively impoverish the world.

Without going into details, I would like to add two further remarks: The first is that we are here at the very heart of what scripture means by the HIERATEUMA HAGION— the holy priestly ministry exercised by the people of God. This is usually called, incorrectly, "the universal priesthood". This doctrine—so deeply connected with that of election— formulated by the OT (Exod. 19: 6) and quoted several times by the NT (1 Pet. 2: 5 and 9; Rev. 1: 6; 5: 10) is a doctrine which explains, in terms of a mediatorial priesthood, the mission, place and ministry of the Church in the world. This has nothing to do with the problem of Church ministries (as if "universal priesthood" meant the priesthood of every-one). It is easy to forget that what is here in question is a doctrine of election elaborated in the OT. Now this royal priestly ministry exercised by the people of God is exercised quite specifically in the cult which thus assumes, on behalf of the world and through the Church which gathers together to practise it, a mediatorial significance.

The second observation is of a more pastoral character: when the Church celebrates the cult it is not withdrawing, decrepit and frail, into a cultural past now grown musty and anxiously cherished only by a few old women and cranks. When the Church celebrates the cult, it is, on the contrary, turning towards the future of the world, it is hastening towards that future and is already enjoying as much of it as can be enjoyed in this earthly life. It is fulfilling its purpose as the APARCHE KTISMATON, the first fruits of the creatures (Jas. 1: 18).

The future of humanity is most truly symbolized for us, not by the event of Hiroshima, but by the worship of the Church. "Seen from the standpoint of the end, the glorification of God which begins here on earth in the life of worship practised by the Christian Church is the decisive event which is in the abiding purpose of God: it is the process already marked by an eschatological validity, a process through which the lasting, unshakable eternal Kingdom of God breaks through into this transient world" (P. Brunner).

(b) *The cult as the expression of the mystery of creation.* I have felt somewhat hesitant about this rather flamboyant subtitle, but, all things considered, I think that this is what must be said of Christian worship: in this world, perverted and disorientated as it is by the sin of man, the worship of the Christian Church, based on and flowing from the reconciliation effected by the death of Christ, is the sphere where the mystery of creation, that is, the mystery of man and the mystery of things, finds the most authentic expression it can attain before the manifestation of the Kingdom. That is why worship—and by worship I mean that Christian worship which proclaims the reconciliation of the world by the cross of Christ, and makes of it a eucharistic anamnesis permitting men to feed on the flesh of the Son of God "offered for the life of the world" (John 6: 51)[1]—is the locus at which the

[1] It is extraordinary to see to what an extent ch. 6 of St. John's Gospel gives to Christ's sacrifice and its eucharistic anamnesis a

whole world is reorientated, and finds afresh its true meaning, becoming itself once again.

That is why the Church's worship is the centre on which is focused and whence radiates not only social life, law, medicine and the public service, but also the discovery, the exploitation and the expression of the world, that is to say, science, industry, and art. Here is actualized what is the first and last and eternal meaning of the created order: to receive the glory of God so that it may fall on and be reflected by His creation, and shine and fill the whole world, in order that God may be all in all. The cult is thus the sphere where —certainly in a broken, sporadic and ambiguous way but none the less truly—there begins that eschatological metamorphosis of which the apostle speaks when he says that "we all with unveiled face, beholding the glory of the Lord, are being changed into His likeness from one degree of glory to another; for this comes from the Lord who is the Spirit" (2 Cor. 3: 18).

This mystery of creation is expressed in worship, in the first place, on behalf of those creatures called men. It is there they become fully themselves, because there they re-emerge before God in the freedom which flows from divine forgiveness. It is there that they find their true being once more because there they rediscover their true destiny and vocation (this is why it is so important, as we shall see in more detail when speaking of the participants in worship, to diversify the liturgical ministries and reject a monopolization of celebration by the pastor alone). As K. Barth (*Dogmatics*) observes: ". . . in the cult, and nowhere else in so direct a manner—the Church's task of provisionally representing the sanctification of humanity in Jesus Christ becomes a really serious concern". Provisionally, because the Kingdom is not yet manifested.

But if it is first and foremost men who rediscover their true life in worship, they also discover their solidarity with the whole of creation, which also finds in the Christian cult the most authentic expression of itself that there can possibly

central implication for the whole life of the world! Cf. too the dimensions which the Eucharist assumes in Justin, *Dialogue to Tryphon*, ch. 41.

be in this world. And that is why the things of this world seek admission to the sphere of Christian worship, that they may there express the truth that the whole earth is full of the glory of God (Is. 6: 3), that they may find there the means of celebrating their own worship. Because man has been guilty of resigning his position as leader and priest of the world, a resignation told of in the story of the Fall, the song of the world is now perceptible only as a sigh. But in the cult, because there man has found again in Christ—the KEPHALE of the cosmos—his original function and ultimate end, the sighs and groans of creation can be transformed into singing.

To refuse to open the doors of the Christian cult to the world is not to love the world, not to pity it; it is to despise it on the basis of a Marcionite dualism, to doubt the sanctifying power of the Word of God and of prayer, the possibility of transforming all creation into a song of thanksgiving (1 Tim. 4: 4) if we forbid the forms, the colours, the accents, the rhythms of the world, to have any contact with the sphere of Christian worship. This point is fundamental: it is not man who is invited, in a more or less disguised pantheism, to join in the song of creation, but it is non-human creation which claims its right to worship by joining in that of a regenerated humanity, by making its worship compatible with the latter's. The very common idea that it is nature which is the true priest and worshipper and so the priest of humanity—and therefore the idea that man, to join in true worship, must walk in the forests and on the snow-covered mountains—is altogether false: it is man who is the priestly servant of the world and it is man's worship of God in which nature seeks to join.

The cult as the expression of the mystery of creation! We noted above that the cult is for the world, and because it challenges the world, a prelude to the Last Judgment. Here it must be said that Christian worship implies also for the world a prelude to eternal life. For the world it is not merely a threat, it is also a promise. Not indeed by a trick of dialectics, but because of what happened in that heart of the mystery of things which is the death and resurrection of Christ, because there it was manifested that God did not wish to destroy what

73

He condemns, but to save it, and further, that He has saved it.

(c) *The Christian cult as the pardon and the fulfilment of non-Christian cults.* In the corresponding paragraph of the preceding section we have noted how the Christian cult forms a vigorous protest against non-Christian cults, that there is the same incompatibility between them as there is between truth and the falsehood, that is, that the one must be given up if we are to enter the other. Here we are to forget nothing of what we said then. But at the same time we must remember that the protest of the Christian faith against the world, its condemnation of the world, is one of its missionary aspects: the Church does not condemn for the sake of condemning, it does not renounce for the sake of renouncing; it condemns and renounces in order to reveal and to make an appeal. To reveal the object of what it condemns, of what it renounces, to make clear that the world as such, withdrawn into its own self-centred rightness, has no other future but perdition; but also to appeal to the world to find anew its life in a rightness and a fulness of life beyond itself, in the Church which is the guarantee of its future.

That is why the Christian cult is not merely a radical protest against non-Christian cults: it is also a promise addressed to them, a promise of which they cannot avail themselves except through self-renunciation, except along the way of mortification and self-renewal which baptism implies. Baptism kills; but it also makes alive, and the things which it makes alive are those which it has killed. In baptism there is no more loss of identity as between the slain and the resuscitated than there was between the Crucified of Good Friday and the Risen One of Easter Day; it was Jesus indeed who was raised.

Similarly, when a nation welcomes the Gospel and begins to respond to it by conversion and self-consecration (this normally happens through a minority group, which becomes a sanctifying power permeating the whole nation), it is this particular nation and not any other which makes the response. Thus it has the right, and not only the right but the duty, to respond to the Gospel in its own way, according to its own special genius, and on the basis of its own culture, that which gives it its own "look" and means of identification, and consequently, on the basis of the response and the religious art which were characteristic of it before it renounced them to give itself to Christ. It is because of this identity, preserved through baptismal death and resurrection, or rather condemned by that death but justified by that resurrection, that on the basis of the same dogmas there can be various dogmatic structures; on the basis of the same institutions, varying ecclesiastical systems; on the basis of the same means of grace, diverse liturgies. It is in this that is rooted and justified that legitimate diversity of Christian cults of which we must speak later.

For the sake of brevity, let us end by the following three considerations.

The Christian cult implies firstly the pardon of non-Christian cults. In forgiving them, it excludes them. For forgiveness does not justify but eliminates sin. This means that once a nation has become Christian, it must completely give up the celebration of previous pagan cults. Although Jesus Christ—since His triumph over them by the cross—holds in check the demons who have perverted the original cult to their own advantage—whether to assure their own glory or to obtain by this means control over mankind—these demons, powerless as they are, are not yet dead. To play with them, to make folk-lorist obeisances to them (as in the Carnival), to restore some of their lost prestige by taking them as mythological types symbolizing the life of men (as in the Festival of the Vinedressers), is to play too risky a game: not only because of the virulence of these demons, but because such manifestations arouse a longing for the time of "Egyptian servitude" when surrender to Christ had not yet been made. It is not by chance that scripture likens the lapse into these cults to an act of adultery, and here again we must remember that some kinds of adultery can be consummated simply by a glance.

But the Christian cult is also the fulfilment of non-Christian cults. The latter have therefore nothing to lose by self-renunciation, by consenting to die in Christ. What they have perverted will be reborn, will arise again in a purified state and their deep purpose, their appeal, their

75

readiness to give themselves, their summons to the materials of the world that the latter might be made to serve art and culture—all that, cleansed, reborn, redirected, will be restored to them. With due reserve—for the Israelite cult is the only one which had not been perverted, which truly constituted a first stage and a transition towards the real cult, and yet, it too had to renounce itself—one might say that the Christian cult fulfils the pagan cults just as it fulfilled the OT dispensation: there is still a line of demarcation between what has already and what has not yet conconsented to election, but it is baptism, not circumcision, which marks it now: there is still a meal marking membership of the covenant, but it is no longer the Passover, it is the Eucharist; there is still, on earth, a place where the Lord is present, but it is no longer the temple at Jerusalem, but the Body of Christ; there is still a guide for the people of God pursuing its pilgrimage, through history, but it is no longer the Law, it is the Holy Spirit; etc. Once again, for pagan cults, the fulfilment is much less direct: it is secondary, whereas for Israel it is primary; but, since Christ is the Recapitulator of all things, He is also the One in whom the forgiven pagans, with all that they have and are, find their peace.

To conclude, it must be said that this fulfilment of pagan cults in and through the Christian cult remains an enterprise full of risk so long as the demons which raised up and surrounded these cults are as yet no more than dethroned. It is in the Kingdom that there will no longer be any danger in welcoming the nations and their glory (Rev. 21: 24). So long as this world lasts, the presence, even the pardoned presence, of these cults can be a snare and a temptation (we might think of the temptations of the Israelites to assume fully possession of the Land which the Lord God had allotted to them). And that is why, in certain moments of weakness, just in those moments when it would like to give them more room because of a hidden liking, or a cooling of its love for Christ, the Church must be free to remind them, by its severity and exclusiveness, of the Last Judgment rather than of the Kingdom. But there may also be moments when, were it only out of concern for the sighings of creation, the

Church has the right and the duty to forgive these cults and to permit them, through that forgiveness, to contribute to the fulness of adoration of the Father, Son and Holy Ghost, and thus to share a foretaste of the Kingdom.

4. Cult and evangelization

It might be asked whether what we have been pointing out so far—and what we have still to point out—does not reveal a profound ignorance of the situation in which the Church finds itself today i.e. an essentially missionary situation. Does not such a situation require the Church to abandon liturgical forms, cherished perhaps or wished for, so that it may appeal to the world with more forceful directness?

(a) To put this question, in my opinion, suggests not merely the awareness of evident uneasiness, but especially a deep misunderstanding as to the aim and purpose of the cult. For to whom is the cult addressed? to God or to the world? Evidently if the cult were addressed to the world, then indisputably it would have to be adapted to the world's capacity of understanding. But the cult is addressed to God, and that is something—we must recognize it, alas!—which we have been apt to forget, as a result of the overemphasis on sermons, and the underemphasis on the sacraments, which has characterized the form of worship traditional in our confession. We have thus forgotten that the Church has a twofold orientation: towards the world in the movement we have called the diastole, and towards God in that of the systole; and it is a deep liturgical mistake which P. Brunner, in a somewhat different context, goes so far as to call a "heresy", to try to confuse these two orientations as it would also be to try to separate them so as to occupy a position exclusively related to God or to the world. The Church, the Body of Christ, the sacerdotal people, fulfils in the world a mediatorial function. That is why worship must not be confused with evangelization or with service, and why, in consequence, any ulterior motives of evangelism have nothing directly to do with the celebration of worship. Let the Church seek—and today more so than ever—to reach contemporary man, to go out to meet him, to go with him two miles rather than one: that is essential. But it is not through the cult that it must try to do this. The cult is something quite different: it is the sphere where finally, step by step, the Church will bring together in adoration, praise and thanksgiving those whom it has reached by evangelization. The Church's worship is not the worship of men in general: as long as this world lasts, it will be the cult of the baptized; that is to say, of those whom the Gospel has reached, converting them, turning them to God and gathering them into the Church whence they will be able both to confront the world and to encounter God.

(b) It will, of course, be objected that the worship of the Church is not without a deep and vital link with evangelism, since in the cult not only are the faithful offered the sign of their salvation in the Holy Communion, but are also addressed in the proclamation of the Word of God, read and preached. Even if it is the act of the baptized, Church worship has an evangelistic aspect which we do not propose to call in question; it is the aspect which appears in the first part of the service called the Mass of the catechumens, which is not, however, merely for them, but is that part in which the catechumens (in the sense understood by the ancient Church, i.e. those who are preparing for baptism) worship together with the faithful, who also, ever afresh, because of their very presence in the world as strangers and pilgrims, need to be brought together and led back again and again to the cult in the real sense.

If the Roman Church does not require of its faithful that they should participate in the Mass of the catechumens, and if therefore it thinks that their presence at the moment of the elevation of the Host is sufficient to mark their Christian obedience, not only is it dealing a terrible blow to liturgical preaching which thus loses its force because it loses its necessity, but it is once more forgetting that the Church—even in its worship—is not yet the Kingdom, and that even the most dedicated Christian has constantly to struggle against the world, which tries to cast him back into the pre-baptismal stage among those who have everything to learn.

However, even if the cult may have a phase in which evangelism is a conscious concern, even there it is not this concern which is primary; in the cult the primary concern throughout is to enable the Church to find its orientation towards God and to live it out. That is why, not in its worship, but alongside it, the Church has an absolute obligation to pursue an evangelistic effort in which it goes out to seek men and bring them back to the Lord, that they may live in His joy. If living in the Christian period has made us largely forget the duty of evangelization, or if it has located evangelization chiefly in the cult, the end of the Christian period must not lead us into the opposite error of forgetting the necessity of the cult for its own sake.

(c) Moreover we must not dispute the fact that the cult in itself, without any direct evangelistic concern, and by the mere fact of its celebration, and because it is a power radiating joy, peace, freedom, order and love, becomes an evangelizing force, and hence something which impinges on the surrounding world. Not that the celebration of the cult is sufficient to evangelize the world, not that we should try to justify the cult by reference to this secondary evangelistic intention, when what does justify the cult is simply the fact that God ordains it, makes it possible, approves it. As K. Barth so justly observes: "The Church's worship is the *opus Dei*, the work of God, which is carried out for its own sake. Is it not salutary and consoling to the poor pragmatic man of today to learn that here there is something which certainly does have its pragmatic side, but which cannot be justified for pragmatic reasons, which has its primary justification in the fact that it is so commanded us. And this thing is Church worship." While we must not give up evangelistic effort because of the evangelizing power which the cult has over and above its main concern, we must not either deny that the mere celebration of worship provides a sign which is for the world a challenge and a promise. Thus it has a power of evangelization which is often hardly guessed at. That is why it is so important that the Christian cult should be celebrated with a maximum of theological urgency and of spiritual fervour.

CHAPTER FOUR

THE APPROACH TO FORMS

WE HAVE seen that Christian worship is a recapitulation of
the saving process, that it is an epiphany of the Church, and
that it bears witness both to the end and the future of the
world. The question which we must try to answer in this
fourth chapter is whether the cult can realize all this according to its own interpretation, somewhat haphazardly, or
whether it must, to do so, not only assume shape, but a
certain shape. We shall speak in turn of the necessity and
the limitations of liturgical forms, then of the different
spheres in which liturgical expression has scope and, thirdly,
of discipline and liberty in liturgical formulation. In addition,
we shall note incidentally what one might call the reward
of liturgical formulation, that is the relation between worship
and culture.

1. Necessity and limitations of liturgical forms

If Christian worship recapitulates the history of salvation,
it bears witness that Jesus Christ has reached and has saved
the world, that there has been the event of the Nativity—
and following the Passion and Resurrection—that there has
been the event of the Ascension. In short, all is said in this.
We must, however, explain and amplify it.

(a) We must first speak briefly of the *necessity of liturgical
forms*. If we were to say that the cult needs forms only
because it brings together a group of men, and that there is
no communal life without form, and if we thus proposed to
justify liturgical forms by sociological considerations, we
should be falling far short of what needs to be said, firstly
because in this case we should have to consider forms as a

necessary evil, secondly because, to judge the forms of the cult, we should have no other criterion but that of the best adaptation to liturgical needs: in short, forms would be optional and would not have resulted from obedience.

Now, this is not the case. In worship, the problem of forms is a fundamental problem, since the cult is a recapitulation of the saving process and, since that process culminates in the incarnation. Before being a movement which rises, Christianity is a movement which descends in order to enter, permeate and take shape in the world, and it is only afterwards, after the embodiment has been assumed, that in and with such embodiment the direction is reversed and it reascends. It is the same movement that we have noted in speaking of the diastole and systole; and the movement of Incarnation and of the assumption of the Incarnate basically shows that God does not wish to save souls only but men and the world. "He who has heard the message of the incarnation of the Word", says Asmussen, "can never again attempt to apprehend what is Christian in what is shapeless" and rebellious to form. Thus if liturgical form is necessary, it is because that reflects the process of incarnation.[1]

Now the incarnation, like the Incarnate, is a disputed sign, a SEMEION ANTILEGOMENON (Luke 2: 34). It is an offence because it contradicts all man's natural thoughts and imaginations about God, spiritual as well as materialist. If forms are necessary, it is because God showed us at Christmas that He did not wish to stand aloof from the world and men, that on the contrary He wished to save them. And to save them, He has Himself taken a form, He has hidden Himself among us by becoming visible, audible and tangible in the form of a man. This must be grasped in order to realize that if liturgical form is necessary, and reflects the incarnation, that form will always be offensive. Those who have no faith, it will not enable to see what the Church is seeking to express, while those who have faith, it will constrain to continue trustful in faith, to pray rather

---

[1] May we say that the Church shapes its cult as the Virgin Mary brought Jesus to birth? We shall try to answer this question in the chapter on the elements of the cult, in which we examine their structure.

than to expect to see as they will see when the Kingdom comes.

But the incarnation is not just an offence: it is also an appeal addressed to all whom it reaches, that they will rediscover in and through it a hope and a future. Contrary to what has been so often said when people wish to excuse themselves for not being spiritual, God was not made man because that was for Him the least derogatory way of coming to visit us and the most appropriate to our earth-bound condition. (Docetism would have been much more adapted to our dreams and our desires, and to our sin-laden state, than the Christmas message.) He was incarnate in order to take back to Himself, to heal His creation and His creatures, to show His solidarity with the world and His love for the world, and to summon the world to find again its true orientation. Hence we may say that if forms are necessary, it is because at the Ascension God showed us that the world and men, His creation, had no need to renounce their carnal state in order to appear before Him; what they must renounce was their sin. To forsake or distrust liturgical forms is, then, to contest the very heart of the Christian faith: the visit of the Lord in Jesus of Nazareth and the salvation of the world by His cross, resurrection and ascension.

(b) But we must now add a few remarks about the limitations of liturgical forms. We have seen that, because of the incarnation, forms are not only legitimate, but necessary. "Thus the choice is never between forms and no forms, but always between good forms and bad forms" (W. D. Maxwell). But what are bad forms? Those which lack taste, style, coherence, intelligibility? Certainly these are included, since nothing is more beautiful than truth. But here this aesthetic criterion is not really appropriate. It is to a theological criterion that we must have recourse if we are to know within what limits liturgical formulation remains Christian, hence legitimate and necessary. There are here two rules which must govern our choice: the first more objective, the second more existential.

Firstly, liturgical forms are limited by the second commandment: "You shall not make yourself a graven image . . .

82

nor bow down before it" (Exod. 20: 4).[1] This does not primarily and essentially mean that Christian worship must be radically removed from the worship of pagan gods—this may be taken for granted, at least it should be a matter of course, for it is the requirement of the first commandment— but it means rather that liturgical formulation must coincide with the limit of revelation itself. In fact what is forbidden by the second commandment is not the making of idols representing other gods, but the attempt to imagine the one true God instead of trusting to the image which He Himself gives of Himself. It is the desire to replace His revelation by human imagination. This does not mean that God is beyond all imagination: the prohibition of images is not a philosophical statement about the mode of the divine being (that is, that He should be understood as transcendent and spiritual); it intends to declare how He reveals Himself, and that He reveals Himself otherwise than through the images that men are pleased to make of Him. He reveals Himself— under the New Covenant, we may now say—in the image which He has given us of Himself in Jesus Christ (2 Cor. 4: 4; Col. 1: 15). Thus we see that what limits liturgical forms is also what makes them necessary: the incarnation of the eternal Son of God. To be authentic and legitimate, liturgical form must therefore correspond to what God has taught about Himself, His love and His appeal (as K. Barth would say about His exhortation and His claim) by sending His Son into the world and raising Him to the right hand of power after His struggle and victory. And it must be said that this restriction is no less binding for dogmatic, homi- lectic, and logical formulation than for visual forms. Given that the second commandment does not presuppose that God is unimaginable—which moreover would contradict scripture as a whole—*a priori* one does not run a less risk of infringing it in speech than in gestures or symbols.

Next, liturgical forms are limited by their inherent justi- fication; they cease to be valid as soon as they seek their

[1] Again, this commandment is not a divine rejection of liturgical formulation. Think of the precision with which God Himself gives exact instructions about the form of worship when He ordains worship in the sanctuary (Exod., Lev.) (or think of the serpent of brass).

meaning and their justification in themselves, as soon as they are no longer content to be an echo of the offence and the appeal of the incarnation and seek to become a continued incarnation, to be in themselves salvation rather than a means of transmitting a salvation accomplished once for all. That is to say, that the forms of the cult, important as they are, have neither value nor the meaning, neither the canonicity nor the bearing of the form which God took once for all in coming to dwell among us. They exceed their due limit as soon as they claim to have saving efficacy in themselves, as soon as they are placed not on the level which is appropriate to them, that of the *necessitas praecepti*, but on the level which is that of Christ, the *necessitas medii*. "The shape and the form of the Christian cult cannot possibly have the significance of the form taken by Jesus Christ. All that takes place in Christian worship refers to something other than itself, it refers to the Christ who has come in the flesh" (H. Asmussen). Thus then, both for the necessity and the limitations of Christian liturgical forms, we are driven back to Jesus Christ.

(c) Restricted as it is by the second commandment, liturgical form is necessary because it is God's will not only to take back His creation into Himself, but also to transform creation. One might say that it is necessary not merely because of the first but because of the second creation. In fact the Holy Spirit who makes all things new, transforming whatever He touches (2 Cor. 3: 18; Rom. 12: 2), is not the instigator of chaos. He is the Spirit of peace (1 Cor. 14: 32f.) and order (1 Cor. 14: 40). As P. Brunner admirably says: "When the powers of the world to come irrupt into this transitory life, the point of impact does not become a place of chaos and dissolution, but there takes place rather a new birth, a new creation, a new building-up, the incorporation of a new form . . . The characteristic work of the Spirit lies in eschatological metamorphosis, the re-creation of our whole corporeal existence, as was done for Jesus Christ at His resurrection. The Spirit who works in the Church is the Spirit who raised Jesus from the dead (Rom. 8: 11). Now this Spirit never by His work gives birth to a shapeless spirituality; rather His re-creative power aims at bringing to birth a pneumatic corporeality." And it is this pneumatic corporeality which seeks and must find expression in the Christian cult.

Thus we see that the approach to forms is indispensable to Christian worship because this celebrates the Holy Trinity: the Father Creator who wills to bring back to Himself His creation, the Redeemer Son who fixes, limits and justifies liturgical formulation, and the sanctifying Holy Spirit who wills to transform the creation redeemed by Christ, bringing it from glory to glory until it becomes a new creation.

(d) Before enumerating the various domains in which the formulation of liturgical expression finds scope, it may be worth while to add a brief remark on the theological importance of form, not merely as regards liturgy but in dogmatics, ecclesiology, church law, etc. Why form? It is there to express and protect that which at the same time it supports and encloses. Thus dogma is both the expression and protection of truth. Thus the structure of the Church both expresses and safeguards the nature of the Church. Thus also the formulated liturgy is the expression and protection of the nature of Christian worship: it must convey the truth that the cult is a recapitulation of the saving process, the epiphany of the Church, and the end and the future of the world; but it must also protect the saving process so that it can become truly operative: it must protect the Church against possible deviations and temptations, so that it preserves its character as pure as possible: it must protect the limit imposed on the world by the cult, so that, for the world, it loses neither the severity of its judgment nor the allurement of its promise.

What we note here leads us to understand that liturgical formulation, because it must express as well as protect the nature of the cult, enjoys considerable freedom but has also precise norms which it may not transgress without compromising the nature of the cult. Here, too, we see how false it is to think that the forms of worship are, as people say with contempt, "only questions of form". Certainly many formal liturgical questions are but "questions of form" and do not involve a judgment on the faithfulness of the Church. But it is clear too that in such matters of form the faithfulness of the Church is at stake and much more often than is usually thought in our Church.

2. *The domains of liturgical expression*

The question to be examined here is as follows: in Christian worship God wishes to give Himself to us and to receive us. What spheres does God open up for the realization of this encounter? By what senses does He will to communicate with us in order to give us salvation, and from what spheres of human sensibility does He await, in response, our thanksgiving for what He has done for us in Jesus Christ?

To answer this question, the simplest thing is to consider the transformations which Christ effected in men, as described for us in the Gospels: Jesus opens the mind of those who are slow to understand (Luke 24: 25–27; 24: 45, cf. John 12: 16, etc.), He opens the ears of the deaf, the mouth of the dumb, the eyes of the blind; He also loosens the rigid limbs of the paralytics, and exercises His messianic ministry by touching men and allowing Himself to be touched by them.[1] This list of aspects of human life which are being touched by salvation is at the same time a list of the domains in which worship finds expression. All these domains have not the same importance: a paralysed or a blind man can with less difficulty worship God than can a deaf or a dumb man or a man incapable of understanding. None the less, just as man would be impoverished if salvation did not affect his whole being, so the cult would be impoverished if it did not offer the whole man grace to express himself liturgically. Again, a blind, a deaf, a dumb, or a one-armed person can live, whereas a beheaded person cannot live. But, once more, the healing miracles recorded in the Gospels afford a promise that vast areas are open for Christian worship which we have no right to exclude from it, since the Gospels show that such areas of human life are also capable of sanctification.

[1] Cf. Matt. 9: 18; 19: 15 par.; Luke 4: 40; Matt. 8: 15; 9: 29; 20: 34; Mark 7: 33; 10: 13; Luke 7: 14; Matt. 9: 20ff. par.; 14: 36 par.; Mark 3: 10; Luke 6:19; 7: 39; 24: 39; John 20: 17; 27; 1 John 1: 1; etc.

The spheres of liturgical expression commanded or permitted, can, I think, be reduced to four chief ones: the logical, the acoustic, the visual and the kinetic.

(a) The *logical* domain is that of verbal expression which renders things intellectually comprehensible. It is the effort which gives to the vowels, by means of consonants, a structure and order which changes them from cries into words: then the effort of grasping the exact meaning of terms and their grammatical and syntactical connexion; then that of memorizing or fixing the preceding efforts and so of introducing logical formulation into a transmitted tradition, which is enriched or impoverished, which receives accretions or is cleansed, etc. This might be called "logolalia" —the speaking in words. This "logolalia" is essential not only for the proclamation of the Word of God (reading, preaching, absolution, benediction, etc.), but indispensable also for prayers, hymns, canticles, confessions, etc., for the understanding of the deep meaning of that encounter between God and the Church which is what worship is.[1] A mode of worship in which "logolalia" is changed into cries might possibly allow one to surmise something of what is being celebrated (one may think of the very expressive vociferations of Charlie Chaplin in *The Great Dictator*, or of certain South American melodies), but a vehicle would be lacking, or rather there would be lacking a means (in the sense of "mediator"), which is essential to show that what is in question is an encounter between God and *man*.

This is the appropriate point at which to stop for a moment to consider the problem of glossolalia.[2] Glossolalia is a kind of shout, song or groan, an eschatological frenzy or trance, which is at times manifested in the supreme moments of the spiritual life, at conversion, for example (cf. Acts 19: 6ff.; 10: 46), because what it is desired to express, as at times in the crises of love, terror or sorrow escapes the control of consonants and becomes a cry, howl,

[1] We discuss below the relation of *lex orandi-lex credendi* which here is only touched upon.

[2] Xenoglossia, even ecstatic, which seems to have been the phenomenon of Pentecost (Acts 2: 4, 6, 11) is not to be quite simply identified with glossolali, despite their kinship.

song, or incoherent stammering. Thus glossolalia is not necessarily a creation of the Holy Spirit, but a phenomenon of this world which the Holy Spirit can use to induce AGALLIASIS. It is a physical phenomenon which it is not difficult to produce by other means than the Holy Spirit: torture, caresses, terror, hatred, or the techniques used to induce personal or collective trance are perfectly capable of engendering glossolalia—that language which lies beyond ourselves.

Theologically there are three observations to be made at this point:

Firstly, it must be said that glossolalia is a challenge to the languages of this world, to their confusion, their mutual unintelligibility, their unfitness, because of their very number, to allow men to understand each other; it suggests the "diabolic" character of the languages of this world, which separate instead of uniting. Glossolalia is not then in itself opposed to "logolalia", but rather to the exclusive use of Greek, Latin or French, etc. That is why it is not legitimate, in this present life, to choose any one language and to make it the privileged liturgical language. However, the challenge of glossolalia to human languages is not a means of miraculously overcoming the Babylonian confusion, since, as a rule,[1] glossolalia itself needs to be translated (1 Cor. 12: 10; 14: 2, 9, 11, 13, 18ff., etc.).

Next, without in the least denying that glossolalia can be a charismatic gift (what St. Paul says about this in chs. 12 and 14 of 1 Cor. makes it impossible for us to deny this), we must realize that the apostle does not think glossolalia can suitably contribute to communal liturgy. It is in the realm of private piety that the NT regards glossolalia as valid, and it is interesting to note that while other Churches besides that of Corinth were familiar with speaking with tongues (Ephesus, Caesarea Philippi and Jerusalem) only Corinth wished to make it a normal element in worship. For St. Paul it was a morbid and dangerous tendency, because, if glossolalia can be a sign of divine blessing, it

[1] Cf. the rather incoherent story of Acts 2 where it is uncertain whether we must opt for glossolalia (v. 12–13) or xenoglossia (v. 4, 11, v. 6 and 8).

must not become an object of human desire. There is a basic difference between the ability to express oneself in the language of the angels[1] and the desire so to express oneself; the former is a grace in which one can humbly and discreetly rejoice (cf. 1 Cor. 14: 18), whereas the latter is a matter of envious longing which undermines the edification of the Church.

However, the Church has the right to wish to use not an analytic, broken, abstract, non-figurative language (as we speak of abstract painting or sculpture), but a language transfigured by the Spirit, a language which, while still being comprehensible, is a language of rapture, expressing the wild joys of the spirit. It is the language of hymns and canticles, which, for example, bursts forth in the Letter to the Ephesians or which enables the Virgin Mary, when her Son is not yet even born, to sing, rapturously, that God has overthrown the designs of the proud, has cast the mighty from their seats and exalted them of low degree, that He has filled the hungry with good things and sent the rich empty away (Luke 1: 51a). This style which carries language to its utmost limits and is typical of canticles, doxologies, and pæans of faith, is the true liturgical language, the nuptial style of the Church extolling the Bridegroom and giving herself to Him, and this language is quite different, and must be so, from church language which is addressed to men.[2]

(b) *The acoustic domain.* Liturgical form is not concerned merely with man's understanding; it is also concerned with and makes an appeal to the voice and the ears, the eyes and the limbs. But if we could establish fairly precise rules for the "logical" expression, this is much less easy in regard to the acoustic, visual and kinetic domains, for here tastes change with the times, with the level of culture and racial prejudices. Although it is clear that liturgy does not merely reflect tastes, but rather forms taste, it is hardly possible to lay down rules about the way in which worship finds expression

[1] The plur. (1. Cor. 13: 1) does not mean that angels have several languages but that there are the languages of men and the language of angels.

[2] This also justifies a difference of tone between prayers and preaching.

in these different domains. At the same time it is apparent that we can deduce from the Christian faith general aesthetic principles—vocal, musical, pictorial, architectural, sculptural, choreographic, etc.

We speak of the acoustic domain in these terms because what appeals by the voice is the same as that which is addressed to the ears. It can again be subdivided into three parts: the spoken word, the sung word and silence.

The spoken word may be considered in three aspects: the word read, the word proclaimed, and the word recited; prayers are read, Scripture and sermons are proclaimed (so the proclaimed word can also be read), the Creed, the Lord's Prayer, the psalms, and the responses are recited. At each level the spoken word must find the appropriate tone and rhythm for audibility and for the communal character of Christian worship. Hence we must not be afraid to adopt quite a different tone in preaching from that which we adopt in reading a prayer: when we preach, we act as an individual witness, whereas when we read a prayer we are the neutral mouthpiece of the congregation. All this must be learnt and we should not fear to learn it . . . as if a technique in such matters impaired the sincerity of worship. In particular, we Protestants must learn not to preach the liturgy, but to read it (even if we know it by heart).

The sung word also may be considered in three aspects: the word sung by the congregation, the word sung by individuals, and the word sung to the accompaniment of musical instruments. The last point will be taken up in chapter VI in which the organ in particular is discussed. Singing is the normal and irreplaceable form of communal self-expression, and Christian worship has always had a place for communal singing even if the style of its singing has varied considerably in the course of centuries. But in addition to the singing of the congregation, there is the chanting of the minister or ministers alone.[1] Among all the points to be noted here, I select two:

The music which sustains the singing certainly has to convey the emotion expressed by the melody, but its special burden is the words of the song. It is essentially a vehicle of

[1] It is not a question here of soloists who sing sacred music.

what is uttered and what should be uttered is the glory of
the Trinity and the victory of Christ.[1] The music is there
essentially to serve, and that is why the best liturgical music
is perhaps that which permits the singing of the liturgy, the
psalm and the Biblical canticles without changes in the text
or versification of the text. So the best music for Christian
singing would be as near as possible to the Gregorian chant,[2]
i.e. an application of it to the particular language used,
since the Gregorian chant was invented for the Latin
language. Hence it could not, without violating aesthetic
principles, be used to sing a text written in some other
language. This certainly does not imply a condemnation of
the other types of psalmody and hymnody which have
marked the life of the Church at its great periods: the
Huguenot psalm, the Lutheran chorale, to which I would
like to add those Jordanian melodies (Jordanian in the
theological sense) known as negro spirituals ("I've got a
home on the other side"); but to which I would not like to add
those Anglo-Saxon revivalist hymns which, all in all, are a
betrayal of the cultural responsibilities of Christian worship.

The second point to be considered takes the form of a
question: should the liturgy be chanted or spoken? As is
well known a great part of the Christian liturgical tradition
insists that the liturgy should be chanted. It has been said,
with exaggeration, that it was through Biblical reading that
music and chanting were introduced into Christian worship.
Many arguments have been advanced in justification of this
mode of procedure: it has been recalled that for its prayers
the Church has always had a place for recitative, the
melopoeia taken over from Jewish worship. From a theological angle, it has been claimed that the great function of
music in worship is to be a power making for order, and that
the word moulded by musical tones is capable of exerting a
greater power for order than the word spoken; from the
pastoral viewpoint, it has been claimed that when the liturgy
is chanted, the minister can less easily modify it to his own
taste than when it is spoken; it has also been said, and

---

[1] "Jesus Christ is sung" says Ignatius of Antioch (Eph. 4: 1).
[2] On this problem consult the inexhaustible Vol. IV of *Leiturgia*
concerned with hymnological problems.

perhaps rightly, that Protestant pastors are mistaken in supposing that it is easier to speak than to sing in public . . . provided of course that it is the liturgy, not an opera, that is being sung. And it must be admitted that we of the Reformed Churches have a tendency to exclude from the definition of liturgical singing anything other than congregational hymns, Huguenot psalms, Lutheran chorales, etc.; hence a certain confusion in language. It must also be realized that we have too scanty an experience of liturgical life to be able to appreciate a liturgy which is not spoken: it appears to us ridiculous. There is an anecdote—perhaps invented later?— according to which Zwingli, to show the absurdity of chanted prayers, went to sing to the political authorities of Zurich his petition that the chanted liturgy should be abolished in favour of a spoken one.

Three things should be noted: first, what we have said above about the word being spoken for prayers, refers to something midway between the word spoken and the word sung; next, that we must expect that a renewed and living type of worship will gradually ask of itself an increasingly musical expression; and finally, that the movement must not be hurried. We are too accustomed to sing only in verse (a tradition which comes to us from the Reformation) to leave out the adoption of recitative before learning to sing in prose: we must not follow the example of the sixteenth century and transform into hymns the Creed or the Lord's Prayer. We must begin by reciting them in speech form.

There remains the question of silence in worship. It is important not only because of the Quaker tradition, but because silence is one of the mysteries of the Christian faith: "recollection" within the peace of God, silence before the advent of God (cf. Ps. 37: 7; Is. 41: 1; Lam. 3: 26; Hab. 2: 20; Wisdom of Solomon 1: 7; Mark 4: 39; Rev. 8: 1). Hence it is by no means a question of that deplorable habit which has become common in the tradition of Roman or Orthodox worship of inviting the priest to abandon at certain moments the *vox sonora*, audible to all, or even the *vox submissa*, audible only to those in the choir, in favour of the *vox secreta*, in which he says to God things which God alone is to hear—a practice which obliges him to indulge in "ekphoneses" when he emerges from silence, like a submarine surfacing, to intimate to the people what point has been reached. We are rather thinking of an attitude of receptivity, of calm, of plenitude which seems to suggest that word and chant are a chromatic dispersion of silence just as colours are of light. But on this ground, I am not sufficiently confident to do more than mention the problem.

(c) The visual is the third domain of liturgical expression, here to be glanced at only incidentally, as it must be surveyed in detail in chapter IX in speaking of the place of Christian worship. As contrasted with the acoustic domain, the visual is certainly secondary although it is true that he who does not see while he hears must be missing something of importance. Moreover—and this is not sufficiently stressed among us—the incarnation of God in Christ means that God wills to do more than simply to make Himself heard (for that there was no need for incarnation: cf. Matt. 17:5; Luke 3:22; Mark 9:7; Luke 9:35; John 12;28; etc.): He wills also to be seen (Mark 16:14; Luke 2:26; 19:3; 23:8; John 6:40; 12:21, 45; 14:9; 20; 20, 29; 1 John 1:1, etc.). And let us not forget the Gospel healings of the blind. We cannot even say, broadly, that in worship the visual domain is reserved essentially to liturgical acts by which the Church responds to the grace of God, since God, to act, uses not merely the Word, but signs, such as the sacramental elements and symbolic gestures which explain and give precise meaning to these elements: and at this point we are already in the last domain of liturgical expression.

(d) The *kinetic* domain, that of attitudes, gestures and movements. Here again we shall have to go into detail when we come to speak of problems of worship. Here we can be brief. In the cult, faith must proceed to the use of gestures, and it is rather a docetic tendency than spiritual modesty which at this point prevents us modern Reformed Protestants from agreeing. "Public prayer must be uttered with a very special turning of the heart towards God" say the church ordinances of Julich and Berg dating from 1671, but they at once add: "by kneeling, or standing upright or other external signs of humility".[1] Speaking of prostration—but this concerns the whole kinetic domain—P. Brunner happily remarks that then "the body of man is included in the spiritual response which the human being makes to the event of revelation", and such an inclusion of the body must not be despised. To be sure, the attitude, the gesture, the movement can be devoid of content (just as doctrine can be devoid of faith); but without the attitude, the gesture, the movement, Church worship also risks becoming emptied of its content, for it has no longer a vessel to contain it, or has one that belies the content (as faith runs dry if it is not defined and sustained by doctrine). Thus this concord and harmony between liturgical feeling (faith, repentance, thanksgiving, supplication, adoration) and the kinetic expression of that feeling is not necessarily a source of hypocrisy (although hypocrisy may make use of these kinetic expressions), it is rather a liturgical necessity and it is time that we learnt this truth afresh. "It is curious to note that the kneeling of the congregation or of certain members of it is regarded as wrong in almost all Evangelical churches. And yet there are thousands of the faithful who long to have the right to kneel. We have become enslaved to a false shame, a shame which is rooted in the fact that we no longer dare to confess openly our faith", observes with justice H. Asmussen.

How shall we subdivide this kinetic domain? Firstly there are liturgical attitudes: standing, seated or kneeling. We stand to invoke the Lord, to hear the Gospel, to confess the faith, to greet a newly baptized person, to honour the institution of the Lord's Supper, to sing the hymns. We sit for the readings (with the exception of that of the Gospel), and for preaching. We kneel for prayers and the blessing.[2] So long as kneeling has not been restored to its rightful place, the action and rhythm of liturgical postures will always have something artificial about them, and it is high time

[1] W. Niesel, op. cit., p. 319.
[2] Kneeling was current practice among the Churches of the Reformation. It is known that in the early Church kneeling depended on the season of the liturgical year, but this symbolism has almost everywhere been given up, and for good reason: in principle, the ecclesiastical year should not radically alter, but only colour, normal worship.

that our Church, which claims to possess the spirit of submission, should agree to show this by its attitudes (because the rejection of kinetic symbolism can become a source of hypocrisy as much as, or perhaps more than, can the use of such symbolism itself!) Among liturgical attitudes I will also include the position taken by the minister in worship: facing the people to absolve, to read, to preach, to celebrate the Eucharist, to give the blessing; with his back to the people when he prays in the name of the people. We shall return to this point.

Next comes the question of liturgical gestures. Gesture is the suitable attitude implemented and intensified. It is not merely a form, but a very personal action which reacts upon the one who performs it. It does not merely express an encounter but brings it about. To give up gestures is to weaken the intensity of the encounter between God and His people. Such gestures are many: joining hands or raising them while opening wide the arms for prayers: eucharistic gestures in the fraction of the bread, in the blessing of or in the elevation of the cup, in the humble reception of the elements; gestures of benediction. We must mention too, without pausing to discuss it, the sign of the cross, which, among ourselves, has been ostracized long enough.

Finally there is the question of movement from one place to another, and of processions: the entrance and the departure of the ministers, the movement from the holy table to the lectern or the pulpit, and the return, the procession to collect the offerings of the people (together with the bringing of the eucharistic species?), the movement of the people to receive communion, to say nothing of the method of meditating before the beginning of the service and at its end (in which matters we have much to learn). These matters are not immaterial or a mere formality, they are an integral part of worship and its expression. This does not imply that a hard-and-fast rule can be laid down for them. But it does mean that we should be able to justify theologically the mode of procedure we have decided to adopt.

3. Discipline and liberty in liturgical expression

The question now facing us is whether the nature of

worship may be safeguarded and expressed in many forms, or whether one form alone can do this; or again whether a variety in ways of worship is legitimate within precise norms which must be respected. To answer this question, we shall first examine the norms, then the conditions of liturgical expression, in order to trace the limits of liturgical liberty and to end by reminding ourselves that worship is reformable.

(a) *The norms of liturgical expression.* Christian worship is not founded upon a human need but upon the will of God. It is less a petition than an act of obedience. That is why its expression is subject to certain norms which must correspond with what we have said about the necessity and limits of liturgical forms. What are these norms?

The first, the most important, that which governs and justifies the others, is fidelity to the Bible. Not that the NT contains *in extenso* the liturgy of the apostolic church, although it does contain more liturgical texts than is generally supposed. But the NT marks the limits within which, with more or less felicity and obedience, Christian worship can truly be carried out as Christian worship. These limits are as follows: first, the assembly must take place in the name of Jesus Christ, to celebrate His victory and invoke His presence. The intention of the celebrant must be to celebrate the Christian cult. Secondly, this cult must enable the faithful to persevere in the teaching of the apostles; next, it must enable them, at the breaking of the bread, to communicate with the body of Christ; fourthly, it must gather up the prayers of the Church and offer them to God; finally, it should be an assembly of men and women who are not just juxtaposed as at the cinema, but committed to a way of life in common. These last four characteristics make possible the first. To be Christian, worship must proceed within these limits, and whatever can be legitimately placed within them, whatever is not contradicted by them (for they have not only a power of expression, they have also a power of protection, a polemical aspect),[1] can claim the right of being a *Christian* liturgical expression.

[1] Thus when the cult requires that we should censure the doctrine of the apostles, or adhere to doctrine unknown to them, or contra-

But all is not said in saying this. We have indicated the basis. And this basis enables us to apply, justify and check three derivative norms of liturgical expression, the first of which is respect for tradition (which is part of the communal character of the Biblical cult of which we have just been speaking). When we perform Christian worship, we are part of the Church of all places and all times, and this community binds us. To respect liturgical tradition implies four things:

First, a feeling of gratitude for what God has taught the Church in the past, for the way in which He has inspired and guided it. That is why there exist in Christian worship and its unfolding certain classical forms which have—to use the phrases of Otto Haendler—such a theological and anthropological plenitude, are of such monumental liturgical importance, that the Church never exhausts their vitality, never wears them out, in spite of constant use. They are transmitted and recur from cult to cult, not so much out of filial piety or lack of imagination, but because to abandon them would not be a liberation but a loss. For continental Protestants this is something far more difficult to understand than it is for Anglicans, Roman Catholics or, especially, Greek Orthodox.

To respect liturgical tradition implies, secondly, to be free with regard to it. If a fine doxology of Christian antiquity is golden, it is a gold coin rather than a gold chain. That is to say, that respect for the traditions of worship does not fetter liturgical expression, but on the contrary, enables us to repeat today in a new way what the Fathers said when they assembled to celebrate the mystery of Christian salvation. It is not a question of saying or doing something different; it is a question of not being bound to what is obsolete. Although it is legitimate to have in one's worship some ancient items (just as one has an antique armchair among one's furniture) the cult is not a museum, and if it facilitates access to another world, it is not to a world that

---

dictory to their teaching; or when the breaking of bread is absent, or does not involve the communion of the people; or when prayers are not addressed to the God fully revealed in Jesus Christ; or when admission to the cult is subject to other conditions than baptism, e.g. racial or social, then it breaks its norms, is perverted and ceases to be Christian.

has gone by for ever, but to a world that is to come. We shall meet these problems again: here I do no more than allude to them, without at all denying that the cult, in its formulation, can become a common denominator for very different epochs in this world's history.

To respect liturgical tradition and subject the cult to the norm of tradition, means, thirdly, to understand the cult in the perspective of Christian unity and so in the perspective of love. Thus for ourselves the problem is not to formulate reformed worship, but Christian worship. Over-concern with the confessional side of the cult (among ourselves shown perhaps above all in the erection of places of worship) is an activity that reveals a lack of hope. Certainly, it is not possible to discuss the cult without taking into account those who celebrate it *hic et nunc*, and so without taking into account the fact that for the moment they cannot celebrate it otherwise than within a divided Christendom. But to subject the cult to the norm of traditionalism is to seek, in all confessions, to liberate it from a norm of confessionalism, that the cult itself may be an appeal for and an anticipation of Christian unity. This does not of course mean that the cult has not the right to criticize that of another confession, but what should distinguish it from the cults it opposes is not the abandonment of what in those cults has remained Christian, but of what is heretical, or at the least dangerous to the purity of the faith. *Abusus non tollit usum!* To take an example: the Roman way of celebrating the Eucharist must not make us suspicious of the Eucharist itself.

One final remark about the importance of tradition as the norm of worship: where this norm is respected, while the clericalization of the cult is certainly not altogether avoided, it can be resisted with some chance of success, because the minister who presides over the cult cannot shape it as he pleases but must conduct it as the Church—the sacerdotal people—understands it. The loss of a traditional, churchly liturgy almost certainly involves subjective arbitrariness on the part of the chief minister, and a radical clericalization of the cult as is shown—despite Calvin's attempt to stop the multiplication of variations—by the liturgical development of the Lutheran and Reformed churches.

But within the general framework of Biblical standards the Christian cult is not only to be based on a relation to the past, the tradition of the Church, but also on a relation to the future of the Church, the Kingdom. This point cannot be over-emphasized. The presence of the Kingdom in the cult is an indispensable norm of liturgical expression. Worship is *par excellence* the sphere in which the future puts forth its buds in the present, and it must be able to burst forth, in the structure of worship too, radiating that AGALLIASIS of which the NT so often speaks (cf. Acts 2: 46; 16: 34, etc.). Denis de Rougemont once exclaimed: "O dancing! gesture here receives a soul!" Paraphrasing this, we must be able to say: "O worship! forms here receive the Kingdom!" This presence of the Kingdom, as a norm of liturgical expression, is shown especially in the nuptial character of the cult: in the fact that there men have access to the messianic table, and are reconciled, that is to say, that they are united by the overcoming of the factors which divide them in this world; it is further shown in the part played by liturgical symbols, to which we shall return in detail. Suffice it to say here that symbols in worship have the function of manifesting, as far as possible, the eschatological character of the cult, and that a type of worship, which distrusts symbols is almost certainly in danger of losing its "hopefulness", of no longer being receptive to the future. It is in fact certain that if among ourselves worship leads so little towards the marriage of the Lamb, it is because, for fear of the ambivalence of symbols, we have no longer allowed the Church, if I may say so, to try on its bridal garments. Conversely, whenever there has been a new awareness of the eschatological dimension of the Church it has shown itself automatically in a call for liturgical symbols.

We have seen that, subject to NT norms, the expression of worship is influenced both by the past and the future of the Church. Finally, it must be said that the present also is, in a derivative way, a norm for liturgical expression. In its worship, the Church confesses the *hic et nunc* of its pilgrimage. Hence it has the right and even the duty of expressing itself by prayers, hymns and symbols which ever anew are inspired by the Spirit of God. But, once again, the *hic et nunc*

99

must be confessional only by accident: what is important is that it should encourage the genius of a nation and a period to rediscover and express itself, pardoned, in the worship of the Church. That is why, despite the deep unity of church worship, the latter must not and cannot be uniform. A cult in Madagascar can legitimately be expressed differently from a cult in Scandinavia, or a cult of the twentieth century can find other forms of expression from those of a cult in the third or the eleventh centuries. As is very rightly observed by Otto Haendler, it is important that "he who prays should realize himself to be challenged in his Today, and not in a Yesterday brought back to the surface by a solemn incantation."

This *hic et nunc* has no more right to dominate and absorb the cult than have the traditional past and the future of the Kingdom. But the three derivative norms, the *normae normatae* of liturgical expression, must, in their tension and balance, be applicable to the cult on the basis of that which is common to them, namely, the Biblical norm, the *norma normans*.

(b) *The conditions of liturgical formulation.* Liturgical formulation is subject not only to certain norms, but also to certain conditions, which, although not a *sine qua non*, have none the less their weight. These conditions are those of intelligibility, simplicity, and beauty.

Since worship is a communal action, the congregation should be able to celebrate it, and therefore they must understand it. This *intelligibility* may be considered from three points of view:

The people must understand what is taking place in worship. We shall return to this problem in speaking of the necessary simplicity of the cult. Let us here be content to remark that the cult is perhaps the best starting point or training ground for catechesis. *Lex orandi, lex credendi.* It is in explaining the cult that we can best explain the history of salvation, the nature of the Church, and its mission in the world (to refer back to the themes of our first three chapters). In this matter, we must admit that we Reformed churchmen are terribly lacking in experience, but this must be acquired.

Next, the people must understand the language of worship. Every effort should be made to free the cult from archaic forms so that it can be celebrated in the current speech of the participants. "So in holy assemblies we must not use any foreign language, but all things should be put forward in the vernacular, in language understood by all those of the locality where the congregation is assembled."[1] This may give rise to a certain conflict between the desire to mark, by liturgical language, the unity of the Church in time and space, and the desire to signify, by the language used, that the cult is indeed the act of the congregation celebrating it. It will be remembered that at Jerusalem a day of annual fasting was instituted to ask God's forgiveness for the scandal of the LXX translation, whereas at Alexandria the Jews held an annual feast to thank the Lord for the translation of the sacred books into the language spoken by all. But however that may be, since the apostolic Church did not think that Hebrew was the only sacred language, since, on the contrary, it indicated that any human tongue could be sanctified to become the bearer of the gospel message, it must be claimed that a serious condition of worship is that it should be performed in the language current among those who participate, or at least in a language which they all understand and can handle.[2] To reject this claim is not so much to insist on maintaining the unity of the Church as to insist on maintaining the separation between the clergy who are familiar with the language and the laity who are not. Or between the more cultured members of the congregation who know it and those who do not.

Thirdly, the people must hear what is said in worship. From the ninth century, as is known, certain prayers were offered in silence by the priest, and now such prayers are numerous both in the Roman rite and in Eastern rites. That each member of the congregation, including the minister, should have the opportunity of private prayer and meditation, is normal. But what is wrong is the exclusion of the people

[1] *La Confession Helvétique Postérieure*, chap. 22
[2] Thus in some African or Asian countries the synods must be held either in French or English because these languages are super-tribal. The language cf synodal debates must also be the same as that of synodal worship.

from prayers which form part of the liturgy of the Church. Such exclusion violates the baptismal qualification of the congregation and hence their fitness for worship: it is a profanation of the baptized. That the custom arose and spread at a time when in fact the tension between the Church and the world was bound to find expression in a tension between the clergy and the laity may be understandable. But this situation is no longer current; it is right that at a given moment of the cult the non-baptized should be dismissed, but the baptized have the right to be able to hear and associate themselves with the whole act of worship.

The second condition of liturgical expression: *simplicity*. Certainly—and we shall return to the point—it may be right that urban worship should be more elaborate than that of a village church, or that the cult of those living in a community should include more elements and symbols than that of a parish. The fact remains that simplicity is an important condition of true worship. It is not to be confused with baldness, negligence of forms or a docetic impatience with regard to forms. It is rather a matter of concentration, a determination to base worship on the central issues. We might also say that it reflects a desire to show that the cult in fact sums up the work of Him in whom God has summed up all things: whence come a sense of order, a pruning of what is unessential, a suspicion of all that savours of the baroque. It also produces great vigilance as regards symbols, for their significance and power are well known. Simplicity, the liturgical HAPLOTES, is in the first instance the opposite not of complexity, but rather of diffuseness. In other words, the second condition of true worship is a respect for the structure controlling the relations between the various parts of the cult, in an arrangement which shows that the cult progresses towards its culminating point, and that, having reached it, it is strengthened by it for the purpose of afterwards witnessing in the world. Now, this climax of worship— and we must dare to say it although this contradicts our confessional traditions—is the Lord's Supper. Thus the act of worship will be all the more simple the better it prepares for the Eucharist, and will make it more joyful, more alive, more existential.

Last condition of liturgical expression: *beauty*. I have some hesitation in suggesting this, as beauty can become a snare (cf. Ezek. 16: 15; 28: 17), arousing the envy of supernatural power, and any collusion between aestheticism and liturgy can be dangerous. Yet, I think we must dare to say that liturgical expression must strive after beauty, since it is a process of nuptial preparation, and since the Church of which the cult is the epiphany is called to appear before its Lord "in splendour, without spot or wrinkle or any such thing" (Eph. 5: 27). Only we must be clear that this beauty is for the purpose of making the cult intelligible and is an expression of its simplicity. C. F. Ramuz has somewhere condemned romantic aestheticism because it believed that "to make beautiful, we must make rich". To beautify the cult, we must not enrich it but purify it. True beauty is a school of purgation, it resists everything that is self-centred: it is grace and harmony, severe towards the flourishes and the excrescences of an aesthetic self-centredness. That is why respect for beauty will not lead us to embellish the cult— as one bedecks an old lady with "make-up"—but it will try to show that the cult cannot fail to be beautiful if it is true. For this reason we must be relentless towards "aesthetic embellishments" whether they be interludes of music or singing, or baroque architecture, or a rhetoric which is self-complacent, or a bombastic redundancy in the formulation of the prayers or—*horribile dictu!*—the way in which, I am told, fashionable baptisms are administered in some Presbyterian churches of the U.S.A. where the pastor baptizes the child by letting water drop on to its head from roses that have been previously dipped into the font.

Liturgical beauty is a protest, not only against all aesthetic self-centredness, but also against negligence, coarseness, casualness, and in general against vulgar familiarity. The very fact that the cult is an encounter between the Lord and the Church implies an ennobling of this encounter and a glorification of the Lord who deigns to be present.

I wish to make clear my meaning in saying that beauty is a condition of true worship: I mean that worship, if conducted with faith, hope and love, engenders beauty, and supplies a basis of radical criticism of self-centred aestheticism and vulgarity. The cult can be very poor without ceasing to be beautiful, and it will probably cease to be beautiful if it aspires to become rich. But "poor" does not mean shabby or sad or cheap. "Poor" means to be without, not forms or symbols, but without pretence or self-centredness.

(c) *The limits of liberty in liturgical forms*. The form of worship is both strict and free. Strict, because it is a question of *Christian* worship; free, because liturgy is an "eschatological game" (Romano Guardini), the finest of all the games that men are invited to play on earth. But a game, in order not to degenerate into licence, an orgy or a scuffle, needs to be played with disciplined liberty, and this was true of primitive Christian worship and of the worship of the first centuries to an extent which is as surprising to those who nowadays understand worship to be like a train which would run into disaster if it went off the rails as to those who understand it rather as the rambling exploration of vast plains by means of a Landrover. According to the fine expression of P. Brunner, "we must take seriously both the liberty of those who are bound to the Gospel, and the bonds of those whom the Gospel has freed".

We have already made it clear that the cult, if it is to remain Christian, must be subject to certain norms and conditions. For Christian worship is linked intimately, indissolubly, automatically with the Christian content to which it must give expression. What we must now observe is that these norms and conditions are not a strait-waistcoat; they do not deprive us of freedom of movement.

But within what limits can and must this liberty be manifested? First, in the sanctioning variation of time and place. And this not only in respect to liturgical language, but in respect to the concerns which will be manifest in thanksgiving and intercession, and to the taste which will be revealed in the music, and in the length and the whole unfolding of the cult. It is the immense problem of ceremonies which must show, without spoiling it, the multi-coloured nature of the seamless robe—to use the surprising *rapprochement* which Grégoire d'Elvire made between the robe of Joseph and that of Jesus. Even if the Reformation sometimes excessively insisted on this liberty of "ceremonies", and in a way which sometimes threw doubt on the inextricable bond between form and content, it is absolutely right that the preoccupations, tastes, culture of a place and a period should find expression in the cult. The limits of such liberty—always viewed within the framework of the norms and conditions of Christian worship—are those set by the unity of the Church, a unity which, however, does not imply uniformity.

This liberty concerns us—those of us of the Reformed churches especially—in regard to the authorization of personal idiosyncrasies in the minister. Although it is exaggerating to say that such liberty is legitimate only if we feel really and spiritually constrained to use it, it must nevertheless be said that the free prayers, so frequent with us, spring more often from pastoral pride or clerical pretension than from an obedience to the Holy Spirit. Certainly they should not be excluded *a priori* but the minister must realize that it is his office to conduct the worship of the Church and not to exhibit his own faith. Hence, as a rule he will adhere to the prayers prescribed in the liturgical traditions of the Church—unless he wishes (and this, although not unthinkable, is not to be recommended for obvious pastoral reasons)[1] to introduce into the cult moments of free prayer; for if he wishes to say publicly his own prayers rather than those of the Church, he has no right to prevent the congregation from saying theirs also publicly. But as a rule ministers will be asked to follow what is not only the tradition of the Catholic type of Church, but what was also the good discipline of the early Reformed Church; namely, that the pastor should confine himself to the prayers officially accepted by the Church—for Christians who come to worship have the right to take part in the official worship of the Church; they do not come to join in the individualistic caprices of the minister. It will perhaps be objected that their official prayers are bad, doubtful in their theology, redundant, archaic and too complicated, and much more. This is often

[1] This reason especially: it is likely that it will always be the same ones who pray in public, which will result almost certainly in the danger of spiritual pride.

true. But the Church will have no strong desire to revise them so long as she cannot count on the obedience of the ministers. Moreover all these disciplinary concerns will not be acceptably settled as long as the pastors alone have in their hands the form of worship: in order that they may adhere to the latter, the congregation too should be able to peruse it in a book of public prayers joined to their Psalter.

(d) *The reformability of worship.* The cult as a whole cannot be reformed. The reading of the Bible as such cannot be changed: what one can change is the lectionary. The liturgy of baptism cannot be reformed, for example, by deciding to baptize without invoking the Triune name, or at least the name of Jesus, or by abstaining from the use of water: what can be reformed is baptismal symbolism and its degree. The Eucharist cannot be reformed by changing the species: what can be reformed are the prayers which accompany and sustain it, or the structure of the service. This means that in the cult there are reformable and non-reformable elements. What is reformable in the cult—as we shall see in detail in discussing the elements of the cult and their structure—is what might be called its sacrificial element, the means whereby the Church receives grace and responds to grace. The sacramental aspect of the cult, the means of grace, what the Lord has instituted as the vehicle of grace—the Word and the sacraments—are not reformable.

Thus the reformability of the cult is limited by the liturgical event which must be respected. But the possibility of reform exists, and must be defended with persistence. Not, of course, to multiply essays in liturgy, or to encourage liturgical restlessness, but that the act of worship may be constantly improved to become entirely what it ought to be. Hence the reformability of the cult is strictly subjected to the norms and conditions we have outlined: a controlling fidelity to the Bible, and in connexion with that, respect for tradition, for the eschatological aspect of the cult, respect for its roots in a given culture and time, its *hic et nunc*, respect for intelligibility, simplicity and beauty.

But this reformability is not within the reach of every one: it is a task entrusted to the Church. It is therefore essential that each Church should have an official liturgical commission, whose duty it would be to test the faithfulness of the cult and to propose to its synod measures which, with perseverance would enable the cult to be as perfectly as possible one of the two major expressions of church life, the other being evangelization.

4. The reward of liturgical expression

"Seek first His kingdom and its righteousness and all these things shall be yours as well" (Matt. 6: 33). In the particular kind of search for the Kingdom which the shaping of liturgy represents, there is likewise a reward. This reward is not an aim to be pursued but a grace given, and all would be perverted if it were the reward which was sought after: but all would also be awry if this reward were not received as such, gratuitous as are all the rewards which are of grace, and good and beautiful as they are. This overplus is the power of the cult to inspire culture or to give birth to a culture. In fact this aspect of the cult may not be neglected without committing the sin of ingratitude or the heresy of docetism. When worship is performed as the Lord wills, then it becomes a cultural focus of the highest importance, because it is a power for purification, for expression and for self-committal. By way of example only, and to encourage far wider research than the indications I give here, I would point out only three aspects of this problem.

(a) Worship, firstly, is a *school of taste*. "The liturgy", notes Max Thurian, "is the privileged sphere where is forged the aesthetic expression of Christianity, within the dimensions suggested by evangelical simplicity. Worship alone, truly alive as an act of thanksgiving, made by Christian people, in words, gestures, forms and colours, opens up a free field of action for aesthetic life, and offers it a ceaselessly enriched inspiration, an inspiration which is not merely religious, but universal and cosmic; so true is it that, in liturgy, with the psalms as the background, the whole of creation, with its lights and its shades, is united and offered to Christ as a sacrifice of praise. It is because the liturgy is an act of thanksgiving that it sanctions the development of aesthetic life in the Church. For art is essentially self-giving in the form of beauty."

But if the cult forms the taste of the faithful, it also forms, by its repercussions, the taste of the world outside the Church. The proof of this is that "the history of art is unthinkable apart from its constant tie with the history of the Church" (H. Asmussen). Because it is basically Christocentric, because it testifies to the secret at the heart of all things—their recapitulation in Christ—the cult cleanses human culture of its distortions, its self-centredness, its chaos and disharmony. It is the place where culture is focused, and when the Church refuses to claim this reward of its life of worship, or when the world refuses to be challenged and inspired by the Gospel, then disorder sets in.

Language is purified by becoming a vehicle of the Gospel and a bearer of prayer. The more serious and devout the practice of prayer is, the more prayer ennobles our speech. It is the experience of all those who truly pray, that the words used require to be mastered by an ever-increasing effort. When we pray regularly and seriously, prayer is less and less something which can be taken for granted. We use a more and more concentrated and careful language where every word assumes more weight. For what we have to say, ever anew, and in ever new circumstances, is that we belong to God, that we have renounced possession of ourselves, that we have given ourselves to Him as a sacrifice, body and soul, for time and for eternity. Music is cleansed as it becomes the expression of hymns, psalms, doxology, and praise. Colours are cleansed by becoming a symbolic refraction of the dazzling light of the Gospel. Architecture is cleansed as it becomes the means of constructing an edifice for the living encounter between God and His people, etc.

Why is it then—it may be asked—that the Church can also become the privileged place for the most execrable taste, the most insulting to Christian grace and hope? Bad taste infects worship in two situations: either when the communal faith of the Church is impoverished to make room for a medley of individual beliefs, each with claims, springing from isolation and pride, of its own; or when the liturgy gives up shaping the circumambient culture, and instead makes submission to it, on the pretext of offering a loving welcome to the world's aspirations. In the latter case faith is no longer a filter, but a funnel. If bad taste gets a foothold in a cult, it is because the cult initially is corrupted, either by losing its communal cohesion or by forgetting that there can be no access to the Church without death to self.

(b) Next, Christian worship calls art into its service and justifies it. We have not here to lay down the basis for a Christian philosophy of art; but is not art basically the longing of things for liturgical self-expression, to find their justification in the praise for which they were created? "Is it not true to say that all arts reach a crisis—far more, they are condemned to decay—when they lose their centre, which is essentially liturgical? And is not Church worship the place where arts are judged, and so can rediscover the reality of their being and function? Is not the place which in any case art claims in worship the bond which, by a sign that is also a promise, binds the non-human creation to the Church's praise of its Lord? Is not art in worship to be understood as the sign that the Church eschatologically welcomes the worship of the non-human creation, and so the sign of a deep solidarity between the children of God and the rest of creation?" (P. Brunner). To exclude art from worship, in which it would rediscover its true vocation, implies hatred of the world.

But the cult is not only the sphere in which art is called to rediscover its true function; it is also the mystery in which art finds its justification and liberty. This is not to say that art will therefore be confined to religious themes; poems other than hymns, music other than that of canticles, buildings other than churches, choreography other than that of processions, pictures other than ikons, and carving other than that of pulpits, lecterns and altars, will be possible and necessary, just as there is a Monday, a Tuesday, a Wednesday after Sunday, just as there is human work and joy, struggle and questing, besides the Sunday services. But just as this work and this joy are justified and hallowed by worship, just as the days of the week are justified and hallowed by Sunday, so other expressions of art are justified and hallowed because the arts have rediscovered in the Christian cult their promised land, their true origin and destiny.

(c) Finally, the cult is formative of culture because it inspires political and social life. It is the point of reference for order and freedom, for justice and peace. It is so because it celebrates the true hierarchy of things, because it confesses the Lordship of Christ, and because it attests the miraculous grace that this Lordship of Christ does not absorb that which it controls, but is the foundation of its liberty, and regardful of it. Hence the possibility of diverse but co-ordinated vocations, of care for the weak, of the discovery of the true rights of man, of human understanding and reconciliation. The results of the committal implied by the Church's intercession for authorities, for peace, for the weak and the sick, cannot be measured. And thus it is that Christian worship is something making for order and freedom, justice and peace in the world; to say that it is no trifling factor in this, is an understatement; it is rather determinative. Clearly the world does not know that in attacking the cult it is striking at the very thing that preserves and guarantees its life. But the Church has the right to realize this, not in order to presume on it or derive some advantage from it, but so as to be unwearied in rejoicing in the political and social service it renders the world, directly or indirectly, by its giving of thanks and its intercession.

But once again it is not the formation of taste, or the justification of art, or the protection of the world, that the Church aims at in its liturgical expression. Seeking by its worship to celebrate through the Spirit the love of the Father manifested in the Son, the Church learns, to its surprise, that God rewards this effort by allowing it to become a shaper of culture, and a sphere of beauty and goodness. The Church would be ungrateful not to rejoice in the fact.

CHAPTER FIVE

THE NECESSITY OF THE CULT

A FURTHER matter of liturgical principle is that of the necessity of the cult. The arguments for this are primary; those in favour of its usefulness, secondary. Often, among us, the cult is justified by its usefulness rather than by its necessity. But usefulness in itself does not justify the cult. At most, it recommends it. The arguments in favour of the usefulness of worship, to have weight, must flow from the prior demonstration of its necessity. Finally, we must say something of the obedience which is imposed on the Church by both the necessity and the usefulness of the cult.

1. The justification of the necessity of Christian worship

Doubtless from fear lest the cult should find justification in itself, or from forgetfulness of the dual orientation of the Church—its orientation towards the world in evangelism and service, and its orientation towards God in the inflowing of grace, in adoration and intercession—Reformed theology, especially in Germany and Holland, is marked by a strong reluctance to speak of the necessity of worship. It sees the necessity of worship, rather, in that "indirect" worship constituted by service to neighbour, an attitude which would make direct worship no longer a necessity, but limited to mere usefulness. Rather than refute the arguments advanced against the necessity of the cult, I prefer, positively, to suggest reasons for this necessity. I see four. The cult is necessary (i) because it was instituted by Jesus Christ; (ii) because it is the work of the Holy Spirit; (iii) because it is one of the ways in which salvation becomes operative; (iv) because the Kingdom of God is not yet manifested with power.

Let us take these reasons one by one.

(a) *The cult is necessary because it was instituted and ordained by Jesus Christ.* When the Church assembles for worship, it is inventing nothing, it is performing an act of obedience. In worship, we are not asked to express our needs and possibilities, but we are asked to obey. But obey what command? Essentially that which Jesus gave in instituting the Lord's Supper: "Do this in remembrance of me" (1 Cor. 11: 24, 25; Luke 22: 19). This point is of great importance for it reminds us of two things: firstly that the cult instituted by Christ was not homilectic, but eucharistic; secondly, and consequentially, that the Lord's Supper is the normal culmination of Christian worship. Certainly, the Supper is not the whole of the cult. It is prepared, awaited, and experienced, through other liturgical elements: but these have their obligatory point of reference in the Holy Communion. In other words, to assemble for worship shows only a partial obedience, if worship does not find its fulness in the moment of communion.

We are not of course neglecting preaching, still less ruling it out; nor are we denying that Jesus Christ instituted the ministry of the Word as solemnly as He instituted the ministry of the sacrament (cf. Matt. 28: 19; John 20: 23; Acts 1: 8, etc.). But the ministry of the Word was not instituted directly for the cult, but in order to make possible the cult, to gather together by missionary work the people to whom He would give life through His flesh and blood. The fact that Church worship has always included the Word read and preached as one of its basic and essential elements— and these adjectives must be taken literally if we are not to make the Church untrue to itself—does not mean, as we shall have occasion to stress again, that the proclamation of the Word is in itself a sufficient and complete justification of the Christian cult. The necessary presence of the Word shows that the Church is still *in via peregrinationis*, and woe to it if it forgets this by neglecting or despising the Word. But—as has been well understood by the tradition which distinguishes the "mass of the catechumens" from that of the faithful—if the latter must always join the catechumens in order "to abide in the Word" (1 John 2: 14), they also progress beyond baptism in a very fundamental way in the Kingdom of the Son at the moment of union with Him when they partake of His body and His blood. Their submission to the Word shows that they are still in this world; their approach to the holy table shows that already they can enjoy the heavenly gift. To wish to exclude them from this access, either by reserving the altar to the priest or by not having an altar at all, is to scorn and invalidate their baptism and to disobey the Lord.

If, because of the ambivalent situation of the Church in the world, it is never possible to separate otherwise than liturgically the Word and the sacrament, catechesis and communion, it is as false and as disobedient to reduce the cult to catechesis as to reduce it to communion. The two are integral to the cult; but the latter finds its culmination not in the Word read and preached, but in the Supper prepared by the Word. The cult that is necessary, because commanded, is thus the eucharistic cult (preceded and made possible by the Word). A fortuitous proof of this lies in the fact that the NT never denotes worship by referring to preaching alone. To go to church is not expressed as "going to hear the sermon", but as "meeting to break bread" (Acts, 20: 7).

(b) *The cult is necessary because it is the work of the Holy Spirit*. It is born of the outpouring of the Holy Spirit. Salvation gives rise to praise (cf. Acts 10: 46, etc.). To question the necessity of the cult is to question the work of the Spirit, which is to give to men pledges of the world to come (2 Cor. 1: 22; 5: 5; cf. Rom. 8: 23), to transplant them into the coming Kingdom, that Kingdom which will be an inexhaustible source of liturgical joy. The cult is thus the sphere for the thanksgiving of the redeemed. To deny the necessity of the cult is to scorn redemption, to refuse to rejoice in salvation; it is also to forget the deeply liturgical character of the first creation, restored by salvation.

This necessity for the cult, brought about by the gift of the Spirit, is perhaps best illustrated by the inevitable thanksgiving of those who in the Gospel story were the object of one of Christ's miracles: the healed paralytic

H   113

returned home giving glory to God (Luke 5: 25); the infirm woman whom Jesus cured on the sabbath day stood upright, and began to give glory to God (Luke 13: 13); the only one of the ten lepers who understood the implication of his healing returned "glorifying God with a loud voice" (Luke 17: 15); the blind man of Jericho, once healed, began to follow Jesus, glorifying God (Luke 18: 43). And this joy and thanksgiving did not mobilize only those who were miraculously healed, but also those who understood, when they saw the saving power of Christ, that all things could now have a fresh start, because forgiveness and life were reaching out to the despair and solitude of men to restore to them a future of hope (cf. Matt. 15: 31; Luke 7: 16, etc.).

The same effect is seen in those who recognized in Jesus the Messiah—and this too was the work of the Spirit, since no one can say "Christ is Lord" except by the Spirit (1 Cor. 12: 3)—we may think of the shepherds at the Nativity (Luke 2: 20), or of the centurion witnessing the death of the Son of God (Luke 23; 47). Worship is the requisite way in which those who through the Spirit live by Christ express their gratitude. Forgiveness restores that aptitude for worship which was lost by sin. If it does not give rise to the spirit of worship, it cannot have been received, and those who claim, in a serious or even a religious spirit, that they have more urgent things to do than accept the invitation to the feast will have no part in it. When we realize the eschatological character of the work of the Spirit, we can no longer deny the necessity of the cult.

(c) *The cult is necessary because it is one way in which the historical process of salvation is realized.* Jesus Christ died once for all to save the world. In Him, the salvation of the whole world has a sufficient foundation. But mankind is not automatically saved in consequence. That men may be, we need the work of the Spirit, who transplants us into the Church and maintains us in it. It is thus that the process of salvation is carried on. "The virtual inclusion of all humanity in the crucified body of Christ must be transformed, actualized and fulfilled by the ontological, real, personally accepted inclusion, as realized in the concrete historic existence of each individual" (P. Brunner). Now this transformation of a virtual into an ontological inclusion is not brought about by the cult exclusively, but the cult plays a part in it. It is not effected only by worship (not, at least, by communal worship), because its first mode of operation is the begetting to eternal life through the Word in missionary preaching (which only exceptionally coincides with the preaching in formal worship), and through baptism, which seals the Word and attests that it has been received.

But the transformation takes place also, or rather is actualized and accomplished by worship. The cult is thus an agent in the process of salvation. If it were not celebrated, the latter would cease. In other words, we are reminded here of what we have stressed so many times, namely that it is God who acts in the cult, by the Word and the sacrament, and hence to doubt the necessity of the cult is to doubt that the latter is the *opus Dei*. In a passage in which he explains the whole cult on the basis of the sacraments of baptism and the Lord's Supper, K. Barth notes "the whole worship of the Church is thus embraced, determined and limited by the divine command concerning baptism and the Eucharist. These two in a way provide the necessary sphere of worship; necessary, because it is the only appropriate one. Whatever takes place here must spring from baptism: namely, that the Church is, that Jesus Christ once for all has died and risen for us, that we belong to Him irrevocably, that we are destined to nothing less than to be justified, glorified and sanctified in Him. And whatever takes place in worship, must lead to Communion, to the fact that the Church abides, that we are brought to share anew in His humanity by virtue of being united to God, that our true vocation, which is to be the object of His work, should be repeatedly fulfilled. That which takes place between this beginning and this end, as testimony to the grace of God, as awakening, purification and strengthening of our faith, is church worship." In short, in baptism, "it is a question of the Church coming to be, . . . in Communion, of the Church remaining the Church".

Thus to declare that the cult is optional, that it is not necessary to the continuation of God's work of salvation, is to despise the source of grace, and to forget the words of Jesus: "Truly, truly, I say to you, unless you eat the flesh of the Son of Man and drink His blood, you have no life in you; he who eats my flesh and drinks my blood has eternal life, and I will raise him up at the last day. For my flesh is food indeed and my blood is drink indeed. He who eats my flesh and drinks my blood abides in me and I in him. As the living Father sent me and I live because of the Father, so he who eats me will live because of me. This is the bread which came down from heaven, not such as the fathers ate and died; he who eats this bread will live for ever" (John 6: 53–58).

However, the cult is not necessary merely in order that the process of salvation may not be interrupted, but confirmed and fulfilled in the lives of Christians. It is also necessary in order that the polemical character of this process may remain alive and effective. Ignatius of Antioch gives this essential injunction, which shows the basic necessity of the cult: "Be careful then to meet as often as possible (PYKNOTERON) for the divine eucharist and praises. For when you meet regularly for this purpose,[1] the powers of Satan are crushed, and the threat of perdition which he holds over you is broken by the harmony of your faith." Through worship, that sphere which by the Holy Spirit is liberated from the dominion of the Evil One, remains occupied; it is protected and the world learns that if it is condemned by the very existence of the Church, it is not yet lost, but summoned to change its master and to confess as its ruler the One who is its Saviour. By worship, if not by worship exclusively, the Church keeps open the wound which the resurrection of Christ and the outpouring of the Spirit have inflicted on the self-righteousness of the world, and in this way too the process of salvation is continued. Thus here again recurs the thought which we have expounded in detail in discussing the cult as the "end and the future of the world".

(d) *The cult is necessary because the Kingdom of God is not yet established with power*. The cult as such is necessary because

---

[1] Or "for the cult"? St. Ignatius has recourse here to the EPI TO AUTO of Acts 1: 15; 2: 1, 44, 47; 1 Cor. 11: 20; 14: 23, which denotes in NT language the liturgical assembly.

the whole of life has not yet been transformed into worship. Thus it suggests that the Kingdom exists already, like the leaven in the dough, but is not yet established. It shows that Sunday is other than weekday, that all is not yet Sunday.

Those who deny the necessity of the cult or who see this necessity only in serving and glorifying the Lord through service to neighbour commit a grave chronological mistake: they behave either as though the Kingdom included everything or as though nothing yet belonged to the Kingdom. They fail to appreciate the eschatological situation of the Church in the world. The Church, therefore, shows by its worship that our world has been visited, and continues to be visited, by the Lord, that we are no longer alone and lost, that a place has been granted to us where God waits for us, to give Himself to us, and to permit us to appear before Him as we appeared before Him before the fall of man, and as we shall appear before Him after the parousia.

2. *The usefulness of the cult*

(a) It is only after having established the necessity of the cult that we can as it were stand back and speak of its usefulness. It is not its usefulness which makes it necessary, otherwise this necessity would be questioned.

In his preface to the German mass of 1526, Martin Luther —who happily did not say only this—remarks: "In short, if we establish liturgical orders, it is not at all for those who are already Christians, for the latter have no need of them. Such orders in fact have no intrinsic justification; their justification is in us: we are not yet all Christians, and they are there to make Christians of us. Those who are Christians perform their worship in spirit. If liturgical orders are needed, it is for those who must become Christians or who must be strengthened in the faith; just as a Christian has no need of baptism, of the Word, of the sacrament, inasmuch as he is a Christian—for as a Christian he already has all that—but inasmuch as he is a sinner. And if such orders are necessary, it is especially because of simple-minded and young people, who need to be and must be daily educated and trained in Scripture and the Word of God, so that they may become accustomed to it, skilled and fluent in it, to the end that they may be able to bear witness to their faith and in time may be able to teach others and help to further the reign of Christ. It is for these that we must read, sing, preach and write and make prayers; and to promote this end—were it necessary—I would have all the bells rung, and have the organs played with all their pipes sounding, and everything resound that can resound.''

This imprudent assertion of Luther which denies the necessity of the cult to insist only on its utility, has had considerable influence on rationalists. The latter have seized on the idea to justify their scorn of worship (except for children and those who remain children), and in their opinion true worship is seen much less in the liturgy than in a moral and honourable life and in social works. We must make no mistake about it, this rationalistic idea in practice reflects the average opinion of our church members; to go to church is not an act of obedience but the satisfaction of a need.

In short, divine service does not exist for God but for ourselves. Now, "he who sees in the cult only a means of furthering a missionary work not yet completed, uproots the cult instead of giving it a basis. For, what proves the value of justifying the necessity of the cult is that the justification remains valid even when, basically, the question of evangelization may be regarded as settled" (P. Brunner). But it must be recognized that if we Protestants have found it possible to justify the necessity of the cult by urging its pedagogic (or psychological or sociological) usefulness, this doubtless stems from the fact that we have given central place to the sermon. When the Lord's Supper as a counterweight to the sermon and as the ultimate motive of worship was absent, then the sermon has tended to make us forget that the cult is not a lesson addressed to men, but rather praise addressed to God (with all the homilectic preparation that such praise implies).

It is, therefore, wrong to base the necessity of the cult on its usefulness. But it would be equally wrong not to bear in mind its usefulness, which may be regarded as pedagogic, sociological, and psychological.

(a) Let us begin with the *pedagogic* usefulness of the cult. Worship in fact—and in this matter the Eastern Church should be our example—is the very background for the teaching of the Church. In worship, we learn to be Christian, to encounter God, the world and our neighbour. We learn faith, hope, and love. It is pre-eminently the school of Christianity.

Here we learn faith. *Lex orandi, lex credendi.* As K. Barth remarks, "This saying is not simply a pious dictum, but one of the most intelligent things that have ever been said about method in theology".[1] It is by prayer that we learn the Christian faith, because prayer gives us access to Him who is the object of the faith, and because what cannot be translated into prayer is bad theology.

Here, too, we learn hope. Intercession prevents us from despairing of the world and of men, and teaches us to meet them with Christian freedom and boldness. And the joy of worship prevents us from despairing of things and of creation, because there in worship creation already has a hint of its ultimate destiny—the *soli Deo gloria.*

Here we learn love. The presence of the brethren, respect for the role in worship which each of them exercises, the bread broken with them—all this makes the corporal nature of the Church alive, delivers us from the pride of aloofness, and teaches us to see mysteriously in our neighbour a member of the body of Christ, a Christ-bearer.

(b) But worship has also *sociological* usefulness. It brings men together and gives them the deepest cohesion, the most basic solidarity which can be found on this earth: "Because there is one loaf, we who are many are one body, for we all partake of the same loaf" (I Cor. 10: 17).

This sociological usefulness does not, however, consist merely in its property of cohesion. It implies, further, a personal integration and appeasement, since it imprints on our life a certain style and mode of being, a simplicity, a HAPLOTES, which deliver us from the agonies and the contradictions of the natural man. And it has further a cosmic implication in the sense that the cult, as has already

---

[1] *Das Geschenk der Freiheit*, Zollikon/Zürich, 1953, p. 22.

been suggested, unites men in the only way which does not make of them a solid body, that is, in and for the operation of grace, so that we may go so far as to say that Christian worship stabilizes the world, penetrating it with something which opposes its fragmentation and contends with its chaos.

(c) Finally, the cult is *psychologically* useful. It offers the faithful a refuge of peace and joy. Many attempts have been made to denigrate worship as though it were an escape from the tasks of witnessing, and a shelter from the temptations and commitments which necessarily characterize the Christian life. The accusation may be correct. But also it may often be false since it threatens to confuse the vigilance of the Church with the restlessness of insomnia. If I may be allowed a biological comparison, I would say (while realizing the ambiguity of the comparison) that the cult is as necessary to witnessing as sleep is to living. In order to be able to enter into the fray, one must also be able to withdraw from it. Really to take part in the general life of men, we must also be able to step back to the point of vantage from which we throw ourselves into human affairs; otherwise we risk forgetting that we are missionaries in the world and feel only that we are prisoners there. The existence of worship allows the Church to realize that it is free in the world. We entirely disregard the truth that worship is at the same time "mass" and "eucharist", both a sending forth from and a coming home to the source of power, if we think of worship as being, not a place of legitimate repose, the supernatural spot where the eschatological ANAPAUSIS is already evident, but, if I may dare to use the expression—a funk-hole! Besides, if liturgy and preaching are properly balanced, such a confusion will be simply impossible. To criticize the Church as being the sand in which the ostrich buries its head reveals a complete ignorance of the eschatological situation of the Church which makes worship necessary.

But worship is psychologically useful not only as a place of repose, where those souls who hunger and thirst for what we confess in our third article—the communion of saints, the forgiveness of sins, the resurrection of the body and the life everlasting—can find satisfaction. It is useful also as the

THE NECESSITY OF THE CULT

time and the place where, quite simply, we are able to tell the Lord that we love Him, to pay those vows of which the Psalmist so often speaks, and to dedicate ourselves to His service. To wish to keep people away from the service of the Temple, is to despise them: we are then doing as the disciples did who wished to keep children away from Jesus on the pretext that, being in good health, it would have been superstitious to present them for His blessing. Our services are already inappropriate enough for making acts of private devotion when a congregation is present. No doubt it will hardly be possible to acclimatize among us, suitably to a Reformed church, the custom prevalent in the Orthodox Church where an individual becomes the lectern for the reading of the Gospel, kneeling in the presence of all that the priest may place on his head the book of God's Word; as also it will be difficult to adopt the custom of lighting one candle from another to show one's desire to be joined to a chain of prayer and one's sense of being, by grace, a light of the world. But at least let us not forget that worship is an indispensable auxiliary to every authentic cure of souls.

(d) To these reasons could be added yet others. But those I have given suffice to show that we ought not to scorn the usefulness of the cult. Positively, this means that we must be very careful to show that we appreciate its usefulness for catechesis, communal life and the cure of souls.

This concern will be indicated by fighting against everything that might make worship wearisome, against negligence, incoherence, and improvization. It will also be indicated—and this I hope will soon be done—by putting into the hands of the parishioners the book of public prayers, so that they may take part effectively in the service. Perhaps another result will be the elimination of parishes that are too small, so that a cure of souls will include at least fifty communicants. It is extremely important that church members should not have the impression that they are attached to a concern that is on the decline.[1] But to enter into details here would carry us too far.

[1] "Ex conspectu mutuo laetitia major oriatur", said St. Jerome (Comment. Gal. 4-10, *P.L.* 26, col. 404).

3. *Obedience to the call to worship, and in its celebration*

"Let us not neglect to meet together, as is the habit of some, but let us encourage one another, and all the more as you see the Day drawing near." This injunction of the Letter to the Hebrews (10: 25) resounds throughout the history of the Church, from the time when Ignatius of Antioch wrote: "He who does not go to worship (HO ME ERCHOMENOS EPI TO AUTO) already is showing pride, and has condemned himself, for it is written: God resists the proud",[1] until the present, and including the recommendation of the Later Helvetic Confession: "all those who . . . despise . . . holy assemblies and hold aloof despise true religion and should be exhorted both by the pastors and by the faithful magistrate not to separate themselves out of rebellion, and not to persist in disdaining holy assemblies."[2]

Since this is not a course in the ethics of liturgy, we cannot delay long over the question of the need for attendance at worship, but will limit ourselves to three remarks:

(a) *Liturgical obedience is demanded of us because of the necessity and usefulness of the cult, and because of the salvation which Jesus Christ has wrought for us.* We have seen that the cult is necessary because it was instituted by Christ, because it is the work of the Holy Spirit, because it is an agent of the saving process, and because the age of the eternal Sabbath has not yet been inaugurated. We have seen further that the cult is useful in church life, as regards catechesis, communal life and the healing of the soul. These reasons suffice to justify the affirmation that worship is not something which is meant for our pleasure, but which demands obedience, and that this obedience should not be regarded as a burden, but as a grace: hence worship is composed of songs, not of complaints. In his fine passage on worship as obedience in the Holy Spirit, Peter Brunner writes: "The essential, decisive happening, alike for every one of us individually and for the whole world, takes place in no other way than through the saving event of the proclamation of the Word, and the celebration of the Lord's Supper. If this

---

[1] Eph. 5: 3.   [2] Chap. 22.

decisive happening no longer takes place, it is no longer possible, in any other sphere of our life, to serve God in a way He approves. If this decisive happening weakens, then all other Christian ways of serving God weaken, become aberrant and fruitless."

Negatively, this implies that to neglect the cult is to sabotage the work of salvation, and that is why Ignatius of Antioch spoke of the pride of those who are idle in attendance at the Church's worship. But more needs to be said. In Chapter II we spoke of the cult as the epiphany of the Church, and suggested that in worship the Church is manifest. Hence, it is in taking part in the cult that we confess ourselves to be Christian. Or negatively, not to attend the cult is to injure the unity and the fulness of the body of Christ, to divide and scatter the Church. Here I am thinking of an important, third century text called the *Didascalia of the Apostles* which exhorts the bishops as follows: "When you teach, command and persuade the people to be faithful in meeting in Church (the liturgical assembly); let them not fail, but be faithful to go there, so that no one diminishes the Church by non-attendance or cuts off a member from the body of Christ. Let no one think only of others but also of himself when he hears the words of our Lord: he who gathers not with me scatters. Since then you are the members of Christ, do not get lost outside the Church by failing to go there. For you have Christ as head, as He himself teaches and declares: you are sharers with us. Do not then despise yourselves, and do not deprive the Lord of His members, do not tear and scatter His body" (chap. 13).

To fail to go to worship, then, is not only to withdraw oneself from the operation of the saving process: it is to sin against the body of Christ: much more, it is to deny to Him who has saved us by incorporating us into His body the gift of ourselves, it is to disown His lordship, it is to belie our self-surrender to Him, and to tear ourselves away from His grace. Hence it is, quite precisely, to play the devil's game.

(b) *Liturgical obedience concerns two points: obeying the summons to worship and obeying the invitation to the Lord's Supper.* It is not merely a matter of going to church; we must take full part in worship. It is a question of taking our place in the congregation and doing our part: of listening to the proclamation of the Word when it is read and preached, of confessing the faith of the Church, joining in the hymns of the Church, confirming by our *Amen* the prayers spoken in the name of the congregation, and also, quite as much, of accepting the invitation to the Lord's table. The Council of Antioch (341) had no hesitation in expelling from the Church and subjecting to penance "those who enter the Church and hear the Holy Scriptures without joining in the prayer of the people or communicating at the Eucharist *propter aliquam insolentiam*". It is sabotage and obstruction, as well as ingratitude to the Lord, to believe that mere attendance at worship is sufficient; and that is why, incidentally, it is so deplorable that in most of our churches there are galleries which, instead of concentrating the congregation, seem to invite the presence of mere spectators who are unwilling to commit themselves. We ought to be bold enough to forbid access to the galleries so long as the ground floor pews are not full.

(c) There remains three further remarks to be made:

Firstly, by patient instruction and pastoral work we must uproot the common opinion, spread by rationalism, that worship is not really necessary, that at most it is useful, pedagogically and pastorally, and that in consequence Christian obedience does not refer to the cult. Before being vexed by the indifference of so many of the faithful about public worship, we must free them from the heresy which declares that worship is *ad libitum*, and that the stronger we are spiritually, the more easily it can be dispensed with.

But to succeed in this we must also, by liturgical instruction, about which we shall speak in our conclusion, restore to worship its sacramental plenitude, restore to the people their share in it, and restore to the paschal joy its proper place. It is only in so far as worship is what it ought to be that it will be possible to insist on the regular participation of the faithful. Further, when the cult approximates more closely to the ideal, it will be less necessary to stress these points, owing to the powerful attraction which worship exercises over the faithful. We must not be surprised in fact if services which are mutilated, odd, disjointed, or priest-ridden, services in which any sign of eschatological enthusiasm is suspect, cease to be attractive—unless of course they provide really inspiring preaching (and decidedly not all do this!).

Our last point is more delicate, because it might lead us to think that we need not be too distressed by the ever-increasing indifference to public worship. If it is obvious that we must do everything possible to instruct the faithful in the need for obedience to the summons to worship, we can hardly hope that in the present situation the cult will bring together all the baptized. In relation to the requirements of baptism and the "episcopal" capacities of the pastors, we baptize far too many people. The considerable decline which we have to note must not therefore depress us, nor cause us to indulge in fruitless lamentations; it ought rather to drive us to review at once our baptismal practice, so as to hasten the day when the normal situation of the Church—a situation in which the number of communicants practically coincides with the number of the baptized—will return. Thus, rather than complain about de-Christianization, which is in itself a challenge to the Church to renew its self-awareness, we should do much better to set to work quietly and without restraint, to restore to the cult its fulness and to the Church its true dimensions. If the whole population is the object of missionary preaching, the whole population, as such, is not "baptizable". We must leave aside the interpretation of baptism as a sign of prevenient grace, otherwise we shall confuse the Word and the sacrament.

This then is the conclusion of our first part, which treats of principles. In the first three chapters we attempted a theological definition of Christian worship: it sums up the history of salvation, it enables the Church to be manifest as what it is, it marks the end and the future of the world. Then in Chapter IV we saw that the Christian cult which celebrates the incarnation, passion and glorification of the eternal Son of God, cannot dispense with forms, and that its formal expression is not a painful concession on our part, but a grace and a source of hope—hence the propriety or otherwise of certain forms of Christian worship. And we ended, as a protest against the rationalist idea that the cult is not essential to the life of the Church, by trying to give a theological justification of its necessity. We can now turn to the theological and practical examination of problems of celebration.

PART TWO

PROBLEMS OF
CELEBRATION

In this second part of our study, we shall again have five chapters which deal with the celebration of worship and correspond more or less exactly to the chapters which, in the first part, were devoted to principles.

These will deal with the essentials of what should be said about: the elements of worship, its participants, the day and the place of its celebration, and its structure. I say "the essentials", because the present work does not attempt to do more than sketch the outlines of liturgiology. The reader is invited, on the basis of what we have to say, to pursue his personal researches in whatever domain interests him most.

Problems of celebration are to be discussed, and we shall certainly be dealing more with precise and practical problems than in the first part. But, since this is not a liturgical laboratory, even here we shall have to remain within the bounds of theological study. The chapter numbers follow on from the first part.

CHAPTER SIX

THE COMPONENTS OF THE CULT

IN THIS chapter we have two main problems: we must first list the component parts of the cult; we must then examine critically the various ways of uniting these elements in their interrelation.

Clearly, to carry out this programme as it merits, we should have to devote some time to the study of the history of worship, because we should then be in a position to see how, little by little, the great liturgical monuments of the Church have been built up, what is essential in them and what is merely accidental and decorative, and what is the source of deviations. This historical study, however, cannot here be undertaken. Hence I refer the reader, in a general way, to the works of A. Baumstark, P. E. Mercenier, G. Dix, Rietschel-Graff, J. A. Jungmann, R. Stählin, and W. Maxwell, and the numerous historical parts of *Leiturgia*. We shall take them into account, but as a whole.

1. List of the elements of the cult

By elements of the cult is meant "the forms and the functions through which liturgical reception and liturgical action are carried out and which, in their organic co-operation, constitute the cultic event" (O. Haendler). The Reformed tradition—faithful in this respect to the authentic Catholic tradition—stresses four major components of Christian worship. In expounding the fourth commandment, the Heidelberg Catechism teaches that the Christian must assiduously attend public worship, especially on Sundays, "in order to hear there the Word of God, to participate in the holy sacraments, to invoke publicly the Lord, and to contribute in a Christian spirit to the help of the poor" (question 103; the "responsorial" character of all this is noteworthy). The Later Helvetic Confession in Ch. 22 teaches too "that holy church assemblies are necessary both to proclaim legitimately the Word of God and to make public prayers and supplications, as also to celebrate the sacraments properly (*legitima*): likewise in order to take a church collection, both for the poor and for necessary church expenses". Although slight changes might be necessary, we shall retain these four headings, and say that the elements of the cult are the Word of God, the sacraments, the prayers (in their various forms) and the liturgical witness to the life of fellowship.

(a) *The Word of God*

All Christians agree that the Word of God is an essential constituent of Christian worship. Without it, the cult would not be a living effective encounter between God and His people, but a mere human monologue or dialogue. It would not be a miracle: the service would not be a response, but rather a blind groping, longing and despair: the Eucharist would not be the crown of the cult, but at best an unexplained mystery and at worst a magical act. Hence if we place the Word of God first, it is not because we wish to make it the sole feature, but to stress that without it the cult would be emptied of its substance and indistinguishable from a non-Christian cult.

The whole act of worship is sustained by the Word of God: it forms the texture of the liturgy, it is the light which illuminates the Eucharist, it assures the faithful that the divine presence is not illusory, but real. But it is manifest in various forms. P. Brunner gives six: the reading of scripture, preaching, the absolution, the greeting and the blessing, the psalmody of the Church, and those indirect forms of the Word such as hymns, confessions of faith, doxologies and the collects. It is in the interests of clarification rather than simplicity that we concentrate in what follows on three main forms of the Word: the reading of the Bible, the "clerical" proclamation of the Word, and the "prophetic" proclamation of the Word, i.e. preaching. Since we are dealing with liturgy and not systematic theology, I

130

may be excused from including here a theology of the Word of God.

(i) *The "anagnostic" proclamation of the Word of God:*

We cannot here dwell on the history of the reading of scripture in worship. We may simply recall that the Church took over the custom from Judaism (cf. Luke 4: 16) which seems to have possessed, from before the Christian era and at least for the Torah, a fixed lectionary of pericopes which had to be read on the sabbaths of the year. The reading of scripture also seems to have formed part of the normal worship of the apostolic Church. If the first to attest it clearly is Justin, in his Apology—where he relates that "the memoirs of the apostles (doubtless meaning the Gospels), and the writings of the prophets, were read, for as long as time permitted" (ch. 67), we find also in St. Paul exhortations to read his letters at meetings for worship (cf. Col. 4: 16),[1] and it is very probable that the exhortation to Timothy (1 Tim. 4: 13) does not allude to his colleague's private reading, but to public reading (the OT, extracts from the gospels?), since, in the same breath, he enjoins him to exhort and to teach. What also leads us to suppose that the reading of scripture was an essential part of the Christian cult from the beginning, is that there is nowhere any suggestion that such reading was an innovation, and that, as far back as our exact sources go, it seems never to have been challenged. Hence we may conclude, with all necessary prudence, that the reading of scripture was always an integral part of Christian worship. We shall see moreover that the Church very soon organized such readings.

This tradition was questioned by the Calvinistic reformation. Not that the latter gave up the reading of the Bible, but that, after certain hesitations, it eventually gave up scriptural reading for its own sake, proclamation of the Word of God by such reading alone, in favour of a reading which was a prelude to preaching. J. F. Ostervald in the eighteenth

[1] Is the letter to be read to all (1 Thess. 5: 27) the one which the apostle ends with this injunction, or that sent by the Council of Jerusalem to the Gentile Christians, Acts 15: 23f.? Cff. 2 Tim. 4: 13. Are books to be read during public worship?

century strove hard to restore to the Reformed Church the proclamation of God's word by scriptural reading alone, and if this has generally been accepted by the English and French-speaking Reformed Churches, it has been much less so by those using the German language. Even recently, a young German-Swiss theologian thought that to resist the subjectivism which is apparent in a "preaching service" where preaching is thematic rather than exegetic, by trying to bring back the objective reading of the Bible, is tantamount to driving out the devil by Beelzebub: "The Word of God which has come to us once for all in Jesus Christ and is attested by Holy Scripture wills to meet us afresh today. This means that it should not be recited, put into circulation like dried meat or dried fruits, but that it should be a living event; in short: it must be preached." This point of view seems to me inadmissible not only because it runs contrary to the whole of ancient Christian tradition (which is not decisive in itself, but significant), or because nothing would lead us to think that Paul's letters were preached, rather than read, by their recipients; it seems to me wrong also because it postulates that the bringing to life of written words can only be effected by preaching about them, and this denies the value of any reading; then again it gives preachers the monopoly of understanding scripture—they alone are capable of making it alive, and thus supplant the Holy Spirit—and consequently it denies the efficacy of *all* Biblical reading. If we thus reject the reading of the scriptures in worship in favour of preaching about them only, we clericalize the cult, and strike a mortal blow at private reading of the Bible, depriving it of any promise of blessing.

But this invites us to reflect on what happens when the Word of God is proclaimed by its reading. There takes place nothing essentially different from that which takes place when the Word is proclaimed by exposition and application (although there is a difference between these two events, to which we shall return). We might sum up the event of the reading of the Word by saying that then the Word which had been in chains, imprisoned by the letters of the alphabet, comes alive. The mystery of writing and reading—which might almost be called paschal, a death and a resurrection—

132

is something that has become so common that we have ceased to be aware of it, and that is perhaps why the traditional Reformed attitude towards scripture reading without exposition reveals a certain contempt. It is forgotten that the Gospel is enclosed in the letter of the Bible and must be freed, that to read scripture is to experience the paschal joy;[1] the Lord reappears, He who is the Word, to tell us of His love and His will, to teach us who He is and who we are, to summon us and give us life. But He does not reappear automatically. In deciphering scripture, we can also draw from it a corpse, a dead letter. Hence, the reading of the Bible in worship is traditionally preceded by an epiklesis, an invocation of the Holy Spirit, that the Word may really come alive for us so as to accomplish its work of salvation and judgment. If reading alone had been incapable of this spiritual miracle, if preaching had been necessary to achieve it, the apostles would have written nothing and would have trusted oral tradition alone. The very fact that they buried their witness to Jesus Christ in these hieroglyphic signs that are letters proves that they believed the Spirit-inspired interpretation of these hieroglyphs would be able to resurrect their witness and enable them themselves to remain alive in the Church. "In the reading of the apostolic word, the apostle of Jesus Christ himself appears, with his witness that is basic for the Church, *hic et nunc* at the heart of the community, to feed it with that living Word" (P. Brunner).

But which passages of scripture shall we choose? How shall we choose them, and who will choose them? Today in our Church we usually say that they must be chosen so as to support the text which will be the theme of the sermon, and that the person to choose them is the preacher. If this choice is made in a disciplined way, and following a sound plan, and if as far as possible it takes into account the course of the ecclesiastical year, now that our Church has recognized the canon of scripture, it is a legitimate mode of procedure, although there is always a certain risk of arbitrariness. I have said now that the Church has recognized the canon of scripture, meaning now that the Church has decided which books can be read in worship, for it must be recognized that

[1] See in this perspective 2 Cor. 3: 6.

we owe the formation of the canon in large measure to the reading of the Word of God in Church worship.[1] The reference to the canonization of scripture shows that the Church has every right to choose the texts which it wishes to be proclaimed in Church worship, for in this way it can show what it considers fundamental for Christian instruction, and also can exercise a useful, even necessary, supervision over the teaching of the ministers.

In this choice, the Church—or the minister who decides to take the risk—can proceed in two ways, both of them valid and traditional, and each having advantages and disadvantages: the *lectio continua* which reads through an entire book or epistle as one reads a serial (a method which was much used in the primitive Church and was restored by the Calvinistic reformation[2]), and the *lectio selecta* which takes here and there from the Bible a passage which is a unity in itself, a pericope. The system of the *lectio continua* is more historical, that of the *lectio selecta* more systematic. Generally speaking, it is the latter system which has prevailed, and it is usual in four of the five Confessions which declare their fidelity to ancient tradition: the Orthodox, the Lutheran, the Anglican and the Roman. Among ourselves this method is becoming ever more widespread, as may be shown by the lists of pericopes which are more and more being affixed to our service books, and we must rejoice about it, provided that it does not entirely evict the *lectio continua* which emphasizes more the liberty of God.

The history of these pericopes shows that the Church has never feared a certain liberty and reformability in drawing up the lists. Thus, there are many local variations, into the details of which we cannot enter. Up to the fourth century at least in the East, up to the fifth century in Rome, and the seventh century in the Gallican rites, three readings at least took place each Sunday: of the OT, of the Epistle and of the

[1] Although tradition knows of certain books which have been publicly read without having been canonized (e.g. the Heidelberg Catechism at the time of the Reformation, whose very arrangement into nine *lectiones* implies its liturgical reading), and of certain canonical books which were not used for public reading.

[2] To my knowledge, Prussia alone, in the Lutheran Church, adopted for a time the *lectio continua* in the sixteenth century.

Gospel. Then, except for Holy Week and certain festivals, the OT—of course with the exception of the Psalms—disappeared from the Sunday lectionary,[1] and it would be worth while to conduct an enquiry into the deep theological repercussions which this decanonization of the OT, this "marcionization" of the Bible, has had on the life of the Church, in particular as regards its doctrine of election and its awareness of being involved in the process of salvation. Modern Reformed lectionaries (as also that of the Anglican Church) quite rightly provide for the three major types of witness in the Bible—the prophet, the apostle and the Lord— to be read every Sunday, and this measure should be scrupulously respected, even when the pastor himself chooses the Biblical readings by reference to the text which he proposes to expound in his sermon. The congregation must be sure that every Sunday they will hear passages chosen from these three major types of Biblical witness.

In what order should these readings be made? It might well be supposed that the text to be read last and as a culmination should be that on which the sermon is to be preached. But this procedure produces an artificial gradation. Hence it is preferable to adopt the sequence which is both logical and traditional: the OT, the Epistle, and finally the Gospel, which as Origen said is the crown of the whole of scripture. And it is usual to mark the importance of the latter by additional solemnity. If it would be difficult in our confession to adopt something like the Gospel procession of the Orthodox Church, and even seems impossible to restore the kiss given by the reader to the Gospel book—a kiss which was maintained by Zwingli, on whom liturgiologists have been unduly severe—it is perfectly possible to ask the people to stand for the reading of the words of Christ.

We will not linger over the question of who should give the Biblical reading. The problem will recur in the following chapter, when we speak of the participants in worship. It is enough to note here that in this matter there are several traditions. For some—and it is the case in the Church of

---

[1] The reading of the OT in worship has been maintained in certain Eastern churches, such as the Nestorian, the Jacobite, and the Armenian.

England, and also, now, in the Church of Rome—the Jewish tradition is maintained according to which any man (for the Roman Church, any woman if there are no men present) who is a member of the Church, i.e. baptized—may be called to read the passage of scripture. For others—and this was especially so in the ancient Church—the reading of scripture was reserved to ministers (sometimes even to the bishop alone), or at least to confessors. In my opinion the best solution, and the most reverent, is to have three appointed readers: the pastor and two elders. The pastor will not reserve to himself the reading of the Gospel, but the reading of that passage about which he is to preach, whether it be in the OT, the Epistle or the Gospel. It goes without saying that this reading must take place with the reader turned towards the congregation, and in the tone of a solemn public proclamation, and not from the pulpit but from a lectern placed near the altar. Since there are three readings, it seems useless to encourage among ourselves the custom of distinguishing the Epistle side (the left) from the Gospel side (the right), a custom which became widespread in the West during the Middle Ages. There are some symbolisms which become a dead letter. So long as the elders have no official liturgical robes, we should be concerned to see that their dress is suitable for the office entrusted to them. As is very judiciously observed by Father François Louvel: "It is deplorable to see men sometimes . . . read in public while wearing a mackintosh which is not even buttoned up."[1]

The problem of scripture reading in church also raises the question of the version to be used for the purpose. Unlike other Churches, we have no "authorized version". Until the day when we shall have recovered this normal pastoral discipline—and without wishing to suppress the use of other versions in private devotion—we shall read the Bible in the version which our Church none the less favours, i.e. the one which it gives to catechumens and newly-married couples, that is, the so-called synodal version. Let us add—and we shall return to the point—that a large-sized Bible in this version should be found in every place of worship, and it alone should be found: it is useless to make the ledges of the

[1] *La Maison-Dieu*, No. 60, p. 117.

pulpit a museum of ancient Bibles, and wrong to camouflage the bereft state of the holy table by placing on it, in majestic display, an eighteenth-century Bible which is quite unusable.

A final point remains to be considered: shall we "lay bare" the scripture reading, simply indicating the context of the passage to be read, or shall we "clothe" it, and dignify it with words of introduction, conclusion and explanation? There is no theological choice in the matter, and the decision will depend above all on two factors: firstly, what we shall later describe as the "social" level of the service (village, urban or conventual), then on the necessary presence of an alive congregation, capable of making response to the OT reading by "Thanks be to God!" and by the antiphon of a gradual; to the Epistle by "Glory be to Thee, O Lord!" and the antiphon of the alleluia; to the Gospel by "Praise be to Thee, O Christ!"; capable also of saying antiphonally the beautiful prayers which prepare for the reading of the Gospel. This enrichment of the scriptural reading by responses, prayers of preparation, the gradual and the alleluia is an optional matter, and a type of worship from which it is absent is neither compromised nor impaired in its essentials. Thus it can suffice to say: "The reading from the OT: it is written in the book . . . chapter . . ." "The reading of the Epistle: it is written in the Epistle . . . chapter . . ." "Let us stand to hear the Gospel. It is written in the Gospel according to St. . . ." There is no need to give the verses; it is needless to indulge in the protestant mania for remarks before or after each reading. If we follow this rule of simplicity, we may conclude the readings by some such formula as: "Blessed are they who hear the Word of God and keep it", or "Lord, to whom else should we go? Thou hast the words of eternal life." On the other hand, as we have noted, the scriptural readings should be opened by a prayer of epiklesis. It is this latter especially which form the liturgical vesture of Biblical readings, for it places them in their authentic theological perspective.

(ii) *The "clerical" proclamation of the Word of God:*
By this somewhat ambiguous phrase[1] is meant those

---

[1] I use this term, for want of a better, because this proclamation is reserved to those whose part it is (cf. Acts 1: 17, KLEROS) to

moments when, in the service, the minister, by means of a Biblical formula, declares and gives to the people the *greeting*, the *absolution* and the *blessing* of the Lord.

Let us begin by a few brief historical remarks. In that sort of liturgical pattern which forms the thread of St. Luke's story of the appearance of the Risen Lord to the twelve, the Lord, suddenly appearing, addresses the disciples thus: "Peace be unto you" (24: 36). Later, He eats with them and opens their minds to the understanding of the scriptures, charging them to pronounce forgiveness (v. 47) to the whole world. "Then He led them out as far as Bethany and lifting up His hands He blessed them. While He blessed them, He parted from them and was carried up into heaven" (vv. 50f.). It is this which is repeated in the cult, and that is why it contains at least the greeting and the blessing, and in some liturgical traditions, the absolution. We cannot here go into the history of these liturgical features, which is as complicated and many-sided as that of any other of the features of Christian worship. Let us note only that the *greeting*—for the main Sunday service—is not directly found in any of the great classical forms of the liturgy; that the absolution, as a proclamation of forgiveness, is found only in Calvin; but that all the liturgies have a place for a final blessing. This does not mean that there are not many exceptions to the general rule. Without in the least wishing to question the value of this tradition, it is permissible to examine the problem theologically without, at the start, accepting the solution of the current liturgical tradition.

In the form of the apostolic greeting: "Grace and peace be unto you from God our Father and the Lord Jesus Christ", or some similar formula, the greeting is hardly to be found in liturgical tradition. It is found, however, very frequently, as a preface to the sermon. Elsewhere—as in the Roman mass and the Zwinglian liturgy for example—the minister begins with the words: "In the name of the Father, and of

have received from the Lord an authorization, recognized by the Church, to be ministers of the Gospel. If I do not call it sacramental—which would throw the stress more on what takes place than on the one who ministers to the mystery—it is because the two other types of proclamation have also and equally a sacramental virtue and character.

the Son and of the Holy Ghost" in order to emphasize the fact that the whole service is taking place in the presence, under the authority and with the power of the Holy Trinity. Again, in Calvin we find an exhortation which is also a promise: "Our help is in the name of the Lord: who has made heaven and earth, Amen": an exhortation also found in the Church of Geneva today. We might mention also that this invocation or exhortation is found in the liturgy of the Reformed Church of France, after the greeting, in the form of an appeal to God to be with His people.

What are we to think of this problem from a theological point of view? Let us notice first that an invocation, a kind of *Maranatha*, is perfectly in place on the threshold of the service. Theologically it has a greater significance than might be thought, for it attests that God is not necessarily present, and that His presence can only be an answer to prayer. The fact of a congregation having gathered in the house of God does not automatically guarantee the presence of God, for He is not to be imprisoned in houses made with hands. But this initial *Maranatha* while stressing that the liturgical encounter about to take place is a favour bestowed, and an anticipation of the eschatological divine presence, has also one disadvantage in the sense that it might imply that the Church arrives before God does at the Sunday tryst for worship, and that the initiative in the cult lies not with God but with the Church. This argument which underlines the fidelity of God—and which is counterbalanced, in the course of the liturgy, by the prayers of epiklesis and the eucharistic *Maranatha*—seems to me less convincing than the one which straightaway underlines the liberty of God. That is why, as a rule, the greeting—which is perfectly in place on the threshold of the service—seems to me preferable to the invocation: it is God who begins the liturgical dialogue. In any case we must avoid the illogicality of the French Reformed Church which invites the people to sing: "Lord, be Thou among us" *after* He has manifested His presence by the greeting.

As a declaration of forgiveness, pronounced to the whole congregation, the *absolution* is not found before the seventeenth century except in Calvin's liturgy where it takes the following form: "Let each one of you truly recognize himself to be a sinner and abase himself before God, trusting that the heavenly Father wills to be propitious to him in Jesus Christ. To all those who in this way repent and seek Jesus Christ as their Saviour I pronounce absolution in the name of the Father and of the Son and of the Holy Ghost. Amen." Everywhere else, in the liturgies which have become classic, the absolution, if it is there, is given in a precatory form. We dealt at length with this problem last year in some parochial lectures, when speaking about different forms of confession, and in particular we discussed the possibility and the legitimacy of a communal liturgical confession. Hence, I shall not delay over this except to recall that this moment of the service, traditional especially with the Reformed Churches, is the result of Calvin's effort to put an end to private penitence, without at the same time losing sight of the need for penitence in the Christian life (private penitence becoming once more, as in the early Church, a measure not of personal discipline but of public ecclesiastical discipline). This solution of Calvin's was justified only to the extent to which it was supported by effective and enforced ecclesiastical discipline. Unfortunately, his solution has remained traditional in the Reformed Church, without being upheld by the church discipline which justified it. In spite of that, and on condition that we try quickly to recover the discipline which we have lost I think we must risk, in public worship, declaring the absolution of sins, of course on the understanding that it is preceded by the repentance which is indicated in Calvin's formula. It should not, however, eliminate the possibility of the *confiteor*, to which we shall return.

All the liturgies include the final *blessing*, although its form varies. "May the blessing of the Lord and His mercy come upon us, by His grace and love, now, always and for evermore" says the liturgy of St. John Chrysostom. "Benedicat vos omnipotens Deus, Pater et Filius et Spiritus Sanctus" says the mass. The Prayer Book uses, before the trinitarian blessing, the words of St. Paul in Phil. 4: 7; Calvin, Zwingli and Luther chose the Aaronite benediction (Num. 6: 24ff.) sometimes with small variants, and if Luther chose it, it was because he had the idea that Jesus used it at the time of

His ascension. Contemporary liturgies are familiar with and propose many variants. In traditional liturgies, the blessing is always phrased in the second person plural.[1] Hence it is not a question of an *exoptatio* but of a *donatio*.[2] "A Church which did not dare to ask a blessing except in a precatory form, that is, by using the first person plural, thus one which was not bold enough to bless by direct address, would show but little faith, and would not be obeying the obligation to use the authority committed to it by transmission of authority" (P. Brunner). The blessing is normally accompanied by a gesture. In many confessions this is the sign of the cross made over the congregation. Among ourselves— and this is certainly better—it is the Biblical gesture of benediction, i.e. the lifting up of the hands, which is also the gesture used by Jesus when He separated from His disciples (Luke 24: 50ff.).

What takes place in this "clerical" proclamation of the Word of God, at the pronouncement of the greeting, the absolution and the blessing? Clearly, an event that is brought about by divine grace. The Word of God, perhaps even more than when it is proclaimed in an "anagnostic" or "prophetic" manner, comes into efficacious action with all the power of the divine RHEMA. Asmussen does not hesitate to speak of the "event" of benediction. P. Brunner— referring to the absolution, but the same is true of the greeting and the blessing—observes that this clerical proclamation of the Word of God is, in worship, the closest approximation to the sacrament, it is what most sharply underlines the sacramental character of the Word; we have here "a concentration of the Gospel, in so far as it is the Word, which can only be paralleled by that concentration of the

---

[1] Except with Luther who—by fidelity to the scriptures?—uses the second person singular.

[2] Neque vero haec benedictio inanis tantum sonus verborum est, aut verbalis quaedam imprecatio qua alius alii bona dicit et comprecatur, ut cum dico: det tibi Deus sobolem pulchram et morigeram. Haec verba sunt tantum optativa, quibus nihil alteri confero, sed tantum exopto, estque benedictio pure eventualis et incerta. Haec vero benedictio patriarchae Isaac est indicativa et certa in futurum. Non est exoptatio, sed donatio boni, qua dicit: accipe haec dona quae verbis promitto. (M. Luther, *W.A.* 43, p. 524, cited by P. Brunner.)

Gospel which is actualized in the reception of the body and the blood of Jesus Christ". It is the creative and efficacious Word of God which is then uttered and that is why those moments of the service when this Word resounds are especially fraught with spiritual power. The blessing is a word charged with power, in which God Himself or a man representing Him transmits to persons, living beings or things, salvation, welfare, and the joy of living, and this same power is operative in the greeting and the absolution.[1] In the absolution, it operates as a power delivering us from the chains of sin, in the greeting as a power which sends forth upon us the divine peace. That is why, in the Church, peace is not given "as the world gives it" (John 14: 27), that is, as a wish; it is given as a reality. This establishment of the "radio-active" character of clerical proclamation has two consequences: firstly, that, in worship, it is reserved to those whom God has chosen as His ministers, His ambassadors; secondly, that it is devalued and impaired if the ministers have not the courage to make it in the second person plural. Those ministers who transform the proclamation into a wish expressed in the first person plural are not showing humility, but sabotaging the liturgy, depriving the faithful of part of the grace which God wills to give them. God has chosen ministers to bring into effect the process of salvation, not to impair it.

(iii) *The "prophetic" proclamation of the Word of God:*
    If what we shall say about this clearly falls short of the importance which should be attached to it, this is not in the slightest because of any resentment at the exaggerated part it plays in Reformed worship (exaggerated, not in itself, but relatively to the other components of the cult, especially the Lord's Supper); it is solely because to treat it properly would require a complete study of homilectics. We may therefore say in all sincerity that it is not from contempt. but from respect for it, that we do not propose to discuss it at length here: we are justified in this because it is so important a subject that in theology a whole special discipline is devoted to it, namely, homilectics.

---

[1] Whether this absolution is privately given or is risked conditionally in public worship.

We cannot here begin with a study of the history of the sermon. We will merely remark that the importance—I do not say the place but the importance—attributed to it is the surest barometer of the liturgical fidelity of a Church. The atrophy or the hypertrophy of the sermon—and the history of the Church gives evidence of both—is a sign of disease, and all the periods of health in the life of the Church are also periods when the sermon reached great heights of development. Wherever the Church is faithful—we shall see why—it takes care to cultivate the art of preaching, the "prophetic" proclamation of the Word of God.

What is the difference between this proclamation of the Word and the others? It is twofold. Firstly, in the hands of God, the sermon is a basic means by which there takes place a direct prophetic intervention in the life of the faithful and of the Church, with the object of consoling, setting to rights, reforming, questioning: in short, it shows that the Word of God cannot become the prisoner of the Church (a freedom demonstrated much less clearly by the two other forms of proclamation), but that it is always also external to the Church, a living force which strikes the Church from without. *Viva vox evangelii.* This is what is intimated by P. Brunner when he remarks that preaching has a "historico-concrete, free, pneumatic character". It prevents the petrifaction of the Word of God in the *illic et tunc* of the event in which it was enshrined, of its coming in Jesus Christ, and makes that *illic et tunc* newly operative in the *hic et nunc,* thus showing that the other forms in which the Word is now operative, especially the Eucharist, are not illusions, but reality.

The second difference is that preaching is not merely the sign of God's freedom, it also manifests man's freedom, since it is that phase of worship in which the preacher can bear witness to the truth and reality of what has been proclaimed by the reader of scripture. Thus it introduces into the service an element of witness-bearing. In so doing it expresses one of the deepest mysteries of the love of God: if God gives Himself to us, it is to enter into the depth of our being and invite us to disclose Him to the world, clothed with our flesh. The mystery of preaching reflects the mystery of the conception and birth of Jesus, and there is no deeper pattern for the spirituality of the preacher than that of the Virgin Mary, who receives, clothes with her substance and gives forth to the world, God's eternal Word, true God and true man.

If preaching—at least where certain charismatic manifestations are no longer in place—is the only element of the cult which has the power to bring a wholesome disturbance into the ordered progress of the liturgy, it does not, however, disrupt it, if it remains conscious of its underlying eucharistic intention. The preaching of the Word has in fact always a sacramental purpose, it ever seeks as its end a sacrament which will confirm and seal it, or rather which will prove that it has borne fruit.[1] If it is non-liturgical missionary preaching, it aims at the sacrament of baptism; if it is parochial, liturgical preaching, it is orientated towards the Eucharist. That is why, if the proclamation of the Word of God is necessary to the Eucharist to prevent it from becoming self-centred and magical, the Eucharist is necessary to preaching to prevent it from degenerating into self-centred intellectualism or mere chat. Therefore, the sermon is not an element in worship which exists for its own sake, but is integral to the structure of the liturgy as a whole. It is not the culminating point of the cult, it is not its head and crown; its function is rather to open, to purify and to protect the avenue which leads to the altar. Here, perhaps, lies the danger of having detached the sermon from the structure of the liturgy and made of it a special discipline; while, by so doing, we underline its true importance, we run the risk of confining it within itself so that it tends to absorb the service as a whole, or of allowing it to appear as a disturbing element which should be diminished in importance or even removed altogether.

We have seen that the "anagnostic" proclamation of the Word of God in a sense resurrects the witnesses to this Word, permitting them to repeat, *hic et nunc*, their witness. We have seen that its clerical proclamation makes it operative in a sacramental way. The efficacy of such proclamation is no less when it is a question of prophetic proclamation. Despite the aspect of a human testimony which it also bears, Christian preaching is not simply a meditation on the Word of God.

---

[1] The same may be said of the other forms of proclamation.

It is a proclamation of that Word, it implies a divine miracle. "Preaching is the prophetic word of the Church, mediating and guaranteeing the presence of Christ" (A. D. Müller). And Luther—and with him all true preachers—was able to say, with the fine freedom born of his obstinate individualism: "A preacher has not to say a Pater or to ask forgiveness of sins when he has preached (if he is a true preacher), but he must say with Jeremiah, joyfully: 'Lord, Thou knowest, what has proceeded from my mouth is right and is well-pleasing to Thee' and again with St. Paul and all the apostles and prophets he can heartily say: *Haec dixit Dominus*, it is God Himself who has spoken that. And again: I have been an apostle and prophet of Jesus Christ in preaching this sermon. There is here no need nor is it good that he should ask forgiveness as though he had taught what was wrong. For this is God's word and not mine . . . Whoever cannot proudly say as much of his preaching, let him give up the task, for he is a liar and a blasphemer".[1] It is this which the credal writings of the Reformers mean when ascribing to preaching the power of the keys, and if we can criticize them for anything, it is not for having recognized in preaching this efficacity, it is for not having made equally clear—what is implicit in their writings—that the same mystery inheres in the two other normal forms of proclamation.

Is the proclamation of God's Word through preaching an essential feature of Christian worship? Was Luther right to say: "Where the Word of God is not preached, it is better neither to sing, nor to read, nor to meet for worship"?[2] When it is a question of the Sunday worship of the parish, we must agree with Luther's declaration, which furthermore corresponds to a general requirement of the Reformation and to the practice of the ancient Church. It must be endorsed on the same basis, neither more nor less, as the requirement which demands a celebration of the Eucharist at a service of worship. But why is it absolutely necessary? As a general thesis, I would say that preaching is necessary in worship because the Kingdom of God has not yet come with power.

[1] W. A. vol. 51.
[2] *Von Ordenung Gottes Diensts ynn der Gemeine*, ed. Clemen, vol. 2, p. 424.

It is in the Kingdom that there will no longer be any place for preaching.

One might say perhaps that the liturgy of the Eucharist bears witness to the Church's participation in the process of salvation, whereas the sermon reflects the fact that this process brings the Church into intimate contact with the world. Or again: the Eucharist attests the presence of heavenly joy, it nourishes and fulfils hope, while the sermon attests the continuance of the present aeon, it calls for faith and nourishes faith. Thus, if the sermon absorbs the whole of the service, the Church is forgetting that the Kingdom has already drawn near, and that it can live on the first fruits of the Kingdom, it becomes "de-eschatologized"; but if the Eucharist monopolizes the whole of worship, the Church is forgetting that the world still continues, it is trying to exalt the Church beyond this world and to uproot it from history. Thus, just as the Eucharist is the corrective to a church life which is enclosed in the world (the Church is not *imprisoned* in this world), so the sermon is the corrective to a church life which has shaken off the world (the Church is still in the world).

This twofold necessity of preaching and the Eucharist is perhaps the most powerful demonstration of the dialectical situation of the Church; it is no longer of the world (hence it already has access to the heavenly banquet), but it is still in the world (hence it needs the warnings, the encouragements, the teachings and the consolations of preaching). These two major forms of grace on which the Church feeds in the cult bear witness to the eschatological tension which lies at the heart of the cult. And that is why preaching, although provisional, is so in relation to the eschatological situation of the Church in the Kingdom, not in relation to its historical situation in the world. When the Church neglects preaching in favour of the Eucharist alone, it inevitably tends to identify itself with the manifested Kingdom; and in the opposite case, it is necessarily failing to do justice to the fact that the Kingdom has already dawned within it. This shows that J. A. Jungmann is quite right when he mentions that for many people the sermon interrupts the liturgy rather than advances it. In relation to the worship which centres on the Kingdom, it is certainly alien. But God has willed that preaching should be a constituent feature of worship and the Church must will so likewise, lest the cult should lapse into self-centredness or the danger of illusion. If the Eucharist connects the Church with the future, the sermon roots it solidly in the present. Hence it is the most powerful corrective to one of the major temptations of the cult, and that is why it is not only necessary, but deserves to be treated with respect and to be developed with the greatest care.

(b) *The Lord's Supper*

We now come to the second normal feature of Christian worship. We might just as well have described it as "the sacrament of the Word of God"; but seeing that we are here dealing with parochial worship and not with baptism, we shall discuss the Lord's Supper only.

But there is a second reason why we speak of the Lord's Supper (or of Holy Communion or the Eucharist) rather than of the sacraments: the term sacrament—an ambiguous Latin translation of the Greek MYSTERION—is not used by scripture to supply an explicit common denominator for baptism, the Eucharist and other liturgical actions of the Church (which arose later), but its implications are much vaster, and cover, as K. Barth finely observes in connexion with patristic theology, the whole field of revelation (*Dogmatics*).

Just as above we did not attempt to give a theology of the Word of God, so now we do not propose to give a theology of the Eucharist (or of the sacraments), which would be the concern of systematic rather than of pastoral theology.

In speaking of the Word of God, we had to take into account three modes of its proclamation. The Lord's Supper has not different modes of celebration, although we might specify in it the phases of the memorial of Christ's passion, of the irruption of the ESCHATON, and of communion. But if these three phases can be distinguished, they cannot be separated without impairing the character of the service as a whole. In fact if we isolate the memorial aspect, we tend to slip into an essentially sacrificial idea of the service which can then be celebrated with no communicants other than the priest, or which can be celebrated with a special intention, as though it were circumstantial evidence produced in court to obtain a hearing from God. Again, if we isolate the aspect of communion, we are threatened with its becoming a fraternal meal, an agapé, for which the species cease to have any special validity, as Zwingli sometimes leads one to suppose, and as is the case with liberal protestantism which has never known quite what to do about the sacraments and which is challenged more strongly by the sacraments than by anything else. And if finally we wish to isolate the eschatological aspect and its joy, we are threatened with having no further use for the species of bread and wine, and thus with dissolving sacramental life either into the silence of the Quakers, or into a collective ecstasy, or into mysticism. Hence we shall do well, at least in a liturgical study (it is a different matter in systematic theology), to take the Lord's Supper as a whole, the fulness of which must be expressed at every celebration.

To limit our subject further, we must point out that the study of the species will not be attempted here. We shall find this question recurring when we deal, in Chapter IX, with the sanctification of space; and it is not until the last chapter that we shall consider some practical problems of celebration. The question which concerns us here is that of deciding how far the Eucharist is an integral feature of the cult, whether its celebration is necessary or not to render the worship of the Church truly Christian.

To answer this question, theological considerations do not suffice. We must see how the Church in normal practice has answered it. We must glance at the history of the Church to see how it obeyed the command of Jesus: "Do this in remembrance of me."

Of the first Christians it is said that they persevered in the doctrine of the apostles, in brotherly fellowship, in the breaking of bread, and in prayer (Acts 2: 42). Hence the meal was of regular occurrence. It is also reported, incidentally, that the Christians of Troas, on the first day of the week, had met together "to break bread" (Acts 20: 7) and here there seems to be an almost automatic bond between the "day of the Lord" and "the breaking of bread". In the First Letter to the Corinthians, nothing suggests that the meetings were not normally eucharistic. On the contrary, it is in a context where he is speaking of what takes place when they meet (SYNERCHESTHAI) that the apostle accuses the Corinthians of no longer taking the meal of the Lord (KYRIAKON DEIPNON) because of the way in which they celebrate it (1 Cor. 11: 20). All these indications and others suggest that the Supper is an integral part of each Sunday assembly. This exegetic deduction has been disputed by the invoking of a pagan text of the second century, the letter of the governor Pliny the younger to the emperor Trajan, where he reports on Christian worship what he has learnt from tortured deaconesses. He alludes to a cult "of the Word" as distinct from a meeting with a meal (taking place the same day).[1] With that preference for pagan texts over against NT texts which historians of early Christianity often show, it has been attempted to deduce from the text of Pliny that there were two sorts of cult in the nascent Church: a "synagogal" cult without the Eucharist, and a "Jerusalemite" cult, a cult of the Temple, with the Eucharist. This idea which at once implies a sacrificial interpretation of the Eucharist, has enjoyed great favour, so much so that Oscar Cullmann who contests it describes it as "one of those pseudo-scientific dogmas which the manuals vie with each other in repeating and which are eventually accepted without consideration of whether they would stand up to an examination of the texts". But Cullmann seems to me to have established that this "dogma" has no basis in fact, at least as far as the Sunday cult is concerned. Indeed in the whole of

---

[1] Has he not misunderstood? Were there not already two phases of the cult by which the non-baptized and excommunicate were excluded at a certain point? This hypothesis does not seem to have been sufficiently considered. Another hypothesis could be that the tortured deaconesses said, after a first questioning, that the Christians came together for praying and singing, and that after a second and more severe torture they admitted that they came together for a meal. The torture-report, or Pliny himself, did not notice that the deaconesses spoke of the same Christian gathering, but that after a worse torture they revealed more about it: the meal. But as this meal was among Christians protected by secret discipline (as J. Jeremias has shown) they remained strong enough to specify that this meal was just an ordinary one.

the ancient Church there is no intimation of Sunday worship being celebrated without the Eucharist.

Up to the fifth century, it was taken for granted that all the baptized who were not excommunicate would communicate each Sunday. But for various reasons, and in particular because of a lack of balance in the development of eucharistic doctrine—which, especially in the West, favoured the memorial aspect to the detriment of the aspects of communion and parousia—the communion of the faithful became ever less frequent, until about the ninth century it was on an average an annual communion; and this indifference threatened to become a matter of total abstention, so much so that the Lateran Council required the faithful to communicate at least once a year at the season of Easter. The Eucharist was still everywhere celebrated each Sunday, but the celebrant was almost alone in communicating. Thus, broadly speaking, communion had been divorced from the Eucharist.

Such was the situation which faced the Reformers. They found too, at least in central Europe, other features. In fact, from the end of the Middle Ages, especially in cathedral churches, there had grown up, alongside the mass, homilectic cults, called the *Pronaus*, the ministry of which in the sixteenth century was entrusted to certain priests who played a decisive part in the German-Swiss and Alsatian reform movements. It was this cult without Eucharist which became in a way the background for Reformed worship, at least that of the Germanic type.

At the Reformation, Luther maintained the Sunday Eucharist, and normally the Anglican Church did likewise. The Reformed Churches were alone in giving it up. Why they did so, is rather a difficult question. Perhaps it would not be too hazardous to suggest three tentative reasons.

Perhaps the basic reason was their realization that a true Eucharist implies the communion of the faithful, and because of age-long habits it was not possible to make them pass without more ado from an annual to a weekly communion. In such circumstances the Reformers were content, provisionally and pedagogically, to bid the faithful communicate four times a year, at the great festivals, in the hope that the number of communion services would gradually increase. It would seem that it was for this reason that Calvin at Geneva accepted with a good grace, though with reservations that are well known, the Bernese *Diktat* regarding four annual Eucharists, at Christmas, Easter, Whitsuntide and the first Sunday in September. This politico-pedagogic reason was perhaps the more admissible in the eyes of the Reformers since, in view of the geographical proximity of Roman parishes, it was necessary that Reformed worship should appear, externally, to be very different from the mass.

Perhaps, too, they gave up the Sunday Eucharist for a second reason springing from a psychological uneasiness. In French Switzerland, at least, the Reformation involved a change of minister; not in all parishes, but in most. There was no problem raised about the preaching of men concerning whose sacerdotal ordination the members of the Church had no precise information. Itinerant preachers, who exercised no ordinary parochial ministry, were known throughout the Middle Ages. But, in the eyes of the people, not in those of the ministers who never doubted their authorization, was it to be taken for granted that they should be allowed to celebrate the Eucharist? Did they not run the risk of being regarded as usurpers by a people who, at least to begin with, still felt a certain nostalgia for Roman Catholicism? In this situation, was it not necessary that the greatness of the feast (Christmas, Easter, and especially Whitsuntide) should in the eyes of the people overcome any hesitations about the standing of the ministers? It would be worth while some time making a study of this chapter in the history of religious psychology.

A final possibility is that they may have given it up for a reason that is much less admissible, but which, in view of the later tradition, must not be at once brushed aside: namely because of a theological (or perhaps philosophical) indifference to the sacrament itself and its necessity. Let us recall the idea, scattered through the writings of Calvin, that the sacraments (and the means of grace in general) show a kind of divine condescension to the childishness of our faith, our incapacity to rise to the level of spiritual beings, with the result that the sacraments eventually came to appear, not as something calling us towards the future but as something enslaving us to the past. A misunderstanding, says K. Barth, even self-induced, when he complains: "How was it possible so to misunderstand the Reformed Church, and for her so to misunderstand herself, that later she came to be regarded as a Church without sacraments, and even a Church hostile to sacraments?"

But whatever be the truth of the matter, it is the fact that, despite hesitations which were never lacking,[1] the Reformed Church, alone among the great liturgical traditions, excluded from its Sunday worship the celebration of the Lord's Supper. For us then the question of the necessity of the latter is especially urgent. And it is so much the more vital because, happily, it has ceased to be academic and has become existential.

Is the Lord's Supper necessary for Christian worship to be truly Christian? Let us first consider two negative replies. The first argument suggests that the Lord's Supper adds nothing to preaching. If we have preaching, we have all that is essential. In the Protestant sphere, it is a discussion similar to that current in the Roman Church about the need or otherwise to communicate in two kinds. Without going so far as to declare with a Luther who was temporarily astray, that preaching "is the only ceremony or rite which Christ instituted to enable His disciples to meet, practise it and thereby live in unity",[2] it is claimed that since the *effectus verbi* is nothing other than the *effectus ritus*, the Word suffices to make the cult all that it ought to be. Such people then energetically protest against the idea that the cult would be lacking in something essential, in fact in its major element, if the Eucharist were not celebrated. This attitude, it is thought, betrays a culpable distrust of the virtue of preaching. They do not ask themselves why, now and then,

[1] The proof is that in the sixteenth and seventeenth centuries there were attempts to keep the faithful in touch with eucharistic life: at Basle or in Scotland they could communicate every Sunday, but in various parishes in turn; at Strasbourg it was possible to communicate in the cathedral each Sunday, and once a month in the other parishes; in the Palatinate, they could communicate once a month in the town parishes and every other month in those of the country; and the ordinances of Julich and Berg state that four Sundays a year are the minimum.

[2] *W.A.* 6, p. 231.

the ordinary service is augmented by the addition of the Eucharist, but they do wonder when it is right to add this sacramental excrescence, and propose Maundy Thursday, Good Friday, a Sunday in Lent and a Sunday commemorating the dead!

The second negative reply to our question rests on another argument which I confess I have found advanced only by my colleague J. Dürr who teaches at the University of Berne. In this case it is admitted that the Reformed cult, from which the Eucharist is normally absent, is indeed mutilated: but this is felt to be a cause for rejoicing, in that thus the cult escapes the vice of self-centredness and the Church is prevented from withdrawing into itself: "Precisely because it is thus mutilated, in its very incompleteness and lack of balance it can bear witness to the deep meaning and the task of Christian worship far more so in fact than can a type of worship which is liturgically more complete and rounded." In fact, it is urged, "the reason why a cult cannot be enclosed within itself is that the congregation realize that they are in the world, called to serve there and to serve others. Just as the body of Christian people must remain open to the world, so their worship also must remain open to the impact of the world". This text, it is true, is found in a context where the incompleteness of the cult is underlined not with reference to the Eucharist, but with reference to the wealth of liturgical ceremonies. Hence we must not hastily conclude that the author means more than he in fact does. But, and this is proved by the following page, he also has in mind the usual absence of the Eucharist, and that is why his remarks are so grave. For he implies that the presence of the Eucharist confines worship to its own interests, condemns it to self-centredness and that Jesus who ordained the Eucharist did not fully understand the relations between the Church and the world. Moreover the Church has more than one open window: if it is open to the world through its apostolic ministry, it is open to heaven through its liturgical ministry. It is only because of this dual opening that there can come from it something orientated towards the world, namely the Gospel, and something orientated towards heaven, namely thanksgiving and intercession. In fact, if I may be so bold as to use the metaphor, it is like a tin of condensed milk: if you wish to make it flow, you must pierce two holes. This double orientation of the Church is something that we have enormous difficulty in understanding and experiencing in our Church, and it is doubtless for this reason that we do not dare to practise truly and freely either evangelization or liturgy: on Sunday mornings we get a mixture which is spoiled for either purpose.

But we must give positive replies to our question: if the Eucharist is necessary to worship, why is it so? I will try to give three replies.

In the first place it is essential to worship, quite simply, because Christ instituted it and commanded the Church to celebrate it. Hence it is a matter of simple obedience, for we must not forget that the rite which Christ instituted was not the mediaeval *Pronaus* of Central Europe which furnished the background to the normal worship of the Church which claims to be reformed "according to the Word of God"; what Christ instituted was the eucharistic rite. His command to carry the Gospel to the whole world, if as basic as the other and complementary to the other, is not a liturgical command, but an apostolic one.

The two other reasons are of a theological kind. At the beginning of our study, when we were expounding the Christological basis of the cult, we pointed out that the latter reflected the two great stages in the life of Christ: the Galilean which was focused on the proclamation of the Word, and the Jerusalemite which was centred on the cross, and we then cited the thesis of M. Kähler who so rightly says that the Gospels are "histories of the Passion prefaced by an ample introduction". The life of Jesus leads inevitably to the cross. Apart from the cross, His prophetic and teaching ministry is emptied of its authentic substance. But the prophetic and teaching ministry is equally necessary to His sacerdotal ministry, not only to make it intelligible but to supply it with motive power and make it possible. Similarly, one may say that the Eucharist is as necessary to preaching (the sacrament of the Word) as the cross is necessary to the ministry of Jesus. Without the cross it would be blunted, lacking in focus, sectarian and moralizing. A liturgy without the Eucharist is like the ministry of Jesus without Good Friday.

Finally, the Eucharist is necessary to the cult because it enables us—unless we have lost all sense of church discipline[1] —to mark the difference between the Church and the world in a way which is not subjective, self-centred and moralizing, but objective. Listening to the Word is for all; but communion is for those who have not only listened to the word, but have received it and keep it; and I am convinced that if in our Church there is such confusion about the theological interpretation of the relation between the Church and the world, it is because our sacramental life has become so atrophied.

Let us hear what P. Brunner says: "The Church welcomes those from outside and also young people not yet confirmed, to join in its main service as far and as long as possible. It permits all to hear the edifying word, proclaimed at the heart of church life, and evoking the anamnesis of Christ. But because of Christ's own institution, it must mark a frontier which defines the exclusive nature of that anamnesis which is evoked by the celebration of the Eucharist." Hence the Church makes a progression from the anamnesis of the Word to that implied by the Eucharist: "Those who cannot cross this frontier must be made to feel that there is something decisive which is lacking to their worship. The caesura (between the two phases of the cult) must seem to them like the interruption of an action not yet complete. But those who cross the frontier know at once that they are caught up in a unified movement of anamnesis which terminates only with communion."

Hence it is no exaggeration to say that not only is the Eucharist necessary to the cult, but that the abandonment of it is an abandonment of the very substance of the cult. And we can without hesitation follow K. Barth when he

---

[1] I do not mean that the Eucharist automatically guarantees the maintenance of church discipline. The Swedish Church, which has the Eucharist but not the discipline, contradicts such an affirmation. But it is clear that it is not with reference to preaching that discipline can be exercised, but with reference to sacramental life. If among ourselves discipline has disappeared, it is largely because of the atrophy of sacramental life; and if it is so difficult to restore, it is because its point of reference is normally lacking.

declares that the Eucharist is the point, the spearhead (*die Spitze*) of the cult (i.e. "the latter is blunted and lacking in focus when the Eucharist is absent from it") (*Dogmatics*) and when he says that worship without the Eucharist is a theological impossibility and that we have not received from God the right to make this liturgical amputation, we have usurped it. J. Dürr uses a striking image to characterize the usual type of Reformed service. He says it ends not with a full stop but with a colon, the function of which is to introduce what is to follow. And after this pause, 48 Sundays out of 52, we are left hungry and thirsty. And this absence of the Eucharist, as we cannot over-emphasize, also compromises the full significance of the other sacrament, that of baptism, and even invalidates it, since we are thus treating the baptized as though they were catechumens, because we are denying them their right to communicate. All in all, the absence of the Eucharist shows contempt for grace.

But—and this is a question already asked—if the Eucharist is indispensable to the full Christian character of the service, does it give more than is given in the ministry of the Word? Let us reply as briefly as possible to this embarrassing question. It does not give anything different from what is given in preaching, since it gives the Gospel and with it life. Nevertheless—and this is why we cannot console ourselves for the absence of the Eucharist by saying that it adds nothing to the Word—when the Eucharist is celebrated something different takes place from that which takes place when the Word is preached. What takes place is this: namely, that those who accept the invitation can show that they accept it. There takes place, in action, a proof of the welcome given to divine grace. In this sense there does take place more than is implied in the preaching of the Word; the existential communion for which God waits can be manifested, and to God's self-giving, there can correspond, visibly and in a way which commits the communicant, the self-giving of the faithful. There is a transaction which at once excludes any intellectualist misunderstanding of worship. The communicant is wholly committed.

Certainly he can, and should, be equally so by the mere hearing of the Word of the Gospel; but in the Eucharist he is called upon to give himself in turn: "In communion with Thy Son Jesus Christ, our high priest who ever intercedes for us, we present to Thee, O God, our sacrifice of praise and the homage of our hearts, and together, we dedicate ourselves, all that we are and have, to Thy service, as a living and holy offering." But to understand this, we must admit the presence in the Eucharist of a sacrificial element, and it is perhaps because, in order to combat the over-emphasis of this element in mediaeval eucharistic doctrine we have tried to eliminate it altogether, rather than reduce it to its true proportions, that we have so much difficulty in understanding the necessity of the Eucharist, for now it seems to offer us no more than the preaching of the Word. The Eucharist is not merely a "mass" as the Word is a "mass" (i.e. an endowment with spiritual strength and benediction to be sent out into the world in the name of the Lord). It is also a service in which we are invited to present ourselves before God that we may dedicate ourselves to Him as a holy and lively sacrifice, praising and blessing Him by the gift of ourselves. It is because God in His grace wills that the cult should be an exchange, an exchange of pain for joy, of wretchedness for thankfulness, an exchange of love, that the Word does not suffice to render the cult fully Christian, that it needs also—as well as the elements of which we have still to speak—the Holy Communion.

(c) *The prayers*

It is not our intention to set forth a doctrine of prayer, any more than it was in the case of the Word of God or of Holy Communion. H. Asmussen remarks that, to his knowledge, a theological study of prayer has not yet been undertaken in the Church. This remark is not quite accurate, at least in essence: for every authentic theology is a theology of prayer, since it is not possible to be a theologian without living a life of prayer, since—as the Orthodox Church says— the theologian is not so much one who knows the history and technique of theology as one who knows how to pray. Thus prayer is—as is noted by the Heidelberg Catechism (question 116)—"the chief part of that thanksgiving which God requires of us".

Of the first Christians it is said that they "persevered in the teaching of the apostles, in brotherly fellowship, in the breaking of bread, and in prayers" (Acts 2: 42), and this continuance in prayer has governed the life and history of the whole Church in a way that is not sufficiently emphasized. For what is the history of the Church except that of the answering of its prayers and especially of the thousand variations of the admirable prayer of Acts 4: 27ff.: "For truly in this city there were gathered together against Thy holy servant Jesus, whom Thou didst anoint, both Herod and Pontius Pilate, with the Gentiles and the peoples of Israel, to do whatever Thy hand and Thy plan had predestined to take place. And now Lord look upon their threats, and grant to Thy servants to speak Thy word with all boldness, while Thou stretchest out Thy hand to heal, and signs and wonders are performed through the name of Thy holy servant Jesus." Prayer—like the proclamation of the Word, the celebration of the sacraments and the life of fellowship of which we shall speak below—is an element which is fundamental to the unfolding of salvation.

Prayer is necessary not only to the individual life of the Christian but also to church worship. The NT unceasingly exhorts us to practise it and Jesus has commanded it. Hence it is, first of all, not the expression of a religious need, nor a technique by which we seek to coerce God, but an act of obedience. So when Jesus is questioned by His disciples on the subject of prayer, He does not give them instruction about it (this He gave elsewhere, cf. Luke 18: 1–8), He teaches them a prayer, the Lord's Prayer, and commands them to make it their own (Luke 11: 1–3; Matt. 6: 7ff.) and very soon this prayer was to become the rhythm of the daily life of Christians.[1] But, from the start (cf. Gal. 4: 6; Rom. 8: 15), this prayer was to be used in the worship of the Church. What characterizes it—as is true also of every authentically Christian prayer and especially of the *Maranatha*—is its eschatological note: in it the Church asks that grace may come, and that the world may vanish away[2] and

---

[1] Cf. Didache 8: 5.   [2] Didache, 10: 5.

that, with such an expectation, the Church may already know in Christ the joy of the Kingdom. We might perhaps say that, during the week, the Church, in offering the Lord's prayer, is praying for Sunday, and on Sundays, by this same Prayer, is asking God to manifest with power that of which on Sundays He gives a foretaste. Thus prayer is not only an act of obedience, it is also an act of faith and hope which hastens the coming of the day of God (2 Pet. 3: 12).

In Christ this prayer is possible. It becomes even the "supreme privilege of Christians that God has granted them in raising them to the status of sons. Prayer is possible only in God's family. Prayer is the exercise of filial rights in God's family. The sons are heirs, and that very fact makes them responsible sharers in the whole economy of the family. In the Father's family the sons have the right to make their voice heard. Hence prayer is God's authorization to His children to speak in matters which are His concern. This authorization to pray is the form in which God makes His sons even now participants in the dominion of His only Son. The fact that the Church is the royal people of God is shown precisely in this, that it has the right to pray and that it uses this right" (P. Brunner). It is with justice that in the canon of the Mass (a feature which has been repeated by so many other liturgies) the Lord's Prayer is preceded by: "We are bold to say".

This prayer which we are commanded to utter and which is henceforth possible becomes in public worship that of the whole congregation. That is why—and we shall return to the point—it is for the congregation to say the closing Amen, whether it has been recited in the name of all by the minister or whether, exceptionally, prayer has been freely offered by one of the faithful (cf. 1 Cor. 14: 16). The Church, consisting of non-interchangeable individuals, is presented before God in worship as a fellowship of persons and, whatever their form, its prayers are the prayers of all, otherwise they have their place elsewhere than in the worshipping congregation. Hence worship is threatened if it becomes a collection of prayers of the revivalist and individualist type. Not that personal prayer has no place in worship, but the latter is not an exhibition of different specimens of individual prayers: it is a communal work. In worship, we say, not "My God", but "Our Father".

In the history of the Church and in liturgical practice prayer has taken many forms. Attempts have been made to classify them, which is proper, on condition that the classification remains an external help towards intellectual clarification, and that we remember the necessarily artificial character of all such classifications. For the lines of demarcation between the various types are often difficult or even impossible to draw. If in what follows we distinguish the major forms of prayer, it is done solely for the sake of clarity, and not by any means to impose a possible classification to the exclusion of another one which might be equally possible theologically. Our categories will be defined by reference to the content of the prayers rather than to their psychological motives (e.g. repentance, love of neighbour, gratitude, etc.).

In his *Traité de Liturgique* R. Paquier gives a suitable classification, which I take advantage of. His point of departure is that in I Tim. 2: I Paul speaks of DEESIS, PROSEUCHE, ENTEUXIS, EUCHARISTIA, the first of these terms being probably generic, and he classifies prayers as prayers of aspiration, supplication, intercession, and thanksgiving. But as this list is not exhaustive, we shall speak afterwards of confessions of faith and hymns, terminating by a note on glossolalia.

Under the rubric PROSEUCHE, let us begin by the prayers which, in liturgical tradition, are called collects. We have here a term stemming from the Gallican liturgical tradition, and it denotes a prayer which was more developed in the West than in the East, the West having a much greater wealth of "proper" prayers than the East where clearly the "ordinary" takes first preference. It is usually a short, concise and precise prayer, which gathers up (*colligere*) and expresses some need of the Church or the world, putting it before God that He may hear it in the name of His Son. In the liturgical tradition subsequent to the fourth century— before that and even after, sometimes, it was often improvised by the priest—it is a prayer which is subjected to certain precise "poetical" rules. This discipline confers upon it its simplicity, its lack of verbiage, and its terseness. The result is, traditionally, the following pattern: (1) Give (2) us (3) we beseech Thee (4) O Lord (5) Thy salvation; the fourth part, i.e. the mention of the one to whom the prayer is addressed, being often made explicit by a relative clause as in Acts 4: 24: Thou who . . .". Such prayers can be repeated in the service and their "relative proclamatory character" connects them with confessions of faith.

The ENTEUXIS, i.e. petition, solicitation, intervention in favour of, intercession, is traditionally better known as the litany.[1] This type of prayer which the Germans call "the general prayer of the Church" usually includes three major parts (with the various details which are called for), namely, intercession for the Church, its ministers and members, intercession for the world and its authorities, and intercession for all those who are weary and heavy laden, those whom the Saviour came to seek. It may be expressed in three different ways: either the minister alone recites it, in the form of a prayer and slowly that the people may associate themselves with it in silence. It is this form which we usually have in our liturgies. Or secondly, it may be recited by two ministers, the deacon indicating the person or subject of the intercession, and the principal minister making the intercession itself.[2] Or thirdly, and this is the most traditional form, widespread in the West from the fourth century, the minister announces in the form of an exhortation the subject of the intercession, the people responding, after a moment's silence, by "Lord, have mercy" or KYRIE ELEYSON. This form seems to me preferable to the others because the whole congregation are audibly involved.

The EUCHARISTIA, the thanksgiving, the prayer which is traditionally said at the moment of the *preface* in the Holy Communion and which, in our services without communion, has become the so-called prayer of adoration. When part of the whole Christian liturgy, it is the prayer which after the *sursum corda*, declares that it is indeed meet and right, necessary and salutary, to worship the Lord and to

---

[1] LITANEUO—LISSOMAI, to supplicate.
[2] The order—deacon-priest—may be reversed.

give thanks unto Him for all that God has done in the creation and the salvation of the world; and by this thanksgiving, which becomes specific in accordance with the feast or the season of the ecclesiastical year, and then takes on a form approximating to a confession of faith, the Church rejoices that she can share even now in the adoration of heaven. Thus with the angels, and all the powers of heaven, with the spirits of just men made perfect, and with the whole Church militant here in earth, in one movement of common all-embracing joy, the Church sings to the glory of God the eternal hymn praising and acclaiming Him and saying: "Holy, holy, holy, is the Lord God of Hosts! Heaven and earth are full of His glory."

Once again, it is for the sake of convenience only that I have grouped the main types of prayer according to the traditional scheme of the collect, the litany and the preface. This does not imply that a type of worship with a different grouping of prayers is less faithful. The essential thing is that it should provide a place for these three types of prayer, and that the service should have definite prayers, intercessions and thanksgivings.

But are these all the prayers which are normally part of Christian worship? No indeed, and before concerning ourselves more especially with confessions of faith and hymns which are in many ways akin to prayers, we must pursue our enumeration.

First, as the crown of all prayers, the collect of all collects, of all litanies and of all thanksgivings, there is the inexhaustible example of prayer which Jesus Christ has taught us in the Lord's Prayer. It does not belong to any particular type, since it sums them all up and is the inspiration of them all.

Then, akin to the collect, there is the epiklesis, the invocation of the Spirit. The importance of this has already been sufficiently indicated; we need now only note that its special feature is that in it the Church confesses the sovereign freedom of God, and hence confesses itself to be the servant of the Lord; and secondly that it asks God to make the action of the liturgy in itself a granting of prayer, to transform the cult into an answer to prayer. Hence the object of its petition is limited to the great moments of the service: the proclamation of the Word and the real presence of Christ in the Holy Communion.

Thirdly, there are the prayers which take the form of acclamations or doxologies, in which the Church glorifies its Lord, and responds to the psalms and prayers—I think for instance of the ancient doxological response to the Lord's Prayer—by which, also, so to speak, it leaps over its usual confession of faith and already shares in the epiphany of the Lordship of Christ, and in which therefore it shows—and this is the essential point—that, so long as this world lasts, it is a "protestant" Church; a Church which testifies to the glory of its Master and in consequence protests against the usurpers of the power that belongs to God alone. Thus these acclamations and doxologies, which are scattered already throughout the NT have a considerable proleptic virtue. Already they celebrate as a valid and manifest fact the still hidden victory of Christ. In this sense they decisively illustrate the Christian doctrine of prayer, for they show that Christians really believe what their Lord said: "Whatever you ask in prayer, believe that you receive it and you will" (Mark 11: 24). They show that if Christians already pray as they do with that formidable eschatological assurance which inspires all Christian prayer, it is because they know that in Jesus Christ God has already granted all their prayers.

If we compare our enumeration with the normal structure of worship in the Reformed Church, we note that one all-important element is missing—namely, the confession of sins. The conspicuous part it plays in our tradition is well known. We do not propose to enter into historical details here. For one thousand years, the universal Church had no confession of sins in its Sunday worship, because Sunday was the joyous and glorious day which commemorated the Risen Christ, and because the Christian congregation of early times thought of itself as the holy and redeemed people, that community of priests and kings which had already obtained mercy. This tradition seems to conform with the NT, although the Lord's Prayer, which was recited in the cult, includes the petition for forgiveness.[1] But ancient liturgical

[1] The text of the Didache (14: 1) which speaks of a confession of

documents show in fact that a special confession of sins by the whole congregation was absent not because Christians had no need to ask forgiveness, but because the cult—we may think here of the eucharistic communion and the holy kiss—begins *after* divine forgiveness, presupposing that the latter has already been obtained (cf. Matt. 5: 23). Hence the confession of sins was introduced into the liturgy as a preparatory prayer and prelude to the Eucharist.

Among ourselves, it has been established as part of the service under the influence of Calvin, who placed it at the very beginning of worship in order that it might supplant sacramental confession, and in order to train in all necessary penitence those of the faithful who were blameless from the point of view of church discipline.

We shall return to this problem, and will content ourselves here with noting the following points: first, it is indisputably clear that to perform the act of worship we must appear before God, and that to do so His pardon must have washed us clean. Worship cannot be celebrated without our seeking and obtaining God's forgiveness. The covenanted forgiveness of baptism is not enough as long as we are in this world; it must be confirmed ever afresh in response to an ever renewed penitence.

Next, let us notice that the right moment for the practice of this penitence and the obtaining of absolution is not necessarily Sunday worship, which should rather be the moment when the faithful, returning, for the Eucharist, from the world into which the Lord had sent them, are content to sing of their felicity, declaring joyfully: "Lord, even the demons are subject to us in your name!" (Luke 10: 17). The confession of sins, individual or communal, may then find its appropriate place *before* the cult proper begins. And if Reformed piety is so often lacking in eschatological exultation, if it is so suspicious of liturgical joy, it is probably due in large measure to the fact that Calvin taught us to begin the cult, with no other preamble than an invocation, with these words: "Brethren, let each one of you come

sins before the breaking of bread does not say clearly whether it is done communally by the worshipping assembly or whether it is done in private beforehand, following Matt. 5: 23ff.

before the face of the Lord, confessing his sins and following from his heart my words: 'Lord God, almighty and eternal Father, we confess and unfeignedly recognize, before Thy holy majesty, that we are miserable sinners, conceived and born in iniquity and corruption: prone to evil doing, useless for any good, and that by our own fault, we ceaselessly transgress Thy holy commandments. By doing so, we draw upon ourselves, through Thy righteous judgment, ruin and perdition.' " Even if later the congregation beseeches God for "the help of His grace in their calamity", the tone is nevertheless struck which threatens to become the predominant tone of the whole liturgy, and it is certainly not the tone of the AGALLIASIS so characteristic of the early Christian liturgies!

But let us note that an invitation to repentance, a reminder of the unworthiness of the faithful to enjoy the presence of the Lord, a liturgical use of the fifth petition in the Lord's prayer (just as the other petitions are made use of in worship) is by no means out of place in the service which would otherwise be in danger of rushing, without check, into an eschatological exultation which would belie the fact that the Church is still in the present age and hence exposed to the snares of the devil. If the Church triumphant is also to be found on earth, this is only true in a dialectical way.

On the other hand—and for this reason we shall return to the problem—since the considerations for which Calvin gave this degree of importance to the confession of sins (the rejection of obligatory sacramental confession, and the restoration of public church discipline) are no longer so relevant to our situation, confession may now legitimately assume the character of a preparatory prayer, of mutual help, which it has in other traditions. None the less, our current practice need not therefore be condemned. However, if I may use the comparison, Christian worship is normally celebrated in a banqueting hall rather than in a laundry, and the festal garments must be put on *before* we present ourselves for the festal meal (cf. Matt. 22: 11ff.).

Among the prayers, in the broader sense of the term, we must include the confessions of faith, which P. Brunner so rightly calls "the Amen of the congregation showing their acceptance of the prophetic and apostolic Word"; in its own words, the Church gives back to God in its wholeness that Word which He addressed to it in the Gospel; in its wholeness, that is to say that the Credo is not merely the response of the Church to the Word partially proclaimed during a particular service, but to the whole Gospel, which could not have been proclaimed to it during that particular service (we cannot read through the whole Bible every Sunday!). To use the language of the Heidelberg Catechism (question 22), it is a question of "all that is promised us in the Gospel and which the articles of the universal and undoubted faith of all Christians sum up, in the Apostles' Creed". Let us examine this more closely:

By this confession of faith, the Church commits itself, promising to serve God in the world. The Church thus declares itself ready to shoulder all the consequences of this confession and even the final one: that of dying for the faith. In fact, *credo* does not mean only: "I admit the existence of what I am about to enumerate" (this kind of faith is also that of the demons: Jas. 2: 19), but it means "I risk my life, I stake my existence on the truth of what follows: that is my life and I renounce all else". One might say that in the creed the Church gives itself to the Word which it receives, as in the communion it gives itself to Him who gave His life for it.

Because of the importance of what takes place in such a confession, the text is not a matter of *ad libitum*; it is, with more or less precision and breadth, a church text. Too much is here involved for improvization or approximation to be in place. Hence we must say a few words about the formulation of this feature. Which creed shall we use? Let us begin by saying which creed we shall not use. We shall not use those cocktails of Biblical passages which have recently been introduced into our Reformed services under the name of *Biblica*: first for a reason of principle (their object is normally to reduce to silence a whole series of Biblical affirmations regarding the birth of Christ, His return, and the Christian hope, or to invite the Church to stop its ears when God has anything to say to it which is irritating to rationalism); next for reasons of form (a confession of faith is not a series of irresponsible parrot-like repetitions but the free response of free men).

If, then, we are to forsake these *Biblica*, there remains a choice between the Apostles' Creed and the Nicene Creed.[1] Traditionally, it is the Nicene Creed which has tended to be usual in the Eucharist, until the Reformation at any rate, when the Apostles' Creed began its liturgical career, at least in the continental Protestant Churches, without however quite displacing the Creed of Nicaea. This Reformed tradition seems to me personally a good one, and that for two reasons: first because the Apostles' Creed is not polemical, but a simple summary of the Word which is the basis and the inspiration of the Church. Secondly, because it is the confession of faith which governs instruction of catechumens, and so is the expression of the faith which they make their own at the time of their reception into full communicant life.

But if the Apostles' Creed seems to me to be the one which should normally be used, this does not exclude the occasional use of the Nicene Creed (which could in any case find an appropriate place at services where the whole body of the faithful are not expected; the Sunday evening services, for example, where we have those who wish, in Christian liberty, to deepen their knowledge of their faith and of the spiritual life). But shall we choose the original text of the creed or the one which was modified by the Carolingian West; that is, shall we add to the creed accepted by the oecumenical Council of Constantinople in 381 the *filioque* which was introduced, at first in Spain, in the eighth century? It is well known that the Lutherans and the Anglicans have accepted this addition, and it is the same with the Reformed liturgical tradition, although our confessions of faith have never specified which of the two texts of the Nicene Creed they desire to recognize.[2] I think that we should do well to abandon an addition which was never admitted in a truly catholic manner by the whole Church, and which perhaps

[1] The Athanasian Creed has never been highly rated from a liturgical point of view.

[2] It would be worth while for a reformation historian to examine whether the *filioque* played a consciously marked part in our theological tradition. If so, it would be the only point where we join issue with the Orthodox Church.

finally caused the schism of western Christianity in the sixteenth century.

The confession of faith is not the moment in the service when the congregation listens to the personal testimony of its pastor, but that cardinal moment when the Church, united in faith, hope and love, responds to the Word of God by its own words. Hence, like the Amen which closes the prayers, the creed should be recited in common by all present. As soon as we have understood that, we shall no longer be afraid of that monotony which so many worshippers seem to dread. And this requirement of recitation in common is a further reason for preferring to all other creeds the inexhaustible and sufficient Apostles' Creed.

The Church, however, has not always confessed its faith in a liturgical creed, and it has even been possible to say that the communion prefaces quite validly replace it. But if the creed has not always been a part of the Christian cult, the latter has always included, in one way or another, confessions of faith. Such confessions in the East from the fourth century, in the Mozarabic liturgies from the sixth century, in the Roman liturgy from 1014, assumed the henceforth traditional form of the Nicene or the Apostles' Creed. Of course Christian worship is not invalidated if the faith is confessed in a different way; but I see no valid grounds for questioning the traditional form, especially since the motive prompting such changes, whatever the alleged reasons, is not the increase of the faith of worshippers, but a minimization of the faith as a declared statement. Such a position would in the end lead to the suppression of the Creed in public worship. We must agree with H. Asmussen when he says: "Parishes and churches in which the creed is no longer confessed find themselves as a rule already outside the pale of Christianity. For the reason for this omission, is, as a rule, not a formal reason, but the collapse of the Christian faith. With regard to such parishes, no words need be wasted about the urgent task of rediscovering the form of worship. Their ministers should be replaced and the parishes evangelized."

Under the general heading of prayer it is also possible to include hymns and canticles. But once again, we must recognize the purely arbitrary and artificial character of the classification, which we give here for purposes of clarification only. Hymns might equally well be classed among the liturgical attestations of church life, since by them the faithful edify and encourage each other (cf. Col. 3: 16; Eph. 5: 19). "And in truth, we know from experience", said Calvin, "that hymns have great power to move and kindle the heart of men, stimulating them to invoke and praise God with more vehement and burning zeal." But seeing that the line of distinction between hymns and prayers and confessions of faith is difficult to draw we prefer to mention them, very briefly, at this point.

The Church has always used hymns and canticles in its worship,[1] and their importance for the cult is notably illustrated by the number of those which are quoted in the NT. They are in fact quoted rather as the NT quotes the OT, which proves that this form of prayer was considered not so much as springing up from man's heart, but as being inspired by the Spirit. Hence we must not be surprised to find the NT speaking of ODAI PNEUMATIKAI (Col. 3: 16). The history of hymnology, into which we cannot enter here, shows not only that it has experienced times of glory and times of degeneration, new movements and reforms, false starts and true returns, but especially that hymnological production can be a faithful index of the life of a Church, as well as a blessed refuge for spiritual vitality, when dogmatic thinking becomes bogged down or petrified (I am thinking in particular of German Lutheranism in the seventeenth century).

As in the case of liturgical prayers properly so called, there are different types of hymns: those of acclamation and confession (for example the Amens, the Alleluias, the Kyrie, the Sanctus, the Agnus Dei and the Gloria); those which Thurian describes as meditative and which form a transition between reading and prayer (the Psalms, the Biblical canticles and all such matter as exploits the same vein of spirituality, and which forms the greater part of our Protestant psalters); and those which assist the unfolding of the

---

[1] For the NT, cf. Rom. 15: 9; 1 Cor. 14: 15; Eph. 5: 19; Col. 3: 16; Jas. 5: 13; Rev. 5: 9; 14: 3; 15: 1–3; cf. also Matt. 26: 30 par.

liturgy, such as introits, offertory hymns and responses, etc.).

Generally speaking (and there are of course exceptions) this aspect of worship marks the eschatological hope of the Church and foreshadows the "new song" which will resound for ever in the Kingdom (cf. Rev. 5: 9; 14: 3; Ps. 33: 3, etc.). Hymns are manifestations of joy (Jas. 5: 13) and proclaim the victory of Christ (cf. Rev. 15: 3). "We know that in heaven we shall do nothing other than ceaselessly repeat Amen and Alleluia, with insatiable satisfaction" said St. Augustine in a sermon,[1] and the Church on earth is invited in its canticles to share in this heavenly joy,[2] a fact which rightly imparts to true Christian hymns an exultation that enhances the faith and the solid life of the Church. P. Brunner, in a way which links him with the so rightly orientated thought of the Orthodox Church, thinks it possible to declare that the hymn is the ultimate form of theology, since it here and now gives the Christian the opportunity to express his theology as he will do in the felicity of the Kingdom.

Should we then place canticles on the same level as glossolalia, which can be accepted on the fringe of Christian worship? They have, indeed, eschatological exultation and anticipation in common with glossolalia. But we should not merge the two, since hymns are a necessarily communal form of paschal joy and favour mutual edification, whereas glossolalia, unless translated, edifies the speaker only (1 Cor. 14: 4). None the less, canticles and hymns take over from glossolalia certain easily understood forms (the Hebrew Alleluia is sung in all churches!), and are sometimes very close to glossolalia, for the words of him whose heart overflows with joy jostle each other as they come tumbling out (cf. Matt. 12: 34); but canticles give ordered form to this exultation, canalize it, and above all enable all the faithful to share it.

What we have been saying furnishes a criterion to judge the value of the canticles, and so to choose the canticles which are to be sung: it is not a question of listening to the

---

[1] Sermon 362, 29, *P.L.* 39, 1632ff.

[2] "Alleluia enim vox perpetua est Ecclesiae, sicut perpetua est memoria passionis et victoriae ejus" said Luther.

flutterings of the soul, but of praising the Lord and entering into the choirs of the angels. "It should always be remembered that the music of hymns should not be light and sprightly; it should have weight and majesty, and thus there should be a marked difference between the music which is played to delight men at table and in their homes, and that of the psalms sung in church in the presence of God and His angels", remarks Calvin. We have already spoken of liturgical music. Hence here I shall only observe that words and music should be matched, and that the music should not delight in itself but rather in the grace of God. Fr. Gelineau pertinently remarks: "a canticle is worn out so much the more quickly when it is richly ornate, and wears better if it is plain and simple. Baroque stuccos peel off and the colours fade, whereas the stone of cathedrals lasts and grows more beautiful with the passage of time."[1]

(d) *The liturgical witness to Christian fellowship*

"They persevered in the teaching of the apostles, in brotherly fellowship, (KOINONIA) in the breaking of bread and in prayers", it is said of the first Christians, and faithfully echoing this, the Heidelberg Catechism, in enumerating the basic features of the cult, speaks about Christian contribution to the assistance of the poor, alongside preaching, the Holy Communion and prayers (question 103). But the offertory which, for the Heidelberg Catechism, seems to seal the prayers just as the sacraments seal the proclamation of the Word, is not the only liturgical manifestation of the fellowship of Christians. To it must be added the mutual exhortations and encouragements, and whatever attests the unity of the Christian community, on the one hand; and on the other, the notices and instructions to the congregation. Just as we refrained from expounding a theology of the Word, the sacraments and prayer, so here—since we are not engaged in systematic theology—we must approach our theme not from the theological but from the liturgical angle.

If it is doubtless possible to look at the offertory from the point of view of a confession of faith, as a positive sign of self-dedication to the Lord's service—hence the rightness of

---

[1] *La Maison-Dieu*, No. 60, 1959, p. 147.

placing it at that moment in the service when the sacred elements are brought to the altar—it is also, in its intention, a sign of Christian unity and brotherhood, for its aim is to help the Church to live in such unity and brotherhood. Here we might think of the importance which St. Paul attached to the collection he made in the churches he founded, a collection intended for the benefit of the mother Church of Jerusalem. So important was it for him that he gladly risked his life in order to go in person and offer it to Jerusalem (Acts 21: 4, 11–14); or again we might remember the theological importance of the community of goods which marked the life of the first Jerusalem Church, as described in Acts. And in fact such an offering, serving the spirit of brotherhood, has normally been a part of Christian worship from the beginnings[1] up to the present day. Hence its place is not at the end of the service, but during the service, and to my mind there is no objection to taking it when the eucharistic elements are brought to the altar.[2] It should be taken from the pews during the singing of a hymn, and brought by two elders or deacons to the altar that it may be consecrated.

Mutual exhortations and encouragements are also a liturgical expression of Christian fellowship. Reminding the reader once more of the arbitrary nature of this sort of classification, I would mention at this point the following elements:

The antiphons. These were known to the Jewish cult, and were from the start taken over by the Christians, who created others beyond those culled from the Psalms. If the antiphons are often prayers, they are a form of prayer which in a remarkable way bears witness to church fellowship, for then "the one so to speak takes the words out of the other's mouth. Both parties are animated by the same Spirit, both are caught up in the same impulse of confession and praise . . . The idea that the congregation should confess and praise

---

[1] Cf. 1 Cor. 16: 2; or the fine text of Justin, *Apology*, 1/67, 6.

[2] Is it to avoid the sacrificial savour which in the NT clings to such collections (cf. Heb. 13: 15–16; Phil. 4: 18; Acts 4: 35, 37, 5: 2 where TITHEMI PARA TOUS PODAS TON APOSTOLON is undeniably sacrificial), that the Reformed Church has for so long excluded them from the service, thus uprooting them from their true Christian atmosphere and making them a worldly burden?

God with one mouth is perfectly realized not when they sing the same words together but only when there is this alternating chant and response. In this duality, the unity of confession and praise finds an unsurpassable expression." This statement of P. Brunner may be somewhat exaggerated, but in truth all who have used antiphonal chants know that it is in principle correct. All the more so as the antiphons, more perhaps even than the Lord's Prayer, the Creed and the Amens, carry an implicit protest against the clericalization of the cult. It must further be recognized that where they have been maintained, the people have in other respects too taken more part in the service than where—contrary to the good example proposed by Zwingli, in whose view the antiphons play a fundamental part—they failed to survive the Reformation.[1]

Second, encouragements to mutual spiritual aid in which, again by antiphons, Christians as it were greet each other during the course of the service and give each other their marching orders: for instance: "Lift up your hearts: We lift them up unto the Lord. Let us give thanks unto our Lord God: it is meet and right so to do", or again the salutation: "The Lord be with you: And with thy spirit", which often forms a prelude to the prayers. Because of its Semitic form (cf. Gal. 6: 18; Phil. 4: 23; 2 Tim. 4: 22; Philem. 25) "which sounds rather strange to our modern ears", R. Paquier fears to see this kind of thing being reintroduced into our worship, and would prefer us to be content with the apostolic greeting which is answered by an Amen.

It must in fact be recognized that as Reformed Christians we have been growing unaccustomed to it for four centuries, but we must ask ourselves whether in losing the greeting we have not lost something far more than a mere formalist introduction: whether we have not lost touch with our duty of brotherly encouragement at the moment when we are to appear before the terrible face of the Lord, and, in addition, the proof of spiritual cohesion and solidarity. For "at no moment of our worship is our wretchedness so apparent as when we pray. Then a searching question may be asked: will

[1] Zwingli justified by the antiphons the distinction between the seats for men and those for women in church.

the Holy Spirit intervene to bring our prayers immediately before God, or will our prayer consist of a merely formal recitation the effect of which will only be to stir the air a little? That is why it is so appropriate that before praying, the minister and congregation should bless each other by mutual salutation" (P. Brunner).

It is, I think, from this point of view, that we should understand the spread of the *confiteor* in Christian worship from the tenth and eleventh centuries: not as a common confession of sins (as in the Reformed tradition) but in the form of a mutual service rendered by the priest and congregation to each other, that they may then, in the Eucharist, appear before God clothed in the joy of forgiveness. The minister comes before the congregation confessing before it and before God that he is a guilty sinner, and he beseeches his brothers to implore for him God's forgiveness. The congregation replies, addressing the humbled minister in the second person, and says that it accedes to his request and will pray to God for his forgiveness. Then the congregation asks of the minister, for itself and in the same terms, the same service which is rendered to it in the same way. We should do well, were it only occasionally to restore this practice, which is so adapted to curb clerical pride, and to supply a normal and authentic example of mutual spiritual aid. Moreover it enables us to see how precipitate is the accusation which we make against the Church of Rome, alleging that it is so priest-ridden that the laity have lost their rights and duties. As far as worship is concerned, it is among ourselves that clericalism has prevailed most, and it is no consolation to say that in the administration and activities of the Church we give a leading position to the laity: this proves, not so much that we respect the rights of the laity as that our Church is uprooted from the soil which would make it something other than an organization, namely an organ of the Holy Spirit.

We must mention here a ceremony which has fallen into disuse since the Middle Ages, at least in the West, but which was taken for granted in apostolic times,[1] and which strikingly

---

[1] Cf. Rom. 16: 16; 1 Cor. 16: 20; 2 Cor. 13: 12; 1 Thess. 5: 26; 1 Pet. 5: 14.

showed the unity and brotherhood of worshippers: I mean the kiss of peace which has its place in the communion service whether it comes before the preface, as in the East, after the Lord's Prayer as in the West, or after the offertory as in the Gallican liturgies. Doubtless originally it was a sign of mutual reconciliation and unity rather than a means of transmitting life (cf. 2 Kings 4: 34). Hence, before the Middle Ages the kiss with which the celebrant had kissed the altar, the gospel book, the chalice or the host was not repeated by the congregation, but—in an increasingly stylized manner—there was a mutual embrace when one of the clergy invited those present to give each other the peace of Christ. This was possible without impropriety since men and women were segregated. No doubt it would be impossible at present to restore this practice, even on Easter Day, or to transform it into a handshaking ceremony and it is thus preferable to leave to the clergy alone the ceremony of exchanging a salutation. It is a pity to have abandoned it, because the kiss of peace shows that all the reasons for which men oppose each other in worldly relations vanish through the encounter with Christ, which crushes human pride. But even without the kiss of peace the Church can show in its cult that it is but one heart and one soul (Acts 2:32), since it has the canticles, the Amens, the confession of faith, the Lord's Prayer, the offertory, and, above all, the Holy Communion, as proof.

A final feature which reflects the fellowship of Christians in worship is the notices. Often we do not know where to place them; often too, by reason of a dangerous false spirituality, or for fear of impairing the dignity of the service we feel nervous about them, as though the Church were suddenly ashamed of bringing together men and women who wish to marry, who have children, who lose parents or friends, or of grouping men and women who have a special task in the world and who must be given instructions about their witnessing or about the way to prepare for it. Hence the notices should not be pushed aside by being placed before the invocation (which would be tearing the church life away from its centre); nor, on the other hand, should they be overemphasized; if the choir is organizing a theatrical evening it may be enough to say that its programme will be distributed as the congregation leave; it is not necessary to announce that the play will be "Friend Fritz" by Erckmann-Chatrian! These announcements—which we shall do well to place after the sermon and before the great prayer of intercession (if only to supply the latter with some concrete concerns)—are the proof that if the Church disperses between the Sundays it does not therefore disappear, but that it continues to pray, to bear witness, to hear the Word of the Lord, to live and to die under His watchful gaze.

2. *How to articulate the elements of worship in relation to one another*

We can answer this question in two ways. Either we can show, historically, how the Church has proceeded to this articulation, in which case we shall examine the numerous traditional liturgical *ordines* and consider the best and most seemly *ordo*. But we postpone this answer to the last chapter. We can also answer it by trying to give a theological interpretation of the possible articulations, which are various, and do not conflict with the elements of worship, and thus survey the whole richness of the latter. This is what we wish to do here. Three types are possible; these do not contradict each other but are complementary.

(a) The first facilitates a formal interpretation of the problem of articulation.

Let us begin by the most external aspect: the circumstances of wealth or poverty in which the various elements of the cult are presented. This is what we might call the social level of worship. I mean that the various elements of the cult—the Word, the Eucharist, the prayers and the liturgical attestations of community life—although all of them may be present, may be manifested with splendour or simplicity. Thus a village service may be more austere than that of a big town parish, whose resources in men and money are much greater. This greater wealth does not in any way invalidate the austere country service, but neither does it give it an advantage, for if it is not exposed to the same temptations as the more ornate service, it is not for that reason shielded from all liturgical temptation. In the same way, a festival service may have more solemnity and grandeur than, for example, that of the eleventh Sunday after Trinity, and this is normal. Such "social" differences, without impairing Christian unity, can legitimately serve to distinguish one local church from another; and if the German Swiss insist on shrinking from the beauty of worship, let them live in peace with their fears . . . provided that they do not immediately suspect of quasi-idolatry those who claim the liberty of rejoicing differently at the presence of the Kingdom.

There is, however, in this matter one thing to be recommended. The "social" level of the cult must correspond to its spiritual level, otherwise the worship strikes a false note; it prevents the church which celebrates it from truly confessing itself and it ceases to be a genuine epiphany of that church. In practice this means two things: if the spiritual life of a church is poor, an ornate type of worship becomes either a source of illusion and pretence, or a prison in which what remains of true spiritual life feels fettered, incapable of movement and expression, like David in the armour of Saul. It also means that if the spiritual life is rich, it is not right—otherwise we shall insult the grace of God, which has quickened and fortified the Church—to continue to live in an artificial and spurious poverty, for in that event, instead of rejoicing in the grace of Christian liberty, we should be behaving as if we were entrapped. We have no right to appear poor when in reality we are so no longer: that is why our generation, which God has richly blessed in inspiring it to rediscover the force of His living Word and of His Spirit, the quickening reality of the body and blood of Christ, and the freedom implied in our growing recognition of members of other Christian communions as brothers, is called to reform its worship and to reveal by its worship not its ingratitude but its thanksgiving for so many blessings.

Still with regard to the formal interpretation of the diverse elements in the cult, but at a much deeper level this time, is the classic articulation dominated by the two major phases of the cult, the proclamation of the Word and the eucharistic communion, the first preparing the way for the second. This articulation, which divides the cult into two halves, is

M

perfectly valid, and the tradition which distinguishes the mass of the catechumens from that of the faithful is a loyal one. We may perhaps regret the terms used, which have resulted in Christians supposing, in Western Catholicism, that if they are among the "faithful" and no longer catechumens, they may legitimately be content with attendance at the second part of the cult whereas in fact it is the whole circle of worship which is meant for the faithful, the catechumens being admitted only to its first phase. As we have already noted this distinction reflects the two phases in the ministry of Jesus—the Galilean and the Jerusalemite—and anticipates the two phases in the last things, namely the last judgment and the Messianic banquet. We shall return to the point.[1]

(b) The second type of articulation favours an eschatological interpretation of the cult. Its elements are then considered with the object of noting whether they witness to a "not yet" or an "already", as regards the coming of the Kingdom. And although basically the articulation of Word as opposed to sacrament is here present, the distinction is not an easy one, because all the elements of worship partially reflect the simultaneity of the two aeons, none being exempt from the joy of the future, and likewise none altogether escaping the limitations and ambiguities of the present. If the ministry of the Word makes the balance tilt in favour of the "not yet" and the ministry of the sacraments in favour of the "already", neither of them is pure expectation, or pure joy; but, in their reciprocal balance, and the inner balance of each, they show, in conjunction (and this is why they must remain united), the situation of worship in the saving process. They show that the health of the Church depends on the inclusion of all the elements enumerated.

(c) The last type of articulation and the most interesting theologically, enables us to discern the way in which God works in and through the cult. In this regard there are

[1] Formally, we might also distinguish the fixed from the free improvised elements, over the whole scale, from a liturgy fixed in every detail with the exception of the text of the sermon, to a liturgy where all is improvised except the eucharistic species.

several propositions to be made, which are not mutually exclusive.

First, we can distinguish the objective elements in the cult, that is, "those in which the revelation of God draws near to man", from the subjective elements, that is, "those in which man draws near to God's self-revelation" (O. Haendler). The distinction is found, in other forms, in many authors, and in this connexion we wish to recall the sermon of Luther on the occasion of the dedication, in 1544, of the Church of Torgau: "My dear friends, we have now to dedicate and consecrate this new house to our Lord Jesus Christ, and it does not depend on me alone. You also must grasp the aspergillum and the censer, so that the house may be exclusively ordained to this end: that our good Master Himself may speak to us here through His holy word, and that in our turn we may speak to Him in prayer and praise".[1] Hence there are the means by which God speaks to us and gives Himself to us, and the means by which we reply, addressing Him and giving ourselves to Him: the cult then involves the way in which God serves us, and the way in which we serve Him. There are many variations, of which I will quote only the following five:

In the view of L. Fendt, God serves us (objective elements) by the irruption of His Kingdom and its activity in Christ and the Holy Spirit, while we serve God (subjective elements) by the proclamation of the Gospel in its various forms, by the setting forth of the sacraments, by hearing and reception, by confession and prayer, thanksgiving, self-dedication and blessing.

In the view of K. Barth, God serves us by His work, which institutes and demands the cult (the basis), which leads the Church from baptism to the Eucharist (the content), and which must respect the elements chosen by God: water, bread, wine, Word (the form); we serve God by our obedience to this will of God (the basis) by hearing (the content) and by sincerity and humility (the form).

In the view of O. Haendler—who fails to underline how God is at work also in the subjective elements—God serves us by the symbol of our faith, by the sacrament and the

[1] *W.A.* 49, 588.

Word, and we serve Him by meditation, gestures, prayers and canticles.

In the view of W. Hahn, God serves us by addressing us and arousing our response, by being among us in Christ, by acting upon us through the Holy Spirit, and by making the Church a community of mutual service; and we serve God by our response and collaboration, by preaching, by sacrament and liturgy, and by the joy of knowing that worship is the heart of the whole of parochial life.

Finally, in the view of P. Brunner, God serves us by the Word and the Eucharist; and we serve God by obedience, prayer, confession and aspiration towards the Kingdom.

Thus we see how legitimately varied can be the explanation of the objective and subjective features of the cult.

If the above distinction raises no problem, another classification—which covers much the same ground—arouses some uneasiness: the distinction between the sacramental and sacrificial elements. This distinction is drawn from ch. 24 of the Confession of Augsburg, which gives the following definitions: "sacramentum est ceremonia vel opus, in quo Deus nobis exhibet hoc, quod offert annexa ceremoniae promissio . . . Et contra sacrificium est ceremonia vel opus, quod nos Deo reddimus, ut eum honore afficiamus".[1] If we carefully respect the last explanation, which suggests that the *sacrificium* in question is by no means a *sacrificium propitiatorum* (excluded by the sufficiency and uniqueness of the cross) but a sacrificium EUCHARISTIKON,[2] I see no objection to this distinction. Then the sacrament is the means which the Holy Spirit uses to convey Christ and His salvation to us, and sacrifice is the means by which the Holy Spirit gives us to Christ and incorporates us into His salvation. By the sacrament, the Holy Spirit binds the Christ to us; by sacrifice He binds us to Christ; the Holy Spirit being at work in both. To take an example, we might say that the annunciation is the sacramental moment, and the *fiat* the

[1] *Die Bekenntnisschriften der evang. lutherishen Kirche*, Göttingen, 1930, p. 354.
[2] *Ibid.*

sacrificial moment in the mystery of the Incarnation. Again, the sacramental moments of the cult are principally two: when the Word of the Gospel regenerates and leads to baptism, and when the Word of the Gospel edifies and leads to Holy Communion. Hence we find three types of sacramental elements: the Word of the Gospel in its power of regeneration or edification, baptism and the Holy Communion, or, in the normal Sunday worship: the proclamation of the Word of God and the distribution of the eucharistic species. And we might say that the sacrificial aspect of the cult is found in the expression which the cult gives to faith, hope and love: in the confession of faith, prayer, praise and the offertory.

If there is reason to distinguish in the cult between objective or sacramental elements, and subjective or sacrificial elements, it is a distinction which has precise limits. For the truth is that in worship an element is never purely objective-sacramental nor on the other hand subjective-sacrificial: "The service which God renders us in the cult and that which we render Him interpenetrate each other, and what God does in our favour, He does only within, in unison with and in the course of the service which we render Him" (W. Hahn). Hence the various articulations of objective and subjective elements which we have described above, legitimate as they are, must be treated with caution. For if it is true that a certain aspect of the cult or a certain moment in worship highlights the idea of sacrament or of sacrifice, the distinction can never go so far as to effect a divorce between them. But how shall we interpret this constant conjunction, which exists despite the differing sacramental or sacrificial emphases? Three explanations are possible:

Either we may, with K. Barth, make use of the Chalcedonian Christology, and understand this conjunction in the light of the two natures: subjective and objective elements, sacrificial and sacramental elements are reflected in every aspect of the cult, despite the difference of emphasis, and are "without confusion, mutation, division, or separation". In this case the elements of the cult recall the mystery of the burning bush (Exod. 3), the sacramental element being the fire, the sacrificial the wood. We might also adduce the example of the annunciation where the eternal Word of God becomes flesh in the Virgin Mary.

Or, with W. Hahn to whom the Chalcedonian interpretation is suspect, since the cult cannot repeat the absolute uniqueness and the perfection of union between God and man in Christ, we have recourse to the eucharistic doctrine of consubstantiation: *in, cum et sub* our service of God, God Himself is at work. This removes both a falsification of the truly human character of the cult (e.g. transubstantiation), and a hesitation to affirm God's work in and by the cult.

Or else—and this seems to me to describe best the inextricable intertwining of the two elements of sacrament and sacrifice—we can have recourse to the nuptial theme, which is basic to patristic liturgiology, and which reminds us that throughout the liturgy the Lord and the Church meet to give themselves to each other and to welcome each other.

But if the distinction between sacramental and sacrificial elements must never lead to their divorce, it is none the less useful, because it offers the possibility of reforming the cult, of making it ever more faithful or bringing it back to fidelity; because, too, it enables the cult to be made truly relevant to the present, and to express the concerns of the Church which is celebrating it *hic et nunc*. In fact, if the Church has no liberty in regard to the sacramental aspect of the cult (it has not the right to modify the Gospel by eliminations or additions; or to suppress the Eucharist or to invent other sacraments; or to choose other sacramental elements than water, bread and wine) it is free—free in obedience to the Holy Spirit—in so far as the sacrificial aspect is concerned. Hence the cult can be more or less faithful, receive with more or less obedience the sacrament. It can also vary from one culture to another, from one epoch to another, and thus seriously become an epiphany of the Church in a particular country or century.

(d) To sum up, the consideration of the possible articulations of the various elements in the cult yields us basic information about its nature.

Worship commits man in his totality, in his mind and body.

This we have been taught by the formal distinction between the Word and the sacrament.

Worship is the moment of encounter between the two aeons, the world to come and the present, it is the moment when, with the two comings of Christ, the simultaneity of the two aeons is most plainly apparent. This we have been taught by the temporal distinction between elements of this world and elements of the world to come.

Worship is the moment of encounter and unity between the Lord and His people who give themselves to each other, receive each other, in the joy and liberty of communion. This we have been taught by the theological distinction between sacramental and sacrificial elements.

This last point leads us directly to the theme of the next chapter, in which we have to speak about the participants in the cult.

CHAPTER SEVEN

THE PARTICIPANTS IN THE CULT

WE HAVE noted that the cult is the place and the time of the encounter between the Lord and His people. Thus those who participate in it are God and the faithful (with their different liturgical rôles). But this encounter involves also other actors: on the one hand, the angels, and on the other, the world which longs to be re-orientated towards the glorification and praise of the Lord. It is these four partners in the liturgy which we have now to describe.

1. *God.* God's participation is so much a matter of course that He is often overlooked in naming the participants. It is God's command which makes worship something greater than desire and longing. It is His presence which makes it more than an illusion. It is His action which redeems it from vanity. It is His glory which makes it other than spiritual blindness. It is His love which makes it other than spiritual onanism. It is His liberty which makes it other than spiritual blackmail. God, Father, Son and Holy Ghost, is both the subject and the object of Christian worship, He who serves and is served by the cult, He who commands and He who welcomes the service, He who speaks and He who listens, He whom we implore and He who grants our requests.

All that we have been saying so far presupposes to such an extent the presence of God, His operation and His welcome, that it is not necessary to affirm more than this: were it not for the presence, the action and the welcome of God, the Christian cult would become a criminal farce, an atrocious lie, a seductive power, which would have to be opposed by every means. But the Church, through faith— and intermittently by miracles which engender an almost

184

visual conviction[1]—knows that its worship is neither criminal, nor mendacious, nor seductive, because it is God who calls the Church to worship that He may give Himself to the Church and take the Church into His embrace.

2. *The Faithful*. These are the baptized. But we shall have to take into account also two categories of "partial participants", namely catechumens and the excommunicate.

(a) For the baptized, the grace of being able to worship is both a right and a duty; for them alone, because the cult is an eschatological event in which only those share who have been transplanted by baptism into an eschatological situation. If, according to the unanimous teaching of the NT, baptism is not necessary for the hearing of the Word of God, it is necessary—and this is a further proof that worship is not exhausted by its homilectic aspect—for communicating in the body and the blood of Christ. Nowhere does the NT imply that one might be a part of the Church and hence share in its worship, without believing in Jesus Christ and having been baptized in His name.[2] This is attested also by the oldest post-apostolic texts[3] and it is the undeviating practice of every faithful Church: the baptized alone are qualified for the cult and authorized to celebrate it. This of course does not at all mean that the cult is reserved to a "picked élite of people of refined culture and capable of appreciating the charm of ancient incantations . . ." or that it is a "society of the perfect . . . who have disciplined themselves by long ascetic practices and led a life of con-

---

[1] Church history shows us that the temple at Jerusalem (cf. Is. 6: 1ff.: Acts 22: 17ff.) is not the only place of worship where visions occur.

[2] One proof among many is that apostolic preaching asks the faithful to prove their salvation by a way of life worthy of their baptism.

[3] "Let no one eat or drink of our Eucharist without having been baptized, for it is about this that the Lord said: 'Give not what is holy to dogs'" (Didache, 9: 5). "Only those may share in the Eucharist who believe that our teaching is true and have been washed by the bath which leads to new birth through remission of sins, and who thus live according to Christian tradition" (Justin Martyr, *Apology*, 66: 1).

templation". On the contrary, the liturgical assembly—and we have only to think of Paul's letters—"is the scratch collection of cripples, hoboes and beggars who have been recruited from the crossroads and 'forced to come in'"; it is precisely because of its demands as a liturgical assembly, but still more because of the grace active within it, that "this unlikely mob of ragamuffins, where all and sundry are welcomed, can be transformed into a company of saints, a royal and priestly procession".[1]

But if the baptized have the right to celebrate the cult, this right must be respected. It will be so in proportion as the following conditions are fulfilled:

Firstly, each Sunday the Church should celebrate a cult which includes all the elements enumerated in the preceding chapter. It shows contempt for the grace of God and is an insult to the liturgical dignity of the faithful to invite them to a mutilated form of worship. The Church has not the right either to sabotage the gifts of God by conjuring them away or to invalidate the baptism of its members by forcing them back into the situation of catechumens, and she does this as much when the ministers alone communicate as when there is no Eucharist for any one at all. She does it too when she avoids the prophetic proclamation of the Word of God. I have sufficiently insisted on this point to make it unnecessary to dwell on it here, except by way of reminder.

To respect the liturgical rights of the faithful, we must secondly ensure that all the baptized (with the exception of the excommunicate, about whom more later) can share in the whole act of worship. This means that our western practice which excommunicates part of the baptized, not because they are notorious sinners, but because they are children, is faulty. In scripture there is not the slightest indication that childhood as such is sinful; on the contrary, we have an explicit attestation that the bread of life is meant for children also, since at the first miracle of the feeding of the multitude there were "about five thousand men, besides women and children" (Matt. 14: 21). That is why the whole ancient Church—and it is a practice which has been maintained by the Eastern churches—admitted children also to

[1] G. A. Martimort, *La Maison-Dieu*, No. 20, 1950, pp. 157ff.

communion. In the West this practice was lost, especially after the definition of the dogma of transubstantiation (it was felt that it would be a risk to admit children who might slaver while communicating and thus be guilty of blasphemy). The Reformation, while rejecting the doctrine which formed an obstacle to the communion of children, nevertheless maintained the exclusion of the latter (which evidently points to uneasiness about generalized paedo-baptism and shows that the theological tradition of baptism had been changed, since, being identified with the Word, it was understood not so much as a demonstration of grace received but rather as a sign of prevenient grace).

It seems to me quite wrong to safeguard the generalized practice of paedo-baptism by refusing to the baptized, until they reach years of discretion, that access to the Lord's table which is their inalienable right. And if we run the risk of authorizing the baptism of children whose parents are Christian (which seems to me absolutely legitimate) we must also run the risk of permitting them to live on the spiritual food of the baptized, otherwise their baptism is falsified. Hence it is useless to imitate the practice of some American churches which welcome children for part of the service only, arranging for them a special service afterwards; it is also false theologically to make the admission to communion depend on a confirmation of baptism, a practice which depreciates the sacrament of baptism. We must restore to children the right to communicate, and we must insist on it so much the more because children are unable to claim for themselves a right which is theirs. To expel children because they are children is to make the church congregation a club for respectable citizens, a fortress, or a school for intellectuals. Moreover, it is introducing into the life of the Christian community segregations based on false categories. If such subdivisions are appropriate in regard to catechism work or pastoral work, they distort the nature of the Church when applied to the liturgy, which is intended to unite all the baptized. To restore to children access to the Eucharist would also make superfluous those special services for children and young people, and instead of these continuing to foster the rationalist idea of the cult (namely that it is a pedagogic instrument for guiding and instructing the young and hence concerns only children or adults who are infantile) by collecting mainly children whose parents do not obey the summons to worship, we should have at our services children accompanied by their parents. If we wish to maintain the exclusion of children from communicant life, then we must also exclude them from baptism.

Thirdly, to respect the liturgical rights of the baptized, we must allow them to celebrate Christian worship in the fulness of their manhood or womanhood. "Every act of worship is performed by living men. And they can perform it only in so far as they are fully human, with all that is in them, so much the more because one of the essential features of worship is its power to penetrate the whole of man's being" (O. Haendler). Jesus Christ did not cure deaf people only, but also the dumb, the blind and the lame. Hence the baptized—and it is by baptism that we become truly and fully human—must be able to share in worship with their ears, their voices, their looks and their gestures. This does not mean only that the language of the service should be understood by all the participants, but also that their looks and attitudes[1] should be allowed self-expression in worship.

According to all Biblical anthropology, the sexual polarization of human beings is also an essential part of their full humanity: it is men and women who take part in worship and not a-sexual beings.[2] I will not go so far as to say that the respect for this sexual differentiation in and by the cult implies that the elect will be resurrected as men and women (in the Kingdom, each having reached his limit, it will no longer be necessary to proceed with decisions such as that of marriage, cf. Matt. 22: 30 and par.) although baptism, that sacramental resurrection, is not a castration, since it is the sexed body of the faithful which is the temple of the Spirit (1 Cor. 6: 12–20). Moreover it is as a male (aner) that the

---

[1] Must we add: their sense of smell? It is rather the divine sense of smell, if I dare say so, which is directly concerned (cf. Phil. 4: 18; Rev. 8: 3, 5; Luke 7: 37; John 12: 3), that of the faithful only indirectly.

[2] I make only a few brief remarks here realizing that to justify them an exegetic and historic enquiry would be needed which we cannot undertake here.

Risen Lord, bridegroom of the Church, governs His people (2 Cor. 11: 2).[1]

We cannot here go into details and must be content with a few brief remarks. This sexual differentiation is manifest from a liturgical point of view in the fact that certain liturgical functions stem from it, since certain of these functions are reserved to men: we never find in the NT a woman proclaiming the Word of God, with that solemnity imparted by a commission from the Lord; we never find them baptizing; nor can we suppose that they might preside over the Eucharist. The liturgical administration of the means of grace is not for them. The reason for this is not at all a question of the prejudice which existed against them in those times, but lies rather in the doctrine of creation of which Paul reminded the Corinthians: "The head of every man is Christ, the head of a woman is her husband, and the head of Christ is God" (1 Cor. 11: 3). There is an order which is willed by God and according to this it is man who constitutes the link between the Lord and woman. Hence it is men who must be consecrated and ordained to the sacred ministry. It is not their virility as such which qualifies them for liturgical functions, it is their consecration. But their virility is the condition of their consecration. Biblical thought is deeply opposed to the pagan and romantic idea, which is reflected also in the sentimentalism of the odious "Mothering Sunday", that woman is the mediatrix of grace. This does not imply any disqualification of woman, liturgically, but it does mean that her feminity precludes her from representing the Lord in church and from acting publicly and authoritatively in His name.

The cult in fact does not overthrow or annul the order of creation, it confirms and restores it: if we deny this then we are following Marcion who set the Saviour over against the Creator, and it was not a coincidence that it was in the Marcionite sect that women first received authority to administer the means of grace. This sexual differentiation which reserves certain liturgical functions to men, was very

[1] The only consolation to be derived from the tiresome dogma of the Assumption is its implication that the Virgin Mary, resurrected before the time, was exalted to heaven as *woman*.

early manifested (and perhaps even from the start) in the fact that the sexes were segregated in Christian worship: men were placed on the one side, women on the other, as also there was a place for the ministers, for the catechumens, for the penitents, etc. Doubtless we have here a matter of decency and good order, intended to maintain the proprieties and to show that the Christian congregation is not a chaotic body but an organic structure. Hence this separation of the sexes was rarely taken advantage of liturgically. In fact, to my knowledge Zwingli alone tried, in his eucharistic liturgy, to justify the segregation by allocating most of the antiphons to *die man* on the one side and *die wyber* on the other. But if our contemporary feeling—and here it is a question of prejudices characteristic of an epoch—alas! authorizes a mixed seating of men and women, this lack of differentiation should not be taken to justify us in not maintaining the Biblical and traditional rule according to which the cult, just because it enables human beings to express themselves most fully, reserves to men alone certain liturgical functions or rather certain ministries necessary to worship. When we rediscover the truth that this datum of revelation respects woman rather than depreciates her, a great step foward will have been taken towards delivering the Church from its feministic agitation: but to make this rediscovery, we must restore to the laity, both men and women, the whole of their liturgical functions, and we must also get rid of the modern idea that differences of vocation imply value judgments of the persons exercising those vocations.

To respect the right of the baptized to participate effectively in the whole celebration of worship is also to recognize that there are different ministries which must be fulfilled, without giving rise to disorder and without allowing some to absorb others. The Christian community, by the variety of the gifts and ministries which it discloses, is an ordered whole. Both its diversity and its order should be manifest: all are not to do everything, nor must one person alone do everything. The more the community is liturgically alive, the more this diversification, this distribution of functions will be respected.

In this connexion, we might notice that the case of the Corinthian church, whose charismatic effervescence threat-

ened to destroy liturgical order, is not exemplary and, in
particular, does not constitute a norm for the liturgical
situation of the apostolic Church. It is an extreme case
which caused St. Paul obvious concern; it is by no means
an *optimum* which a local congregation should aim at as the
most valid expression of worship. And hence, although we
must respect the marginal legitimacy of such exuberance, I
feel that in treatises on NT worship it is given far too
canonical a significance. By doing this we foster a guilt
complex and an uneasy conscience among communities
which are devoid of such enthusiasm, whereas in fact they
ought to rejoice in their situation. This is by no means to
say that they should be content with a type of worship in
which the minister does everything, but should recollect,
according to the fine phrase of W. Hahn, that "as regards
charismata the essential fact is their eschatological, not
their enthusiastic character". And this eschatological
character is not devalued if it is ordered and calm.

This allocation of parts bears a splendid title in the
Epistle of Clement of Rome to the Church of Corinth: it
speaks of the *liturgies* proper to each officiant. After suggesting a Christian transposition of the various liturgical functions
of the old covenant—those of the high priest, the priest, the
Levites and the laity (HO LAIKOS ANTHROPOS), he
adds: "Let each of you, brethren, be found in his place (EN
TO IDIO TAGMATI) to present the Eucharist to God,
being of a good conscience, serious-minded, and not trans-
gressing the rule attached to his liturgy (TON HORIS-
MENON TES LEITURGIAS AUTOU KANONA)" (I
Clem. 41). Even though later the word seems to have
disappeared, the idea has remained, and of this we have a
curious witness in the fact that in the West at least it was
not until the tenth century that the various liturgical
departments, the epistolary, the evangelistarium, the capitu-
lary (which laid down the passages to be read), the cantatory,
the antiphonary, and the *ordo* giving the rubrics were
collected into a single volume.

These various liturgies which together form *the* liturgy can
be apportioned and history has known diverse ways of doing
this. Without entering into historical details, we may notice

three main "liturgies": that of the head of the community, that of the assembled congregation, and, as an intermediary between them, that of the diaconate. Let us look at the matter a little more closely.

Firstly, there is the *ministry of the head of the community*. How must we call him? PROISTAMENOS (Rom. 12: 8; I Thess. 5: 12), "he who stands in front",[1] or EPISKOPOS, he in whom the Lord visits His people?[2] The term "pastor", which is, moreover, much more episcopal than presbyteral, is perhaps the one that is best fitted. His ministry seems to me threefold: first, he is the commissioned representative of the Lord and in consequence the successor of the apostles. What he does, he does in the name of his Master and with the authority of his Master. His presence at the head of worship is one of the signs of the real presence of Christ among His own.

Hence—and this is the second aspect of his ministry—he ensures the valid Christian character of the worship that is being celebrated. Not, of course, absolutely—for the Lord is free—but with a relativity sufficiently decisive to enable the faithful to have confidence and to be assured that their worship is not invalid. This legitimation of worship by the presence of the pastor, which was so vigorously underlined by Ignatius of Antioch, is a feature also reflected explicitly or implicitly in Reformed credal documents which reserve to the minister *legitime vocatus* the administration of the means of grace: the proclamation of the Gospel and the celebration of the sacraments. To quote only one text, they recall that "if today this Word of God is preached in the Church, by legitimately appointed pastors, we believe that it is the true Word of God which is proclaimed and which the faithful receive".[3] An essential element in the ministry of the pastor is therefore of a juridical kind: because he is there, as the representative of the Lord and the successor of the apostles, the convocation of the people is regular, and they can be confident that they are the true people of God

---

[1] The NT is unaware of the president, he who is *seated* in front!

[2] I think that the term EPISKOPOS stems less from the verb EPISKOPEIN (to inspect) than from EPISKOPE, the "visitation" of the Lord.

[3] *The Later Helvetic Confession*, ch. I.

living by the true grace of God. That is why, as the Reformed confessions of faith are always reminding us, following Christian tradition and scripture, the ministry is essential to the Church if it is to be a true Church.

Finally, a third aspect of the ministry of the pastor is that he must lead the worship, not to do everything himself, but to ensure that all is done which ought to be done and is done in order and effectively. Hence he should not, out of a sense of false humility, lose his identity in the congregation. If he too is a member of the people of God he is so as a shepherd, representing the chief Shepherd (1 Pet. 5: 4). His characteristic ministry consists in fixing the time and place of worship, and summoning the congregation, greeting the latter in the name of the Lord, announcing to it the Word of God (if not in its anagnostic proclamation, at least in its clerical and usually its prophetic forms of proclamation), in celebrating the Holy Communion and supervising its administration and order,[1] in consecrating the people's offering, and dismissing the assembled people into the world with the blessing of the Lord. Usually he is also the mouthpiece of the congregation in their relation to God and hence he must recite at least some of the prayers.

Secondly, there is the *ministry of the people*, who must not, out of indolence, false humility or refusal to commit themselves, shirk their own responsibility. The liturgy of the people is essential to worship, and must not be entrusted vicariously to others, for example, to the pastor or the choir. If liturgical tradition has generally respected the role of the pastor, it has much less respected that of the people, whence the deplorable clericalization of the cult. We must realize, however, that this is due in the first place not to a kind of liturgical voracity on the part of the pastors, but rather to a weakening of the liturgical conscience and self-dedication of the laity. Realizing in fact that the celebration of the cult involves a total engagement, they have often withdrawn and resigned their part. This resignation impairs the whole character of worship: it turns it into a spectacle or a lecture, whereas in fact it is an action, or a game in which all those

[1] He is responsible for the worthy conduct of the communicants, and church discipline in general.

who are present are called upon to play as a team. The ministry of the faithful is normally made up of the following elements (which can be more or less amplified): the respectful hearing of the Word of God, the eucharistic communion, association with the prayers by the utterance of the Amens, the recitation of the creed, the offertory, the singing of the hymns, and the participation in what we have called the liturgical attestations of Christian fellowship (antiphons, *sursum corda*, the greeting, the *confiteor*). The clergy also play their part in this latter aspect of the liturgy in which the whole people of God stand forth as a sacerdotal people.

Thirdly, there is the *ministry of the deacons or deaconesses*. If the ministry of the pastor and that of the laity are indispensable to the cult, the diaconal ministry is very desirable. The great variety of the forms that it has taken historically shows that it is less precisely articulated than the others. Broadly speaking, we might say that it covers the following two domains: the supervision of good order and "the policing of the temple", and assistance given to the pastor as liturgist. If the former aspect is emphasized, the diaconal ministry comes nearer to the people (this is the Gallican and Eastern tendency); if the latter, then it comes into the orbit of the pastor (this is the Roman tendency). In the first view, the deacon is responsible for welcoming the people when they come to church and for seating them; he must intervene if there arises any disorder, he must ensure that the communicants have the right to communicate. It is his function too to indicate to the congregation what it must do—kneel, pray, stand up, sing, etc. Finally—and this is the origin of the Litany—he must advise the faithful on subjects of intercession for their personal prayer. In the second view—and the two are not mutually exclusive—the deacon shares in the proclamation of the Word of God, especially by certain Biblical readings (on this point authorizations have been made, revoked and restored in liturgical tradition) and also assists in the distribution of the bread and wine consecrated by the pastor. The deacons also have usually collected the gifts and offerings of the faithful. It is a ministry which can be entrusted to women. If we apply it to our own Church, we note that it corresponds to what we describe as the ministry of the elders. It should include the following elements: the welcoming and the seating of the faithful, the reading of scriptural passages,[1] the reception of the offertory, the distribution of the eucharistic species.[2]

Should we add to these three a *presbyteral ministry*? On this point the information yielded by tradition is meagre for the period preceding the monarchical episcopate which became general from the fourth century. From that time the presbyteral ministry took over increasingly the pastoral functions which had formerly been reserved to the bishop. For the pre-Nicene period, what we chiefly know is that the presbyteral college (which assisted the bishop administratively rather than liturgically) surrounded the bishop in the place of worship. Hence it has a liturgical place rather than a liturgical function. If at times it intervenes in worship, it is to take part in the blessing of the eucharistic species at the moment of consecration. This custom, which goes back to the second century, doubtless springs from the fact that in exceptional circumstances a presbyter could act as a *locum tenens* of the bishop in his absence, thus enjoying a delegated authority enabling him to preside over Christian worship. But this is about as much as we know of the presbyteral ministry before it becomes almost wholly identified with the episcopal or pastoral ministry. Hence in our own Church constitution—the justification for which we do not examine here—the college of elders should have no other ministry than the traditional diaconal one.

The effect of more concern for the diverse "liturgies"—a concern demanded by the liturgical rights of the baptized—would be to declericalize the cult, and this is so important as to be the essential condition for a renewal of liturgical life. Declericalization would enable us in a large measure to overcome the false problems raised by the dichotomy between clergy and laity. On the one hand, we should not question the specific character of the clergy (the sacred

[1] It would be desirable for two deacons to read the two scripture passages other than the one that is to furnish the theme of the sermon (which would be read by the pastor).
[2] We might add invitations to pray, indication of attitudes, announcing of hymns, provided that it did not result in more disorder than order.

ministry being of divine institution, for it is the Lord who willed to have in His church a DIAKONIA with different orders: cf. KLEROI, Acts 1: 17), but, quite as much, we should not disqualify the laity in favour of the clergy,[1] and should cease to regard the word "lay" as equivalent of "profane". And if the course of history has promoted a kind of sacerdotal concentration on the clergy alone—a concentration which runs parallel to the Christianization of the West, and has favoured the idea that the relation laity-clergy coincides with the relation world-Church[2]—we now find ourselves in a situation where the sacerdotal character of the people of God can flow back from the clergy to the totality of the Church, and so to the laity, since a distinction between the Church and the world is once more possible. Hence it is high time to restore to pastors, the faithful and the deacons their characteristic ministries: no longer need the clergy, not monopolize them, but be the sole order to maintain and preserve them all.

For this reason too we must be very suspicious with regard to what might be called the vicarious representative of the congregational liturgy, namely the choir. The growth of this institution took place from the fifth century, both because the liturgy of the congregation was becoming ever more complex, and also because the faithful became increasingly reluctant to commit themselves to liturgical life. We must basically agree with H. Asmussen when he writes: "A choir as the substitute for the congregation is quite unacceptable"; and that not only because it can upset the normal course of the service, and certainly not because it prevents the community from admitting the mediocre quality of its singing (the congregation should have the courage to admit this mediocrity and should overcome it, not by remaining silent, but by learning to sing better!), but chiefly because it facilitates the congregation's surrender of its liturgical functions. If, then, we wish to have a choir, it should be

[1] In the Reformation period, a flagrant proof of this rejection of the laity is seen in the liturgy of Strasbourg, which precluded the people from the salutation and the *sursum corda*.

[2] Hence a growing separation between choir and nave, and the secret prayers of the clergy, or in the East the concealment of the preparation of the species.

given a precise duty; not that of supplanting the faithful in their characteristic ministry, but of educating them in the fulfilment of this ministry. The choir should thus become the mainspring of liturgical life and worship; it should train the congregation to fulfil their specific ministry. If its effect is to keep the congregation silent, it may be very beautiful but it is false. The same might be said of soloists instead of the congregation singing the creed or the Lord's prayer.

But in order that the right of the baptized to participate in worship should be respected, we must bear in mind the need for their liturgical training. We shall return to the point with specific proposals at the conclusion. Here it is enough to emphasize the need for liturgical training by instruction about the doctrine and history of worship, by pastoral directives, by seminars in liturgy for the pastors, for deacons and choirs, by "liturgical laboratories" capable of making experiments without involving the whole life of a parish, and above all, by systematic practice in the parishes. The time has come when we must not postpone a liturgical renewal, which will not of itself alone bring about a renewal of church life, but which will make a place for and articulate the latter, embodying it in the practice of the Church and not merely that of theology.

We have spoken about the right of the baptized to full participation, according to their order, in the Christian cult. It is not only a right, however, but also a duty, and if we wish the right to be respected, the duty must be also. We need do no more here than allude to it, stressing that the duty will be all the better understood in proportion as the right to full participation is more respected. In fact, one cannot blame Christian people too much for neglecting their Sunday duties if the Church authorities do not begin to demonstrate that they are not truncating the cult or depriving the faithful of their rights: right to the Word, right to the eucharistic communion, right to fellowship in a service full of paschal joy.

(b) Among the baptized, we must include not only the elect present in a particular place, but also the elect of all times and places, for the cult, being an eschatological event, must never allow itself to be fettered by those limitations of space and time to which it must have regard in this world. Since Christian worship is an epitome of the history of salvation, it is a joyful sharing here and now in this whole history, which is interrupted neither by space nor time: as a unity, it is summed up in Christ (cf. Eph. 1: 10), who is the sovereign Lord present in Christian worship. Because Christ is present, all those whom He has saved are present also. Thus the cult is pre-eminently the moment of true community: all those who are hidden with Christ in God are present, and it is not without deep theological reason that, in ancient basilicas— I am thinking, for example, of that of St. Apollinaris of Ravenna—the walls of the nave were covered with frescoes of the saints: we never have Christ without His members: when He is present, so also are those whom He has redeemed. Christian worship is the most emphatic contradiction of human solitude and abandonment.

First, the elect wherever they are situated: those of the parochial family who are prevented by illness or travel, but also those who are gathered in other places of worship to celebrate the same cult, absent in body but present in spirit, we and they are united in virtue of the power of our Lord Jesus Christ (1 Cor. 5: 3). In all confessions, the liturgies constantly declare this, and if here I quote only a few prayers which figure in the Reformed liturgies, it is to emphasize that this assured transcendance of space in Christian worship is not peculiar to churches of a catholic type: "We praise Thee together with all those Christians who are assembled today," says the Liturgy of Ostervald of 1713. "Bless, O Lord, the worship we come to render to Thee, in communion with all Thy Church gathered together this day," says the Liturgy of Neuchâtel of 1904; and according to the *Liturgie jurassienne* of 1955 the Sanctus is chanted "with the angels and all the powers of the heavens, with the spirits of just men made perfect, and with all the Church militant here in earth. . . .".

Further, with the elect of all times: in celebrating the cult, a Christian community localized in time and space draws near—with all the other liturgical communities on earth— "to Mount Zion and to the city of the living God, the heavenly Jerusalem, and to innumerable angels in festal gathering, and to the assembly of the first-born who are enrolled in heaven, and to a judge who is God of all, and to the spirits of just men made perfect, and to Jesus, the mediator of a new covenant" (Heb. 12: 22ff.). Even now the Church shares in that heavenly adoration which will eternally unite all the people of God, from Abel the righteous to the most recent of the baptized. The Church knows this and rightly confesses it in the *memento* which introduces the Canon of the Mass and in which it remembers before God "all those who have fallen asleep in His peace and trusting in His promises of resurrection to eternal life", as also "His witnesses of all times who have glorified Him on earth by their faith and works, patriarchs, prophets, apostles and martyrs" (*Liturgie jurassienne*). The Church rejoices in this at the moment of the Preface which summons the faithful to participate in the *trishagion* chanted in heaven by the angels, by thrones, dominations and powers, and by the spirits of just men made perfect.

Just as a Church, necessarily localized and dated by space and time, is an epiphany of the holy catholic and apostolic Church, so its cult is already a participation in the worship of the Kingdom which will gather together the elect of all places and times that they may live for ever by the grace of the triune God, Father, Son and Holy Ghost, to glorify Him for ever. If true worship is holy because it brings the baptized before the Saviour, it is catholic because it unites, before the Lord, the completed number of the elect. We are not thinking of that prayer for the dead which the Reformation rejected because of the odious commercialization of soteriology which the Middle Ages in the West had fostered, but of prayer with the living of all times and places. Because others of the elect, besides the living who are assembled *hic et nunc*, share in the celebration of the cult, Christian worship prevents a breach in Christian unity: it maintains the communion and continuity of the redeemed.

(c) Besides the central participants, that is, the baptized, there is also a place in Christian worship for what might be described as peripheral participants. We have notably for-

gotten this in the course of Christian civilization because—
the whole population being, in fact if not in essence, composed
of the baptized—the public nature of the cult came to the
forefront instead of its exclusive nature. This public nature
of worship has helped to transform it (I am speaking very
theoretically) into a spectacle, following the Catholic trend,
or into a lecture following the Protestant trend, instead of
allowing it to remain an encounter, in which the Lord and
His church are committed to each other in mutual self-
dedication. Hence, if there are peripheral worshippers among
us, they are no longer the same as they were in the ancient
Church; they are those baptized who have grown lukewarm
through the cares and cupidities of the world. They do not
directly concern us here; they are rather the concern of
pedagogic and pastoral theology.

From the standpoint of liturgical law, the peripheral worshippers are those who are not authorized to share in the celebration
of the whole cult, those who are excluded at a given moment.
This implies that Christian worship is not entirely public.

The preaching of the Gospel is by its very intention a
public act, for the Messianic secret lasted only until Easter
morning, after which, what Jesus taught in private was to
be proclaimed on the rooftops (Matt. 10: 27; cf. 28: 19). If
the public nature of preaching can be disputed, it is disputed
only by the world which desires to silence it (cf. Acts 4: 17ff.;
5: 17–32); it cannot be disputed by the Church. Hence the
worship of the Church has always comprised a public part,
akin to non-cultic evangelistic preaching, and called later
"the mass of the catechumens". But the cult is no more
exhausted by this kerygmatic section than the ministry of
Jesus was exhausted by its Galilean phase. From a certain
moment, the cult is reserved for the baptized: this is its
Jerusalemite aspect. It then proceeds with all doors closed[1]
and is submitted to the discipline of the arcana. Although
such discipline was not as rigid as that which obtained in the
mystery cults, J. Jeremias has shown that it goes back as
far as the apostolic period[2] and was connected with eschato-

[1] In the early Church it was the duty of the deacons to ensure the
exclusion of the unbaptized, and the closing of the doors.
[2] *Die Abendmahlsworte Jesu*, 3rd ed., Göttingen 1960, pp. 118–31.

logical teaching, the Christological mystery (the reason for the abrupt close of St. Mark's gospel at 16: 8), and with the Eucharist (the reason for the absence of any account of the institution in the Fourth Gospel and for the choice of the secret term "breaking of bread" in Acts). In fact we might ask whether this secrecy was not decided by Jesus Himself, who was anxious that holy things should not be given to dogs, nor pearls cast before swine (Matt. 7: 6)[1] and for whom it was axiomatic that if grace is offered to all, it is given only to those who seek it with faith and repentance: salvation is never unconditional.

The peripheral participants are those who take part in the Galilean phase of the cult only. They are not yet, or are no longer, among those called the "offerers" (PROS-PHERONTES). They are of three types.

Firstly the catechumens, the candidates for baptism. It is not known precisely at what date the organized cate-chumenate began, but as soon as it was organized, the catechumens were (one must say: remained) excluded from the eucharistic service, being obliged to join in the first, the homilectic, part of the cult. If, later, they were admitted at least to the preliminary prayers, or if at any rate they were not excluded without being prayed for, they were originally excluded even from the prayers, for the prayers are not a private act of the ministers but a communal act on the part of all those who, being dead and resurrected with Christ, have access to God through Him. Now the catechumens have not yet a right to such access publicly. This exclusion is not due to motives of pride or self-righteousness, and, instead of being irritated by it, we should do better to notice that what is surprising is not the dismissal of the catechumens at a given point in the service, but rather their admission to that part of the cult in which—on account of the continuance of this world and its temptations—the Church deepens the teaching of its members and maintains them in a situation of catechumenate or penitence. We should see in all this not a segregation inspired by pride, but an appeal prompted by love; the Church welcomes the unbaptized for as long as possible in order to show them what should be the true

[1] For its application to the Eucharist, cf. Didache, 9: 5.

orientation of their lives. But those who have not yet publicly consented to redirection through baptism, or whose consent is still being tested, cannot be admitted to that encounter between the Lord and His Church which is the Eucharist, or to the liturgy which is its basis and means of expression. The Christian cult is not a spectacle. And it is in proportion as the cult has ceased to be understood as the act of a community, that it has grown ever more public.

Then there are the penitents. Placed under discipline and so excommunicate, the Church has put them back to the level of the catechumens: they are expected to be present at the "Galilean" phase of the cult and are excluded from its "Jerusalemite" phase. The liturgical rights conferred on them by their baptism have been withdrawn. But their relegation to the catechumenate level is very important for an understanding of the meaning of excommunication. The aim of the latter is not to indicate to the excommunicate that they have irretrievably lost their salvation, but rather to invite them to commit themselves afresh, because their first act of self-committal has been compromised by their lack of faith or their way of life. Were they completely excluded from worship, they would lose all chance of salvation; but relegated to the catechumenal level, they are still called, and what baptism will be for the catechumens, solemn reconciliation with the Church will be for the penitent. Hence it is not without significance that the ancient Church fixed the date of this reconciliation at the special time appointed for baptisms, namely the paschal season. We might add that the early Church placed on the same footing the energumens, that is the demoniacs (especially the epileptics): their demon possession made them unfit for worship with those who were indwelt by the Holy Spirit; but I do not know whether at the paschal season they were submitted to exorcism or whether they had to be content to remain for ever on the threshold of the earthly Church, in the hope of being counted among the righteous at the resurrection.

Among the peripheral worshippers, but to a lesser degree than the catechumens, penitents and energumens, are those whom St. Paul called the "idiots" (1 Cor. 14: 24), that is, unbelievers who came to church out of curiosity or from interest, but who were uncertain whether they would become candidates for baptism or not. For them the first part of the cult corresponds less to catechumenal instruction than to extra-liturgical evangelization. Nevertheless, they are admitted—we might recall the fact that St. Augustine went to Milan to hear St. Ambrose preach—and this again shows the effort made by the Church in its worship to gather in the multitudes in a welcoming and hopeful spirit. But they too are admitted only to the "Galilean" phase of the cult.

We have seen that in worship all the participants must have the ministry appropriate to them. What is the function proper to these peripheral worshippers? From the place reserved to them, they share in one part of the ministry of the faithful: they listen to the proclamation of the Word of God. K. Barth is right when he says: "In the whole world there is no more intensive, strenuous and lively action than that of listening to the Word of God: listening to it, as is right, ever anew, ever better, ever more faithfully, ever more intently". Traditionally this is the only part they can play in worship.[1] To pray—especially to say the Lord's Prayer—to confess the faith, to communicate in the Lord's body and blood, they must cross the threshold, or rather they must pass through the burial implied by baptism, for it is in Christ alone that these elements of the liturgy are delivered from vanity to become authentic. But to understand this, we should have to learn afresh the meaning of the mystery of baptism.

We must add two further remarks. The first concerns the necessity of the "Galilean" moment to the fulness of worship. In speaking of the component parts of the liturgy, we have noted the essential place in it of the proclamation of the Word. Now, the whole of liturgical tradition places this proclamation in the "Galilean" phase of the cult. By this it is not implied that the baptized no longer need it, that their presence at the Eucharist, or even a part of the Eucharist (in which they are non-communicants), is a suffi-

[1] One might say that it is also part of their liturgy to be dismissed before the Eucharist and to show the difference between sin and salvation, the world and the Church.

cient fulfilment of their duties as baptized members of the Church. This is what was thought in the West during the Middle Ages, and what the best Roman theologians of today protest against (with wisdom!). If the proclamation of the Word is placed in the "Galilean" phase of the cult and (at least where liturgical tradition is faithful to the early Church) the faithful are not excused from listening to it, it is because they are, so long as this world lasts, still to some extent catechumens and penitents. To deny the need to attend ever anew the school of Holy Scripture is to deny the continuance of this world and its temptations, it is trying to establish oneself, from pride or impatience, in the world to come. Hence, it is not without grave danger that we have called the first part of the cult the "mass of the catechumens" and the second part the "mass of the faithful", for it is a description which might seem to suggest that the former mass is optional for the faithful. We are not yet in the Kingdom; until we are, the faithful will always have to class themselves also among the catechumens and the penitents.[1]

And yet we already "taste the powers of the age to come" (Heb. 6: 5). Hence it is not legitimate to reduce the cult to that part of it to which catechumens and penitents are also welcomed, and to cheat the baptized of their right to eucharistic life and worship. The Calvinistic Reformation, to the great demerit of Calvin, and without exception, condemned the faithful to be for the most part only catechumens and penitents. This state of affairs has led to a widespread loss of the awareness of what is implied in baptism among Reformed Christians and has also caused terrible injury to Christian worship. Later, attempts were made to repair the damage—I am thinking of J. F. Ostervald in the eighteenth century, of E. Bersier in the nineteenth and of certain contemporary liturgical attempts—by making the "Galilean" phase of the cult more liturgical than it was in the sixteenth century: but this effort contradicted the right tradition which made this phase as unliturgical as possible since it is accessible to those who are not qualified for full Christian worship.

[1] Or rather, as we have noted, the faithful can invite to this part of *their* cult those who are not yet baptized, or those who have compromised their baptism by their conduct.

It was not a wise step: in order to revivify Reformed worship, the first step to be taken is the restoration of a weekly eucharist and communion, and the rest will follow. For it is such a restoration which will once again make of all the faithful PROSPHERONTES, worshippers in the fullest sense of the term. This alone will bring about in a natural and genuine way the joy of the Church's response to the grace of God.

3. *The angels, partners in worship.* In the Preface to the Eucharist, the congregation, after declaring what God has done for the world and its salvation, chants the *sanctus* "with the angels and all the powers of heaven". In so doing it avows that it is participating in the doxology of the heavenly beings described by the Book of Revelation (cf. 4: 8); it draws near to the heavenly Jerusalem where are innumerable angels" (Heb. 12: 22).

(a) But who are the angels? We cannot here discuss in detail the content and the limits of Christian angelology. Let us be content first to note two points. We must agree with K. Barth that the angels, for Christian faith, are "essentially marginal beings" (*Dogmatics*); they surround, they obey, but they have no initiative. They are secondary; but they are real. They are created beings, celestial spirits of whom it may be said—going to the very limit of the definable—that in them "the liberty of the ego and the necessity of the being coincide" (P. Brunner). In this sense they are perfect creatures who already enjoy the immutable state which will be the experience of those raised from the dead. For this reason God can count on them. The definition of André Chamson is well known: "To become a man is to make a vocation coincide with a will."[1] With the angels this coincidence is no longer a programme or a problem, it is a fact; thus in heaven they are the image of what man is called to become, and not only man but every creature.

For—and this is the second point to be mentioned here— the angels do not include only one category of being, the "anthropoid"; they include animal categories also: cherubim

[1] *La Neige et la Fleur.*

205

and seraphim.[1] There are the four-and-twenty elders and the four beasts (Rev. 4: 6–10). Since we have not to defend angelology in this context, these definitions may suffice for our purpose, provided it is borne in mind that the whole of scripture is aware of and bears witness to the existence of angels, and thus warns us against putting too much trust in the rationalist mind, which is blind and deaf to the plenitude of the cosmos, inhabited far beyond the range of our perception and the apparatus at our disposal.

(b) The Book of Revelation shows us quite specially, though not exclusively, that there is a close link between the angels and the worship of the Church. This link is twofold. First, it implies that the earthly worship of the Church is joined to the worship of the angels in the heavenly sanctuary, that worship which is "already the perfect worship of the created order". Certainly "the cult of the Church on earth, as regards its intensity, purity and fulness, is but a pale and broken reflection of what takes place in heaven. The worship rendered by the angels takes precedence in every way over that of the Church on earth. But their worship and that of the Church on earth are not separated by an iron curtain; because they have the same centre, the Lamb that was slain, they are in real communion with each other. This means that the Church on earth is here and now invited to join in the praises sung by the angels in heaven and to beseech God to allow it to unite itself with their *Sanctus*" (P. Brunner).

This communion of the Church with the celestial worship performed by the angels is important, not only because of the joy and exultation which it inspires, but also because it makes clear that earthly worship is not a self-enclosed thing which seeks its justification within itself; for the angelic cult is the prototype, not so much of the Church's worship, as of the worship eventually to be rendered by the whole world and for the moment represented by the Church: "Then I looked and I heard around the throne and the living creatures and the elders the voice of many angels ..." (Rev. 5: 11–14).[2]

[1] This opens up an eschatological future and a hope for the animal world.

[2] Should we again speak here of glossolalia, a human attempt to

But—and it is in this way above all that the angels are our companions in worship—it is not merely that we unite in our clumsy way our worship to that offered by the angels: they also join in our worship. They are present. When the Church is assembled for worship, "it is", as Calvin says, "in the presence of God and His angels". For this reason women must attend veiled (1 Cor. 11:10). We might even ask whether each local congregation has not—like each individual (Matt. 18:10; Acts 12:15)—its special angel commissioned by God to guard and guide it: I am thinking of the angels of the seven Churches spoken of in the first chapters of the Book of Revelation who are perhaps among the guardian angels (though they may be the bishops of these churches); or perhaps they fulfil both functions, so that, as Origen suggests, there would be "two bishops to each church, the one visible and the other invisible, sharing the one task".[1]

Is it possible to be precise as regards the special ministry fulfilled by the angels in our earthly worship? The Fathers did not fail to be so, but prudence dictates to us the greatest caution in following them when they dare to peer into revelations into which perhaps even the angels long to look (cf. 1 Pet. 1:12). In short, we have in this matter only one explicit testimony: the angels have a special ministry to fulfil at the time of the prayers, since they take charge of these to present them to God (Rev. 5:8; 8:3). However, we are not forbidden, I think, to consider not only the presence of the angels, which is constant, but their special intervention at moments when their worship and ours draw closest together, e.g. the confession of the faith and the doxological acclamations. In this respect it is more a question of the linking of our worship to that of the angels than the converse. But I wonder whether one moment of the cult, specially privileged by the presence of the angels, is not that of the sermon, because proclamation is a special and essential function of the ministry of the angels, who are present

---

speak the "language of the angels" (1. Cor. 13:1)? In any case, Paul's warning against it shows that our communion with the angels must remain a pale and broken reflection of their worship.

[1] Homily on Luke 13.

whenever the great works of God have to be proclaimed. They announce the nativity, they announce the glorious resurrection of Jesus Christ,[1] they comment on the ascension, they will announce the parousia (Matt. 13: 31; 24: 31, etc.). To hope, at the moment of preaching, for the help of the angels, is not the least of the consolations attending the pastoral ministry. However this may be, the proclamatory messages of the angels, e.g. the *gloria in excelsis* of Christmas night, "span in fact the whole gamut of what, in Christian truth, can and must be proclaimed" (H. Asmussen).

(c) Let us add further a brief remark on the ministry of the angels. The Epistle to the Hebrews calls them LEITOUR-GIKA PNEUMATA EIS DIAKONIAN APOSTELLO-MENA DIA TOUS MELLONTAS KLERONOMEIN SOTERIAN (1: 14) and the Book of Revelation the SYNDOULOI of the faithful who are called to bear witness to Jesus (19: 10). Hence it is wrong, and K. Barth (*Dogmatics*) is right to underline this, to ascribe to them above all a liturgical function. If they have an evident liturgical function, it is that they are particularly charged with promoting the process of salvation, and the worship of the Church sums up and furthers this. They are essentially—as their very name suggests—envoys. But like Christ, like the apostles and like the Church, they are sent in order to return: to proclaim the work of God, to fulfil that work, and to gather up its results and present them to God in thanksgiving. Like the Church, if I may say so, they pass from the "mass" to the "eucharist". Thus they symbolize the twofold orientation of the Church; turned towards the world, sent out into the world to accomplish God's work: and turned also towards God, present before the face of God, to offer to Him with thanksgiving the fruits of the work for which they have been sent. As with the Church, their first office is only for a time, the time preceding the parousia, but their second office is eternal. But as with the Church—and it is precisely thus that the future is already present—their second office is already being performed. The cult is the answer to the

---

[1] As regards the Passion, their ministry is not kerygmatic, but consolatory (cf. Luke 22: 43).

THE PARTICIPANTS IN THE CULT

missionary appeal, but, because of the simultaneity of the two aeons, the cult is already possible in this time of missionary action.

4. *The world and its sighs.* God and the faithful are the principal participants in the Church's worship. But their encounter is not without witnesses (since the angels are there), nor is it without localization, since it takes place in this time-space world. The presence of the world is then also implied when the Church is engaged in worship. We shall devote the next two chapters to this theme. Hence we can be brief at this point, especially as we have already mentioned the problems which arise here. We shall confine ourselves to mentioning the two points which create a problem in the present context.

(a) First, it must be clearly realized that it is not the Church which participates in the praises and the doxology of the world, but the latter which participates in the praises and doxology of the Church. In the Kingdom, it will no longer be possible to draw this distinction, since the whole cosmos will be occupied in singing a doxology to the Lord. Then it will no longer be unsafe to say that the Church in praising God is voicing the song of the world. But so long as this evil world lasts, in which man has, so to speak, brought about a divorce between worship and the world, in which man has become deaf and blind to the glory of God which fills the universe (Is. 6: 3), has forsaken his role of chief worshipper in the created order and hence his vocation to be the first of creatures (Gen. 1: 1–2: 4), it is not the Church which is invited to enter into the praises sung by the world (which is too distracted to have any certainty of reaching God), it is the world which is invited to enter into the worship offered by the Church. For it is the redeemed, the baptized, who, having themselves been re-orientated, are capable of re-orientating the whole world: it is they alone who are able to lead the world in worship.

Thus Psalm 148, having summoned the heavens and their hosts, the stars, the deeps, fire and hail, snow and frost, stormy winds, plants, animals, peoples and their kings, men and children, to sing the praises of the Lord, gathers together all these praises and sees them focused in that of Israel: "He has raised up a horn for His people, praise for all His saints, for the people of Israel who are near to Him. Praise the Lord!" (v. 14). The Church's worship is thus the floodgate through which pass the praises offered by the world—its appeal for help and its thanksgiving—and that is why the cult cannot tear the Church away from the world, but on the contrary must bring it into solidarity with the world. Hence too the welcome which the Church holds in store for the world, the love which it bears to the world, are manifested in the first instance, though not exclusively, in and through its worship.

(b) What then is the part played by the world in the Church's worship? We might answer that the world offers to the Church its time and its space: it asks the Church to assume the world, liturgically, by sanctifying time (i.e. Sunday and the liturgical year) and by sanctifying space (i.e. water, bread and wine, and the whole jewel-box of stones, wood, light, colours, sounds, space and movements, which envelop the sacramental elements that Jesus has chosen as the signs of His action and presence). And by this day of worship—*pars pro toto!*—the whole of history regains its true bearing, the whole of time re-assumes a meaning; and by the sacraments—*pars pro toto!*—the whole of space rediscovers its orientation, the whole of creation is quickened and given intelligibility. This theme we shall amplify in the following chapters.

In this chapter we have been speaking about the participants in worship: the essential ones being God and the baptized who there come to an encounter, and the attendant ones being the angels and the world who are witnesses and servants of this liturgical encounter between God and His people. In speaking of the baptized we have seen that those who are present in body are not present alone, since Christ is accompanied by all those who belong to Him, and it is impossible to commune with Christ apart from His whole Church. We have also seen that those who are absent by reason of illness or travel are still present at worship in spirit. Their participation is attenuated, since they cannot join in the two fundamental phases of the cult, namely, the hearing of the Word and sacramental communion. One question now arises: can one be a worshipper without being directly present, by participating only through radio or television transmission? Let us reply briefly:

For Christians who are prevented not by indolence, the cares of this world, or the fear of self-committal, but legitimately prevented by illness, age, or distance, an authentic sharing in worship is partially possible by this means. Partially, because there will still be lacking brotherly fellowship, and above all the possibility of communicating with the body and blood of Christ.

Consequently, such transmissions can never be considered a real substitute for the ancient custom according to which, after the end of the cult, the deacons carried to the sick the remaining eucharistic species, in order to associate them effectively with the Church's worship.

Such transmissions of services are ambivalent. On the one hand they are edificatory through the consolation it is their purpose to bring to the faithful who cannot attend service. On the other hand, they help in the evangelization of the world by making known to it the message and the worship of the Church. But it may be questioned whether this way of fulfilling these two tasks is legitimate. In the first case, it is possible that the cult is degraded to the level of a spectacle or a lecture,[1] and in the second, that pearls are being cast before swine. The right Christian tradition, for which the cult consisted of a communal action involving all the participants, did not tolerate the presence of the unbaptized. Liturgical celebration as a spectacle, as a folk-lorist exercise, as a cultural document, or as part of an advertising campaign, would have been abhorrent to it; such would have been considered blasphemy, doubtless rightly.

Can we not then use these modern means of publicity in

---

[1] Since, in Roman discipline, the obligation to attend mass does not imply communion, the refusal to consider such wireless or T.V. services a substitute is feebly grounded: it is the obligation to communicate which is the real grounds for the rejection of them.

the service of the Gospel? Assuredly we can, but we must use them so as not to encourage indolence or contempt. Hence I wonder whether we ought not at first to suppress the radio or television transmission of actual services, which go a long way towards maintaining the ambiguities of western Christianity, and perhaps too the "religious" emptiness of the Sunday morning programmes (consequent upon suppression) would have the effect of bringing more people to church. Then, we would have to see whether at other times it might not be necessary to have Christian talks broadcast, with the object of pastoral guidance as well as of evangelization and catechesis. However, to reach this solution, all the confessions would have to adopt it in concert, and at present, on all sides this new plaything is too keenly appreciated for us easily to give up the delights it permits and promises.

CHAPTER EIGHT

THE TIME OF THE CULT

TWICE over, the seer of the Book of Revelation, describing the new Jerusalem, declares that "there shall be no night there" (21: 25; 22: 5): an eternal day will have dawned, whose light will flow for ever from God and His glory. But the time of that worship which expresses eternal felicity is not yet ours, and in the cult of the Church we have only a proleptic foreshadowing of it. Hence, there is a time for worship.

In this chapter, we shall have three areas to explore rapidly. First, Sunday; then, the problem of the liturgical year; finally, a few remarks on the power of the cult to sanctify time, to claim it for Christ and to dedicate it to Christ.

1. Sunday

It is not possible to deal fully with this theme, because this day, if we try to pierce its mystery, is a kind of summary of all that Christian worship implies: like worship, it recapitulates the whole of the saving process, and it is not too much to say with a contemporary Anglican theologian: "The keeping of the Lord's Day is linked with the holding of the principal truths of the Christian faith".[1] Since we must reduce as much as possible what is to be said, I would like to refer to some recent important works on the subject:

Le Jour du Seigneur, studies from the second Congress of Liturgical Pastoralia, with contributions from, among others, Revd. Frs. Feret, Daniélou, Congar, Romano Guardini, etc. (Robert Laffont, 1948).

[1] H. P. Porter, *The Day of Light: the Biblical and Liturgical Meaning of Sunday*, Studies in ministry and worship, London, 1960, p. 49.

J. Daniélou, *Bible et Liturgie* (Lex orandi, No. 11, Paris, 1951, esp. p. 303–469).

H. Peichl, etc., *Der Tag des Herrn* (Herder, Vienna, 1958).

H. P. Porter, *The Day of Light,* the Biblical and Liturgical Meaning of Sunday (S.C.M. Press, London, 1960).

W. Rordorf, *Der Sonntag,* Geschichte des Ruhe-und Gottesdiensttages im altertum Christentum (Zwingli Verlag, Zürich, 1962).

These are technical studies against the background of patristic literature. It must be recognized that on this problem Protestant continental theologians (like the Reformers) are neither eloquent nor deep, or else appear to be interested in the theme less for liturgical than for social reasons—they are more sabbatical than dominical—e.g. the collective work of J. Beckmann, Claus Westermann, E. Lohse, *Verlorener Sonntag?* (Kirche im Volk, vol. 22, Kreuz Verlag, Stuttgart.[1]

(a) *The Biblical data*

J. J. Stamm remarks that "the history of the Sabbath in Israel . . . is the history of an ever-deepening consciousness of meaning: at first, the social bearing of the Sabbath is recognized; and later, its implications for the saving process and for the cosmos as a whole are understood". The same may be said of Sunday, even if in this case it is not the social implications which were a major factor at first. But if the realization of its significance was slow in developing, if it was necessary to wait several centuries for a true theology of Sunday to be formulated, the NT contains certain basic elements, which must be quickly reviewed.

It is important to begin by a brief note on the attitude of Jesus towards the sabbath. This was His favourite day for the performance of His messianic work: not only did He preach in the synagogues,[2] but He seems to have preferred

[1] Dare I avow that what K. Barth says (*K.D.* III/4, pp. 51–79) seems to me to lack the vigour and interest of his normal teaching? I wonder if this difference does not stem largely from the fact that here he has not listened—not even critically—to the voices of the Church Fathers.

[2] Cf. Mark 6: 2 par.; Matt. 4: 23 par.; 9: 35; Luke 4: 15; John 6: 59ff.; 18: 20.

it for the working of His miracles.[1] It is the day *par excellence* when, like the Father, He works (John 5: 17); when, therefore, He manifests the irruption into this transient world of the world to come. It is the day of which He is "Lord" (Matt. 12: 1–8 par.). Why? Not by any means—as has often been thought—because He wished to oppose Jewish formalism and its officious laws, but because for the OT dispensation the sabbath indicated the goal, the final conclusion of creation, the perfecting of the covenant between God and His people, and because in Jesus Himself this goal was reached. Thus Jesus' attitude to the sabbath is manifestly eschatological and messianic: He shows thereby that the old covenant has reached its conclusion, and that a new order in the process of salvation is now beginning. The Jewish feasts in general and the sabbath in particular were but "a shadow of things to come, the substance being Christ" (Col. 2: 16).

Hence in the attitude of Jesus to the sabbath we see a parallel to His attitude towards the Temple—I am thinking of the expulsion of the merchants, or of the words about His body being the new Temple (John 2: 21)—He fulfils it in His person, He assumes it, and conferring upon it its plenitude, He supersedes it: with Jesus begins both the seventh day and the eschatological ANAPAUSIS. Thus I am surprised that in the exegetical debate on the Messianic consciousness of Jesus, His attitude to the sabbath does not play a more important part, for it would provide a solid argument to those who rightly maintain that He knew Himself to be the Messiah. We have a curious indication that the seventh day, the true sabbath, begins with Him, in the Matthean genealogy which dates the birth of Jesus, as if to inaugurate a seventh age, after six times seven generations. Further there are many indications that Jesus Himself constitutes the eschatological rest: there is the saying in which He promises rest to all who come to Him (Matt. 11: 28ff.)[2] and that about His presence being like the presence of

---

[1] Cf. Matt. 12: 9–14 par.; Mark 1: 21f.; Luke 13: 10f.; 14: 1f.; John 5: 1f.; 7: 23; 9: 14.
[2] This text precedes immediately the one, fundamental for our purpose, about the plucking of the ears of corn.

the bridegroom, when fasting is no more appropriate (cf. Matt. 9: 14f. par.; 11: 17). In a very special sense, too, the time of His presence is that of the forgiveness of sins; hence the time when men, at last obeying the recommendation to enjoy true rest given by Is. 1: 13f., can cease from their self-centred works and allow the Lord to act.[1] The true sabbath is Christ.

But if Jesus is the true sabbath—as He is the true Temple, the true OT sacrifices, the true circumcision—He also puts an end to the sabbath (as to the Temple, to sacrifices, and to circumcision) by fulfilling it. In other words, the day of Christian worship will not be the sabbath day, but a different day: the sabbath is fulfilled and superseded. If this is so, then to maintain the sabbath of the Jews would imply a relapse into the old covenant, as though Christ had not come. And in fact from the start it was observed that Christians met for worship on another day, the day after the sabbath. Let us begin by quoting the oldest indications of this change of day.

The texts most often quoted in this connexion are the following: first it is noted that in Acts 20: 7 the faithful are said to assemble on "the first day of the week" (MIA TON SABBATON) as though this were a matter of course. It is on this day too that the Corinthian Christians are exhorted to show their Christian unity and brotherly generosity by "putting something aside and storing it up" (MIA SABBATOU) (1 Cor. 16: 2). It is doubtless the same day, now called for the first time "day of the Lord" (KYRIAKE HEMERA), on which the seer of the Revelation was ravished to behold heavenly worship (Rev. 1: 10). Hence we find in the NT two titles: the first day of the week and the day of the Lord. Day of the Lord—or, by contraction, simply "lordly" (KARIAKE)—is also found in two ancient texts: in the Didache (14: 1, with no exact theological explanation, but with the statement that it is the day of pardon and liberty) and in Ignatius of Antioch (*Magn.* 9: 1) who says that on this day "our life dawned through Christ and His death", and who therefore specifically connects this day of worship with the resurrection of Christ and its life-giving

[1] This idea was much used by the Fathers.

power for those who believe in Him. Pseudo-Barnabas
speaks of it as the eighth day, the day of the great rest,
source of the world to come, stating that Christians "celebrate,
to their joy, the eighth day, because on that day Jesus rose
from the dead and after appearing ascended into heaven"
(15: 9). As for Justin Martyr, he calls this day "that named
after the sun": Sunday (*Apol.* 67: 1).[1]

If here we have the oldest specific attestations of the
Christian day of worship, we must also mention certain
implicit ones and especially the two following: first, the fact
that Jesus, according to St. John's Gospel, appeared the
second time, not on just any day of the week, but eight days
after the resurrection, i.e. the Sunday after Easter (John
20: 26).[2] Then there is the fact that the fiftieth day after
Easter—which appears to fall on a Sunday—the disciples
are gathered together and receive the Holy Spirit (Acts 2: 1).

It is true that the Acts of the Apostles mentions a daily
meeting of the disciples (Acts 2: 46).[3] Even if this were an
allusion to an initial tradition abandoned later, a sort of
inauguration of the eschatological sabbath, even if it were
also something of a hyperbole, at least with respect to those
who were not apostles, the text is not clear, for the mention
of daily meetings could refer to a frequenting of the temple
for prayer and witness. In any event, very soon, and certainly
in the Pauline churches, the first day of the week was fixed
as the day for the Christian cult.

Why this day? There are various hypotheses. H. Riesenfeld
wonders whether this day was not originally chosen in
connexion with the sabbath, to show clearly that the sabbath
no longer sufficed because it had been fulfilled in Christ.
The Christians first went to the Jewish cult to hear the
reading of the OT or to take part in the sacrifices and prayers
of the temple; then they gathered in their own homes

[1] Cf. the *status dies* mentioned by the younger Pliny (*Epist.* X,
96. 7) implying a day for the cult.
[2] Perhaps also the third appearance by the sea of Tiberias may
have been a Sunday, since the disciples are not engaged in the
Sabbath rest, and this last meeting, with the meal and the missionary
charge, symbolized by the miraculous catch of fish, is so dominical
in character.
[3] We cannot include Acts 5: 42, which does not refer to the cult
(with breaking of bread) but to preaching or non-cultic evangelization.

rejoicing because Christ had given them what the sabbath promised: hence in their homes they persevered in the doctrine of the apostles, in brotherly fellowship, in the breaking of bread and in prayer. "There is evidently a connexion betwwen the attendance at the Jewish cult and the specifically Christian meetings. At first the Temple and its worship were not abandoned in favour of a more or less developed Christian cult, but attendance at Jewish worship was continued in the conviction that it was consummated at the heart of God's new people, which was being constituted on new lines: recitation of the words of Jesus, prayers addressed to the risen Christ, breaking of bread in His memory, and the teaching of the apostles".

This hypothesis, if it underlines the passage from Judaism to Christianity effected by the Jerusalem church, does not seem to me convincing, in that it does not sufficiently insist on the newness of the new covenant. We must rather agree with G. Delling who thinks that the Christians chose this day for two internal reasons: "First, one of the constitutive elements of Christianity was the assembling of a community. Second, Christianity is in its essence a history of salvation, and the cult inserts into this history its celebrants, hence the decisive points of the history become dates for Christian worship." In other words, the very nature of the salvation which had appeared with Christ demanded a cult and a day appointed for it, because the nature of the Church postulates that it will assemble and will commemorate the important dates in its history.

But this hypothesis presupposes that it was the Church which by internal necessity chose and fixed the day of its worship. May we not go further and envisage that this day was not chosen but received by the Church? To be sure, we do not find in the NT an institution of Sunday parallel to the institution of the sabbath in the old covenant. But may we not suppose—especially in view of the Johannine testimony—that it was Christ Himself who, when He rose on the first day of the week and came back to His followers on the same day, implicitly or even explicitly designated that day as the day of His regular meeting with the Church until the parousia?

Let us add a final remark. We have seen that Jesus is the true sabbath because He fulfils it. This fact brought about two consequences in the Church, only the second of which has a direct bearing on the day of the cult. First,with Jesus, has come the true rest, or an anticipation of the true rest (underlined in the fourth chapter of the Letter to the Hebrews). Now rest, for the whole early Church, "consisted not in devoting one day, but every day to God, and in abstaining, not from work, but from sin". It consists in ceasing from our works to allow God to work in us. Since the advent of Christ we are constantly engaged in the sabbath rest. Secondly, and this is our point here, the fulfilment of the sabbath by Christ caused a change in the day of worship: henceforth, it was no longer on the seventh day that the people of God assembled to commemorate their salvation, but on a new day, called sometimes the first day of the week and sometimes the Lord's day.

(b) *The first day of the week*

We have seen that the Christians assembled on the first day of the week (Acts 20: 7), the day on which Jesus rose again (cf. Matt. 28: 1; Mark 16: 1–2; Luke 24: 1; John 20: 1).

Hence the day appointed for Christian worship is a memorial of the resurrection of Christ. Each Sunday is an Easter day. On that day the Church celebrates the great new beginning, the possibility of a future other than death, the victory of Christ over the dominion of Satan. It is a day of triumph and liberty. Right in the midst of this world of bondage and death, the Church by its weekly celebration proclaims and experiences ever anew the significance of Easter. This is the central affirmation.

In the history of the Church, moreover, a second memorial, connected with Easter, has been attached to the first day of the week: the memorial of that first day of creation when God separated the light from the darkness (Gen. 1: 4–5), the memorial of the creation of the world. "Sunday, the holy day, is a commemoration of the Saviour. It is called the Lord's day because it is the Lord of days. In fact before the passion of the Lord it was not called Sunday, but the first day. It was on this day that the Saviour began the first work of creation; and on the same day He gave to the world the first fruits of the Resurrection. Hence this day is the basis of all good: it is the basis of the world's creation, the basis of the resurrection, and the basis of the week", writes an author of the fifth century.[1] In the traditional eucharistic preface, the Church recalls this by reminding us that Sunday is not only the memorial of the new creation, but also that of the first.

(c) *The Lord's Day*

We have seen that the NT calls the day of the Christian cult not only the first day of the week but also the Lord's day (Rev. 1: 10). Is there a slight difference of implication in these two terms? Without wishing to press the suggestion, it appears to us that if the term "first day of the week" connects Sunday with the past phase of saving history, and with its centre in the resurrection of Jesus, and, from that focus, with its initial date in the separation of the light from the darkness, the term "Lord's day" connects it rather with the future. In fact, the day of the Lord—in the OT, the day of Yahwe—has a clear eschatological connotation.[2] Sunday is the anticipation of this final day: it is not only a memorial of the resurrection, but also a foreshadowing of the parousia. This is that eighth day of which pseudo-Barnabas speaks, that day after the end of the world, which played such an important part in the Fathers' theology of Sunday, and which, especially in western traditions, exerted such an influence on millenarianism, and contributed to shape a theology of history. One might wonder whether it is possible to interpret in this way too the miracle of Pentecost, the prelude, according to the prophecy of Joel, of "the day of the Lord . . . the great and notable day" (Acts 2: 20). The day of Pentecost, in fact, springs out of the mystery of the eighth day, since it is the first day to dawn once the seventh day has found its sevenfold plenitude. As day of the Lord, Sunday thus appears to be both a memorial of Pentecost

---

[1] Eusebius of Alexandria, P.E. LXXXVI, 416.
[2] Cf. 1. Cor. 1: 8; 5: 5; 2 Cor. 1: 14; Phil. 1: 6, 10; 2: 16; 1 Thess. 5: 2, 4; 2 Tim. 1: 12.

(that eschatological day when the Spirit, the earnest of the age to come was poured out upon the Church) and an anticipation of the parousia.

(d) *The significance of Sunday*

Accordingly, Sunday has a fourfold significance: it is a memorial of Easter and Pentecost, and—looking back and looking forward—it is a memorial of the first creation and an anticipation of the new, Easter and Pentecost signifying, in time, the restitution of the first creation in all the joy of its goodness and a foretaste of the new creation both in its ambiguity as something still to come and its reality as something already experienced. At the outset we noted that Christian worship is a recapitulation of the saving process. We now see how the day of that worship facilitates and gives meaning to that summing up, and H. B. Porter's assertion is thus verified: "The keeping of the Lord's day is linked with the holding of the principal truths of the Christian faith." We must now amplify this in speaking of the necessity, the ambivalence and the history of Sunday.

G. Delling justifies the necessity of Sunday worship on two grounds. Firstly, the Church is a people and this people must manifest itself by assembling together. A day of worship is thus necessary for essential ecclesiological reasons, and those who doubt this fall into the danger of atomizing the Church and individualizing the Christian life. No Church is possible without the cult, for Jesus promised His presence where two or three are gathered together in His name (Matt. 18: 20). It is with this promise that Christ sends the Church out into the world, and it is with this promise that He gathers the Church to Himself when it comes to rejoice before Him that even the demons have become subject in His name (Luke 10: 17).

But if a day of worship is necessary because the Church is a people, the day cannot be any day: it must be Sunday, a day which is necessary because it recalls Christ's victory over death and the outpouring of the Holy Spirit, because it enables the Church to make a weekly commemoration of those events which brought it into existence; and for Biblical thought, such a commemoration is not an exercise in intellectual recollection, but an authentic participation in the event that is being recalled. On Sundays we participate in the events of Easter and Pentecost.[1]

For this reason the Church could not accept any other day of worship, even if the world were to choose some other day as a day of rest. If for example France decided to fix the weekly day of rest on the day which witnessed the events of 14th July 1789, or if Russia fixed it on the day which saw the outbreak of the revolution of October 1917, or if some African republic fixed it on the day which saw the proclamation of its independence, or if the United Nations were to appoint as a universal day of rest the day of the proclamation of the San Francisco charter, to serve as a weekly celebration of these events; still the Christian Church would not have the right to exchange its own day of worship for these secular days of rest. Were it to do so, it would be denying its Lord just as much as if it had maintained the Jewish sabbath. Were such things to happen, it would have to protest by maintaining its own cultic day even if—as was the case for three centuries—that day were no longer a holiday.

This shows that in Sunday worship the proclamation of Easter is far more important than the element of rest, and to wish to justify the Sunday rest on social grounds rather than by liturgical necessity is wrong and inadmissible. Were it not so, had the day of rest been more important than the commemoration of Christ's victory, then the nascent Church would have adopted the Jewish sabbath as its cultic day. This change of day by the apostolic Church is the strongest proof that the meaning of Sunday is not understood if the social concern for a weekly rest takes priority over the thought of the paschal joy which Sunday evokes.

Sunday is necessary not only because the Church is a

---

[1] We also celebrate creation and have a foretaste of the powers of the world to come. The last element, important as it is in the NT, is not linked to Sunday as much as the memorial of Easter and Pentecost, for Jesus did not promise that He would return on a Sunday. This basic element in the Christian cult could be celebrated on some other day: if it has contributed to the theology of the cult, it has not directly contributed to the theology of Sunday, except perhaps by giving it its name of the Lord's day.

people commanded to assemble for the memorial of that which justifies its existence, but also necessary because the present age still continues, because the day when, indisputably, the name of the Father will be hallowed, His Kingdom come and His will done, has not yet dawned. Sunday is necessary because of the situation of the Church in the world: by Sunday worship it attests the presence, real and actual, of the world to come. It is not merely the communal character of the Church, nor merely the memorial of Easter and Pentecost which require the Sunday cult, it is also the fact that every day is not yet a Sunday, that the "eighth" day has not yet dawned in brilliance and triumph. Thus to deny the necessity of Sunday, the day of worship (and by implication to deny the necessity of worship itself), is to falsify the Church's situation, either by neglecting the presence here and now of the coming Kingdom—which would empty Easter and Pentecost of their reality—or by neglecting the present fact of the historical Fall. This would mean dissociation from the Kingdom of God by denying its real presence among us, or dissociating oneself from the transient world by denying its continued existence. The Church is already assured of the presence of what is future; but it does not yet enjoy its rest otherwise than in the form of a rest from sin, in the form of forgiveness.

This leads us to speak of the ambivalence of Sunday. It is a day like other days, and yet it is different from other days. Like other days it has 24 hours of 60 minutes each, each minute of 60 seconds. Like others it is situated relatively to the seasons and to the moon (as is shown by the dating of Easter). And yet it is different from the others, not so much because it is a day when work ceases or is lessened, as because it is the day of the Church's *rendezvous* with its Lord, the day of Christian communion, and of the new covenant.

To understand this ambivalence, we must recall one of the basic aspects of sacramental doctrine. Just as the eucharistic bread and wine are real bread and wine, they are none the less different from our ordinary bread and wine, for they are restored to their true end, they secretly justify and hallow all the food of this world by the promise of the Messianic banquet which they carry. But he who is without faith sees in them only ordinary bread and wine.

It is the same with Sunday which restores time to its true end, of doxological duration, and secretly it justifies and hallows all the other days. But it does so only for him who has faith. Sunday is thus set in the sacramental context which controls all church life and which, for the believer, makes all allusive to the victory of Easter; under the apparent insignificance of its "matter", it is part of those parables which abandon to their blindness and deafness those to whom the mystery of the Kingdom of God has not been revealed (Mark 4: 11f.). For the world, it is as improbable as the *titulus* of the cross. And it will remain so as long as it will itself last, i.e. as long as the world to come is hidden among us.

Hence we must not be surprised if non-Christians do not quite know what to do with their Sunday, if it is a day which disorganizes and bewilders them; hence too we must ask ourselves whether in our present circumstances it is not a lack of love to continue to impose Sunday on those for whom it can only be an empty day of escape, of solitude and often of suicide. The suspicion that the Church's worship constitutes only a mode of escape is false. On Sunday it is not the Church which is fleeing, but the world. The Church collects and concentrates itself in order to give thanks and to find again the spring of joy, peace and strength for its mission to the world.

The history of Sunday, which is most symptomatic of the degree of the Church's self-understanding throughout the ages, would, if pursued in detail, take us too far. We shall confine ourselves to remarking broadly that there is no time in its life when the Church has not celebrated Sunday, but that it was only from March 7, 321, when the emperor Constantine decreed that the day of the sun should be a holiday, that the history of Sunday became really interesting; for, from that date, a sort of competition was set up between its observance as the Lord's day and its observance as a weekly day of rest. In view of the struggle of the best theologians of antiquity against a sabbatization of Sunday, one must seriously question the assertion of Jean Daniélou who considers as dramatic the fact that, before the fourth century, Christians had to distinguish the day of worship from the day of rest. It was not dramatic at all, and it is rather afterwards that the dramatic element supervened: at the moment when, after the coincidence of the cultic day with the day of rest, Sunday—the day of paschal joy[1]—in spite of the protests of some Fathers, increasingly attracted to itself the idea of a Christian "sabbath", a social day of rest. This tension between the day of worship and the day of rest underwent various vicissitudes and it was in the sphere of Protestantism, especially Anglo-Saxon and Netherland Protestantism in the seventeenth and eighteenth centuries, that Sunday observance most obviously lapsed into a sabbatarian legalism, deeply contrary to the dominical theology of the nascent Church and the early Church. It was from this time, too, that those false problems arose which still worry us today in regard to Sunday observance: that of a sanctification of Sunday by cessation from work rather than by the celebration of worship, and that of a "socialization" of Sunday.

We shall not solve them until two conditions have been fulfilled. The first is that we should learn afresh that it is not the world which, by its protective laws, can sanctify Sunday: it is rather Sunday which, by its worship, sanctifies the world and the days of the world. The second is that we should learn afresh the truth that what sanctifies Sunday is not cessation from work, but worship, and worship in its fulness. Protestant moans on the theme of the desecration of Sunday not only cut no ice, but are stupid, as long as the Church itself profanes Sunday by tearing out its heart: the celebration of the Eucharist. From this point of view it would be interesting to see whether the Protestant sabbatization of Sunday has not been largely due to its being almost constantly deprived of the eucharistic service. Up to about the middle of the eighteenth century, worship was celebrated not only on Sundays but also on weekdays (at least in the

---

[1] Tertullian (*De Corona*, 3) asks that on Sundays people should not kneel, as does also the Council of Nicæa (canon XX). It should be remembered that Sunday is not a fast day, not even during Lent and Advent.

towns). These weekday services, which normally included a sermon, were not very distinct from Sunday services[1]—and that against the advice of Calvin who protested until his death against the abandonment of the weekly Eucharist. In these circumstances was it not necessary to distinguish Sunday from weekday services by other means than that of the eucharistic celebration? And is not this the underlying reason why the distinction was gradually made on a different basis from that of liturgy—namely, on a social basis (especially as the Reformation never wished to put an end to the institution of Sunday)?

This would lead us to think that the best way of exorcising the Reformed sabbatization of Sunday would be to restore to the Sunday service its true dimension by the celebration of the Eucharist. Sunday would not then be necessarily the day of rest (this would depend not on church decisions but on "worldly" decisions); instead, it would be the day of communion. In this case we should also have to oppose the "Catholic" disqualification of Sunday, arising from monastic influence, and which consists in divorcing the Lord's day from parochial communion, not by failing to celebrate the mass on Sundays, but by celebrating it on other days of the week or even on every day of the week. This too falsifies the nature of Sunday. The Protestant falsification of Sunday makes the latter parallel with the days of this world, thus neutralizing the eschatological tension in which the Church lives, and allowing the present aeon to absorb it; while the "Catholic" falsification of Sunday consists in making parallel with it those days which are not yet (if I may say so) days of the Lord, but days of the moon, of Mars, Mercury, Jupiter and Venus; this again neutralizes the eschatological tension of the Church, suggesting that it is already living in the future aeon.

Now it is important that—as the early Church so well understood—this eschatological tension should be respected, by a clear distinction between the eucharistic day and the

---

[1] Although Calvin, for example, tried to distinguish them in that on Sundays he preached from gospel texts, not from OT texts or texts drawn from the epistles (he sometimes made an exception for the Psalms).

non-eucharistic days. This does not mean that the present world is dismissed from view on Sundays—since the sermon reminds us of its continued presence; nor does it mean that the world to come is dismissed from view during the week, since we are reminded of it by private devotions and by the offices. But what qualifies Sunday as Sunday, what gives it colour, is not rest from work, nor even the assembling of the people of God, but the assembling of the people of God for eucharistic communion. This is what makes Sunday Sunday, and if it is forgotten the nature of Sunday is lost. This is the lesson which we must basically draw from the history of Sunday observance.

2. The liturgical year

If Sunday is the day of worship *par excellence*, the Church has none the less, from the most ancient times, conferred on certain Sundays, as on the week that they open, a distinctive character and a special memorial intention. This is what is called the liturgical year, and although it is not entirely without relation to the unfolding of the seasons of the solar year, it shows nevertheless that the Church is something far more than an institution which blesses the rhythms of this world; that, on the contrary, it calls in question this world and its rhythms.

(a) Let us begin by a few brief remarks on the history of this liturgical year. Two questions arise straight away. When did Christians begin to celebrate not only Sunday in general, but some particular Sunday or some special feast? What was the Sunday, or the feast, which formed the point of departure for the ecclesiastical year?

It is extremely difficult to answer the first question, and scholars are far from being in agreement. Is it possible that St. John, in reporting that "the passover of the Jews was near" (2: 13; 11: 55), implies secretly that at the time of his writing there was a Christian passover which fell on another day? We may hesitate to admit this, although the Christians of Asia Minor who in the second century entered into conflict with the Church of Rome about the date of Easter referred expressly to the teaching of John. When St. Paul tells the

Corinthians that he wishes to remain at Ephesus until Pentecost (1 Cor. 16: 8), is he presupposing that they have an instinctive knowledge of the Jewish calendar or is he alluding to a celebration of the Christian Pentecost? There is general agreement that in this context it can be a question only of the Jewish Pentecost. But why then, according to the statement in Acts, does he wish to make haste to arrive at Jerusalem (where he is going essentially to meet the Church) in time for Pentecost (20: 16)? It is very difficult to answer these questions with any degree of certainty, because we have to wait until the second century to find indubitable attestations of annual Christian feasts. It is usually thought that the nascent Church observed only the weekly memorial, and that not until the expectation of an imminent parousia grew dim did it begin to calculate in years. K. Holl affirms: "There is a general consensus of opinion that the major feasts of the Christians were not annual feasts, but weekly ones. The little flock, which impatiently awaited the parousia of the Lord, did not calculate in years."

I must frankly confess that I have never yet found an argument which really convinces me, on historical and psychological grounds, that the apostolic Church lived in the expectation of an imminent parousia: the way in which it organized itself, the surprising patience with which St. Paul pursued his missionary enterprise (cf. Gal. 1: 17f.; 2: 1; Acts 27: 9ff.), and assured a succession to himself (cf. Phil. 2: 21ff.; the pastoral letters), the catechesis which the Church put in hand, and so many other things too, make me feel that the apostles did not teach that Christ would shortly return. This is witnessed by a certain consolidation of the Church (generally imputed to a chilling of Christian hopes) which can equally well mark the progressive steps taken to obey the command to endure to the end. Hence I should be inclined to believe that neither the Jerusalem Church nor the other apostolic Churches allowed the Passover and the Pentecost of the Jews to go by without specially celebrating their own Easter and Pentecost. But it must be admitted that not before the debates of the middle of the second century, about the tradition of dating Easter, do we have sure attestation of the liturgical year.

But if it is difficult to answer our first question and to know from what period exactly we can date Christian festivals which are annual and not weekly, it is, on the other hand, easy to answer the second: it was the feast of Easter which gave a starting point to the formation of the liturgical year. By the feast of Easter the year, as it were, received its Sunday. More time would be needed to enter into the detail of its history, but the liturgical year, contrary to what might be thought, did not weaken its teaching about Sunday, it enabled the Church rather to become ever more deeply conscious of its mystery.[1] The annual paschal celebration was very early set within the framework of six weeks of preparation (Lent, which reached its full development through the organization of the prebaptismal catechumenate) and by seven weeks of exultation ending in Pentecost, the beginning of an eighth week; although it took long to define clearly, in this "great week", the day of the Ascension and that of Pentecost. At the beginning, the Church celebrated, in fact, for a week of weeks, the victory of Christ, His exaltation, and the irruption of the world to come through the outpouring of the Spirit.[2]

To understand the paschal theology of the ancient Church, I think it is very important to stress to what an extent the weekly rhythm influenced the shaping of liturgical tradition; Easter appears flanked by a week of weeks (without Sunday!), a time of fasting and preparation, and by a week of weeks (with Sunday), a time of joy and exultation. It was only much later that the Church began to celebrate the birth of Christ. In fact, the Nativity was not celebrated before the second half of the fourth century, and one has the faint impression that the Church began to celebrate it with a somewhat divided mind. Divided, because it was necessary to choose a date with very little to go on (the choice was influenced by the solar rhythm since, after hesitating about January 6, it was finally decided to adopt a date near to the winter solstice, the time when the unconquered sun started

---

[1] The Christmas cycle is perhaps an exception. See below.
[2] Let us recall the fact that the Council of Nicæa fixed the method of calculating Easter in a Christian way: Easter falls on the first Sunday following the full moon after the spring equinox.

again on its course of life and light). Divided, because there was no weekly recurrence of Christmas, unlike Easter which was commemorated every week despite the great annual Sunday in spring (it is curious to note that the Church did not venture to fix the feast of the Nativity on a Sunday, e.g. the first Sunday after the winter solstice, but chose a fixed date without reference to the day of the cult). Divided, because it was not traditional to celebrate dates of birth (in the early Church birthdays were not those of the first birth, but those of birth to glorification, i.e. dates of martyrdom; and, in addition, scripture did not seem to favour birthday celebrations since it reports only those of Pharaoh and Herod!).

However this may be, it is useful to remember that the Church waited nearly four centuries before celebrating Christmas on a special day, the more so as the celebration of Christmas is with us the pre-eminent Christian feast. Just as Easter had its liturgical casket in the preparatory Lent and the "great week", so Christmas became exalted by a period of preparation (the four weeks of Advent) and a period of rejoicing (the days between Christmas and the Epiphany). It was around these two great cycles—that of Easter, chronologically and theologically having priority, and that of Christmas—that the liturgical year was gradually crystallized. It was subject to changing and sometimes contradictory fortunes, and unanimity with regard to it has never been reached in the Church.[1]

It should be added that from the second century at least (here too the *terminus a quo* is difficult to decide) the Church celebrated not only Sunday but marked out, by the discipline of fasting, Wednesday (the day of the betrayal of Jesus) and Friday (the day of His death), thus commemorating each week the whole of the mystery of salvation. Towards the close of the same century, in parallelism to the annual feast of Easter, it began to give an annual corresponding analogy to these Wednesdays and Fridays, not by instituting Good Friday, which is a much later development, but by com-

[1] Thus, in the West, Trinity Sunday is the Sunday after Pentecost, whereas in the East it coincides with Pentecost, the Sunday after the latter being the feast of All Saints.

memorating certain martyrs in whom Christ continued to suffer, to be betrayed and put to death.

By the close of the Middle Ages, the apparatus of the liturgical year had become so heavy, and so distracting to genuine faith, that the Reformers tried to lighten it considerably. Here again we cannot go into details, but will simply note that the pattern varied from one country to another, from one Church to another: here more conservative, there more radical. Luther, for example—although he wanted to see the feasts attached to the nearest Sunday—maintained all those which could be directly connected with the process of salvation as summed up by the Apostles' Creed. This scheme included not only Christmas, Easter, the Ascension, Pentecost, but also the Annunciation, Candlemas, the Circumcision of Christ, and the Epiphany. He was tolerant also about other feasts: only in 1523 did he suppress Corpus Christi (which had been instituted in 1264), while the same year he asked his followers not to be too hasty in suppressing the feast of the Nativity of the Blessed Virgin on September 8 and of her Assumption on August 15; while in some Lutheran Churches these feasts were continued to an even later date, as were also feasts of the Apostles, of St. Michael and All Angels, and of certain saints. As for the Prayer Book, the *proprium* provides for the celebration of the traditional cycles of Christmas and Easter, the commemoration of the Apostles (including the conversion of St. Paul), of the Evangelists, of St. John Baptist, of St. Michael and All Angels, and of All Saints.

Here, too, it was the Reformed Church which proceeded in the most violent manner. The ordinances of the Palatinate retain only the commemoration of Christmas, New Year's Day,[1] Easter, the Ascension and Pentecost, while those of Julich and Berg, of 1671, mention Christmas, the Circumcision (rather than the New Year), Good Friday (which is new), Easter, the Ascension, and Pentecost. This latter list corresponds to that drawn up by the Later Helvetic Confession which expressly rejects the commemoration of saints, adding: "we admit that it will not be without profit if in a suitable

---

[1] Luther protested against a New Year celebration which was not a commemoration of the circumcision of the Lord.

time and place the people are exhorted, in public sermons, to remember the saints and if the example of the latter is set before them for imitation". It should however be noted that, in some places, attempts were made to eliminate entirely the ecclesiastical calendar, as in Scotland, or to eliminate the feast of Christmas, as at Neuchâtel. Nevertheless, people refused to accept such violent changes, and even if the reasons for their resistance were not perhaps of the highest order, theologically, we must rejoice in this opposition, for the liturgical year effectively prevents a docetization of the Gospel.

(b) In fact we must ask ourselves whether the celebration of the liturgical year is legitimate. At first sight, the NT would seem to cast doubt on this legitimacy: St. John shows Jesus as regularly going up to Jerusalem for the feasts in order to signify that He is their fulfilment and that His coming means that their end is near; and St. Paul, seeing the Galatians observe days, months, seasons and years, fears that he has worked in vain among them (Gal. 4: 10), because, as he says elsewhere, feasts, new moons and sabbaths are only a shadow of the things to come, their substance is in Christ (Col. 2: 16). Often people have inferred from this that the keeping of the liturgical year is wrong. But this is a false deduction: what the apostle is combating is an anachronistic, that is, Jewish, way of observing the liturgical year. He protests against the failure to understand that this anachronistic celebration compromises the Christian faith. I would go so far as to say that the result of this polemic (explicit with Paul, implicit with John) is to suggest that the way of keeping the liturgical year is a test of the faith one confesses, and is clear evidence of what one believes.

The legitimacy of keeping the liturgical year is subject to one absolute condition: the cycle of the year should be a celebration of Christ.

A. D. Müller writes: "The liturgical year cannot be anything but an amplification of the revelation which became an event in Christ, i.e. it must be Christ-centred. But to be so it must take into account the Christology of the letters to the Colossians and Ephesians, which intimate

that Christ is not only the Jesus of history, but also the
Lord of history and the incarnation of all the creative powers
of the cosmos . . . Thus the liturgical year serves to draw
out and make effective, on the vast plane of historic and
natural life, the total content of the Christian revelation. . . ."
In other words, it implies that the liturgical year would
include not only Christian feasts but also such things as
youth, maternity, sickness, the fatherland, harvest, industry
the new year, etc. This seems to me quite wrong and to be
going in the direction of the "new moons" which St. Paul
opposes (Col. 2 : 16). Not that Christ did not become the
Lord of the cosmos; not that the cosmos ought not to be
brought into the Church's worship, so as to regain its true
orientation. But it is wrong for two reasons: because Christian
worship celebrates the process of the world's salvation, and
hence the Jesus of history (who alone enables us to understand the cosmic Christ); and because the cosmos has no
need to be celebrated; on the contrary, it is summoned to
enter into the celebration which praises and confesses Jesus
of Nazareth, the Christ of God. This linking of the cosmos
to the liturgy of the Church is sufficient because church
worship takes place in time and needs bread, wine, sound,
and light to be its true self. Moreover the cosmos and its
powers are implied in the celebration of the Ascension.

The criterion according to which the liturgical year is
legitimate only in so far as it contributes to the celebration
of Christ's saving work permits us, then, to choose and
classify the Christian feasts. It is right to celebrate the birth
of Jesus, His passion, His resurrection, His ascension, and
His sending of the Holy Spirit, with all that immediately
encircles these feasts: the annunciation, the circumcision,
the epiphany and Palm Sunday. It is right too that the
Church should prepare itself for these feasts and rejoice in
them, that the two peaks of the Christian year—Easter and
Christmas—should be preceded and followed by weeks which
enable Christians to experience their meaning fully. But such
a criterion excludes certain festivals which have wrongly
been introduced into the Christian year, and have been
created by our pride or our boredom. We should not ask
ourselves such unchristian questions as "What shall we do

on Sunday?"—as if the keeping of a weekly Easter commemoration were becoming tiring—and then go on to invent a Mothering Sunday, a Sunday for the sick,[1] a Sunday for harvest, a Sunday for the fatherland, and so on. We ought really to have courage to put an end to this abuse, this blackmail, this menace. If the world is bored on Sundays, it is not the business of the Church to sanctify this boredom by prostituting Sunday!

A further question which arises is: does this Christological reduction of the liturgical year cut out any commemoration of the events in the saving process subsequent to Pentecost, whether it be the conversion of St. Paul, the martyrdom of St. Stephen, the death in the faith of all the saints, or the posting of the 95 theses on the church door at Wittemberg (for Reformation Sunday would become very dangerous if it were made parallel with Pentecost rather than being the commemoration of a saint)? To answer this question we must remember that we can never have Jesus apart from His Church, but that His Church does not replace Him. Hence it seems to me that in principle it is not on Sundays but during the week that we should commemorate (in private devotion and the daily offices) apostles, saints, martyrs, prophets also,[2] reformers, angels and archangels (St. Michael) and that, on Sundays, their mention in the memento and the eucharistic preface, where in fact they find their appropriate place, ought to suffice. In addition, we should recall in the sermon the example of the saint whose commemoration will take place in the following week, since "it is not without profit if in a suitable time and place the people are exhorted to remember the saints . . .".[3] It is clear that such commemoration during the week[4] would not bring about public holidays. The abuses of the Middle Ages in this respect are now sufficiently forgotten for there to be no need for us to ask, with Luther, that the commemoration of the great

[1] The sick are found in all the gospel healing stories.
[2] The Feast of St. John the Baptist alone is not enough to keep alive the awareness that the OT also forms part of the history of salvation.
[3] The Later Helvetic Confession.
[4] Reduced to the list in the Prayer Book: but why not add the commemoration of the Reformation, October 31?

witnesses to Christ should be transferred to the nearest Sunday.

We must now consider whether the keeping of the Christian year is useful. In so far as it is understood that this is a matter of church discipline and not of eternal salvation, its usefulness is evident for it provides, in a way, year after year, a *repetitorium* of the process of salvation: it gives the authorities of the Church the assurance that in all the parishes, proclamation is being made of what is the basis of salvation and justifies the existence of the Church, it obliges the pastors to renew the faith and the life of their flocks from gospel sources; it gives the faithful the opportunity to experience the fulness of the mystery of salvation; and the world is repeatedly confronted by the great appeals of the love of God.

However, if these considerations show its usefulness, it does not follow that the observance of the liturgical year should monopolize the fifty-two weeks of the year so that each Sunday draws from it its specific content. Hence we must say that the Reformed Church, with its keen re-action against these observances, has rendered a great service to the Church by refusing to follow the year except for the major feasts, and thus refusing to align itself with the Lutheran and Anglican churches in this respect. Not that its protest has not caused injuries as grave as those which it desired to heal, since one result has been the incoherence and improvization in the choice of texts for sermons. None the less, the protest has shown that the fifth Sunday after Epiphany, or the seventeenth Sunday after Trinity, are not entitled to a respect corresponding to the respect we owe to Easter or Whitsuntide. The keeping of the Christian year must not endanger the possibility of the *lectio continua*, which was familiar to the ancient Church and was restored by the Reformed Church. Hence, it seems to me that it would be wise if its observance were reduced to the cycle of Easter (from Septuagesima or Ash Wednesday to Pentecost) and that of Christmas (from the first Sunday in Advent to Epiphany) so as to allow in the intervals and with renewed authorization year by year, the abandonment of the *lectio selecta* in favour of the *lectio continua*.[1]

[1] Gospel texts between Epiphany and Lent, epistles between

235

One final remark: *the* Sunday of the year is Easter. Easter is the origin, the heart and the justification of the liturgical year. Now, Easter is a festival the date of which fluctuates from year to year during March and April, since, following the decision of the Council of Nicæa, it must fall on the first Sunday following the full moon after the spring equinox. It is often asked whether it would not be well to "immobilize" Easter by appointing for it a fixed Sunday. And it is not only those who depend on the spring tourist trade, or the education authorities concerned about Easter holidays, who ask this question. Luther asked it in "Of Councils and Churches" of 1539, and today Richard Paquier asks it, proposing that Easter should be fixed on "the first or the second Sunday in April, which would obviate many useless complications in the ecclesiastical calendar".[1]

Such a measure would seem to me wrong for three reasons: firstly, the Church should not make too many sacrifices to the spirit of rationalization which, by simplifying the life of the world, tends to make it boring; secondly, because the mobility of Easter introduces into the ecclesiastical calendar (the varying number of Sundays after Epiphany and Pentecost) a certain mobility which removes the danger of rigidity; and lastly and principally, because it is owing to the mobility of Easter that the cosmos can share in the celebration of the world's salvation, since the sun and the moon have their part to play in "marking seasons and days and years" (Gen. 1:14) and thus contribute to the praise of the Lord. The mobility of Easter, in fact, gives life to the Christian year and protects it from a certain docetism: for it does not commemorate a non-temporal idea but an event which took its place in the rhythm of the created world.

Pentecost and the end of August, OT texts from September to Advent. Such texts to be accompanied by two in counterpoint, e.g. OT and epistle when the gospel text was central and the theme of the sermon.

[1] Luther's motives were less pragmatic: he thought that to calculate the date of Easter by reference to Israelite feasts was to Judaize. One knows then the Second Vatican Council and also the Frankfurt Assembly of the Presbyterian World Alliance (1964) agreed in principle with the idea of a fixed Easter day. Alas!

3. The sanctification of time

What we have been saying about Sunday and the ecclesiastical year introduces us into a sphere which goes far beyond the scope of a liturgical treatise: that of the sanctification of time. Hence we shall take only a rapid glance at this.

(a) How shall we define the sanctification of time? To sanctify time means that we recognize as its point of departure and its culmination the mystery of the death and resurrection of Christ, and that, whether it be chronologically near to or distant from this event, we refer it to this central and determinative moment. The thirty hours or so which separate the afternoon of Good Friday from the morning of Easter Day are the mysterious pole, hidden and yet real, of the whole time span, the whole of human history. Central not only to sacred history, which runs from the election of Abraham to the exaltation of the Church—but also to profane history and further, to that which lies behind history and can only be dimly surmised: the creation and the end of the world. Hence all history, if it is to yield its secret, the history of Israel and the history of the Church, the history of nations, pre-history and eschatology—must be interpreted Christologically. The time given to worship contributes to this sanctification of time, firstly, because the cult, being celebrated in time, claims it for the service of Christ, exalts Christ as Lord of time; secondly, because the cult, being celebrated in time, consecrates it and submits it to the Lordship of Christ. Since the cult recapitulates the saving process, whatever the moment of its celebration, it connects that moment with the unique and central event which justifies the whole time process.

(b) But it is not only the moment in which the cult is celebrated that is consecrated to, and claimed for, Christ and hence justified by its reference to the heart of time: the time span of which the cult is the first fruits is likewise so claimed and consecrated and justified (according to the Biblical principle of *pars pro toto*). I mean that the whole week is consecrated by the dominical cult, as the whole year is sanctified by the celebration of Easter, as the whole day is sanctified by those moments of daily prayer which the Didache (8: 3) recommends to Christians and which, in monastic tradition, will be developed into the "hours".

This principle of the sanctification of the whole by this claiming, consecration and sanctification of the past is a principle which lies at the root of the Biblical doctrine of election and which gives to the latter its missionary bearing, and concerns us here for two reasons.

It shows that one Sunday suffices for the week, and that if Sunday is truly celebrated as such, Monday, Tuesday, Wednesday, etc., need not try to ape Sunday, for the latter has sanctified them and so permits them to be what they are, i.e. other than Sunday. What makes Sunday Sunday is the celebration of the Eucharist. If it is celebrated on Sunday, there is therefore no need to celebrate it again on Wednesday or Friday. The dominical Eucharist suffices for the whole week. That it should have its repercussions, that its meaning should be unfolded in the daily offices, whether private or family or congregational: that is good. We cast doubt on the sanctifying power of Sunday when we try to repeat its note by celebrating the Eucharist on weekdays. We are not yet in the Kingdom, and we must allow the week time to be different from Sunday. Thus if the Lord's Supper is an integral part of Sunday, then the dominical celebration is sufficient for the life of the Church and we falsify the nature of Sunday by celebrating the Eucharist on weekdays too.

But what lends to Sunday its special character is not only that the Eucharist is celebrated on that day (the Eucharist understood as the culminating point of the service which we have already described). It is the further fact that it is celebrated in the midst of God's people who are assembled to meet their Lord, to receive Him and to give themselves to Him. This leads us to postulate a sanctification of time not only through the dominical communion but also through the uniqueness of this communion. The doctrine of the Church was injured and impaired when, doubtless for pastoral reasons, Sunday Eucharists began to be multiplied or when it began to be claimed (not before 1517!) that one could fulfil one's Sunday obligations by attendance elsewhere than in one's parish church. If the eucharistic celebration ought to be confined to Sunday, there should also be only one celebration in each parish (as the ancient Church wished)— a celebration which should bring together all the church people of the parish. To multiply the celebrations of the Eucharist, or to consider as other than exceptional that people should make their communion elsewhere than in their parish church, is to jeopardize the essentially communal character of the Church and to suggest that salvation individualizes the faithful, whereas in fact it personalizes them. The Reformed custom of having only one full parochial service per Sunday (with the exception of occasional offices, although these ought rather to be said during the week) is therefore a good Christian habit, which we should reinforce rather than weaken by indulging the indolence of the parishioners or humouring their fancies for changing. The best way of reinforcing it will be to reintroduce the regular weekly celebration of the Holy Communion.

CHAPTER NINE

THE PLACE OF WORSHIP

WE NOW come to an exciting and complicated chapter,
because it is not enough to give a few practical directives for
the furnishing of places of worship: it is a question of
considering the theological legitimacy of such places. I think
the essence of what is to be said can be grouped under three
heads: firstly, we will speak of the presence of Christ and the
signs of that presence: secondly, we shall see that the
function of places of worship is to welcome and present
harmoniously these signs of the presence of Christ: lastly,
we shall make a brief remark on the place of worship as a
basis for the sanctification of space.

1. The signs of Christ's presence

(a) Under the New Covenant, the Lord did not appoint
one place for the manifestation of His presence, in the same
way as He appointed a day, whether explicitly or not, for
the commemoration of the saving event. Even under the
Old Covenant the matter is not as clear as it may seem so
long as we are content to think simply of the Temple at
Jerusalem and all that it signified. The people of Israel were
not without their God when—before Solomon and during
the exile—they were without a temple, and in the great
prayer which Solomon addressed to the Lord at the dedication of the Temple, it is made clear that the Lord dwells in
heaven and cannot be imprisoned in the place where His
name is invoked (1 Kings 8: 27, 30, 31, 34, 36, 43, 45, 49).
There are of course privileged spots which become centres of
worship: those where a divine manifestation has occurred
(Shechem, Bethel, Mamre, etc.) or places marked by divine
choice (such as Jerusalem). But God is not held to such

240

spots: He accompanies His people when they are nomadic (the theology underlying the Ark of the Covenant); He can leave the temple and cause it to be destroyed when His people deceive Him, and He does not in consequence lose His divinity. He can then rejoin His scattered people. The theology of the OT shows that the special place in which God is present is the hearts of the people who invoke Him. It is with His people that He dwells, wherever that people is to be found. And if it is true that there are sacred spots, this is not to suggest that God is exclusively localized there, but to show that God intervenes in the world and claims the whole earth as His own; it is to show also that God calls His people to meet Him *on this earth*.

(b) The New Covenant begins with a Christological concentration and reduction of the presence of God. In Jesus of Nazareth, "the whole fulness of deity dwells bodily" (Col. 2: 9). In Him the eternal Word of God has "dwelt among us" (ESKENOSEN EN HEMIN: John 1: 14). Jesus is fully and totally the temple of God and the locus of the divine presence (John 2: 19ff.) To be with God, we must then be in Christ, we must enter into His body by baptism, so that the body of Christ—a new designation of the people of God—the Church becomes, from Pentecost onwards, the Temple (cf. 1 Cor: 3: 16ff.; Eph. 2: 20–22; 1 Pet. 2: 4–10). Not only the Church in its communal character but each member of the Church, being a bearer of Christ and a bearer of the Spirit, is a temple, consecrated to make known, to reflect and to praise his Lord (1 Cor. 6: 19ff.). Thus the true temple of God is the Body of Christ, the physical body of Jesus, His flesh, that which the apostles saw and touched with their hands. It is on this basic truth, as on a cornerstone, that the whole teaching of Peter and Paul about the Church as the Body of Christ and the Temple of God rests. The place of worship, therefore, is essentially the place where Christ is found. Now Christ is found where two or three are gathered in His name (Matt. 18: 20). Hence the place of Christian worship is the assembled Church. It is not primarily a building but an assembly, and if, as we shall see, buildings made with human hands (cf. Mark 14: 58; Acts 7: 48; 17: 24; Heb. 9: 11; 24) can become places of worship, it is simply because they are intended to house the assembled liturgical people. But it is the people who are the temple.

Before continuing, it may be worth while to make two marginal observations: (i) We must remember, in the first place, that according to the unanimous teaching of the NT, the worshipping Church is always localized, not at first in a building, but in a town: there are the elect at Rome (Rom. 1: 7), there is the Church of God such as it is at Corinth (1 Cor. 1: 2). Thus it is the towns which become, as localities, places of worship, i.e. the place where Christ's presence is experienced. This is important for the understanding of the character of the local Christian assembly which claims and consecrates space. (ii) We must realize further that for the NT the legitimacy of these assemblies is not linked to their dependence on some other particular assembly. They do not stand in any dependent relation to some other place of worship, as the Jewish synagogues depended on the Temple at Jerusalem. They are not synagogues but churches, and what makes them places of worship is not their organization or the unified structure that they may possess, but the presence of Christ in their midst. What qualifies them as authentic places of worship is the signs they show of the presence of Christ.[1]

(c) The Christian place of worship is the assembly in which Jesus Christ, God's temple, is present, in the power of the Spirit. We must now consider at greater length the signs of the presence of Christ which make of a liturgical assembly a true place of worship.

When He left His disciples to be received into glory, Jesus said: "I am with you always, even unto the end of the world" (Matt. 28: 20). How could He, the full epiphany of God, remain present among them? The answer is that He remains present among His own by the sending of the Holy Spirit, who breathes life into those signs which Jesus Christ

[1] In an ecclesiological context we should have to examine the (provisional) role played in the early Church by the liturgical assembly of Jerusalem and the theological relation and difference between a church and a parish.

instituted or appointed as the attestation of His saving presence. Normally the Church is localized where those means of grace are in operation which link us with the saving process and assure its continuance. Let us weigh the terms of this preliminary assertion one by one.

We must begin by enumerating the normal means of grace appointed or instituted by Jesus Christ. There are four: (i) The Word, because he who abides in the Word abides in Christ and Christ in him (John 5: 38; 8: 31; 15: 7; 1 John 2: 14; 2 John 2. (ii) The bread and the wine of the Eucharist, since they are the body and the blood of Christ (Mark 14: 22, 24 par.; 1 Cor. 11: 24f., cf. John 6: 51–58). (iii) The ministers of Christ, since he who hears them hears Christ Himself (Luke 10: 16; Gal. 4: 14; 1 Thess. 4: 8; 2 Cor. 5: 20). (iv) One's neighbour, since he who does good to one of these little ones is serving Christ Himself (Matt. 10: 42; 25: 35–40, 42–45).

Hence, there is a place of worship wherever the Word of Christ is proclaimed, the Lord's Supper celebrated, the minister recognized, one's neighbour helped; or, rather, there is a place of worship where through these means Christians abide in Christ. Normally a church is a church when these four signs are found in conjunction. To be sure, each time that the Word of God is proclaimed, whether in a private house, in the open air or in some place of assembly, its intention is to bring about a manifestation of the Lord, and consequently to bring some part of this world under the dominion of the Lord, to make of it a holy place. Similarly, every time the Lord's Supper is celebrated, even privately in the bedroom of a sick person, its very celebration hallows the place. Similarly, also, a tribunal before which a minister of the Gospel appears to bear witness becomes by that very fact a sphere of Christ's epiphany, hence a place of worship; as does also a hospital where, in the person of the sick, Christ is served; or a shelter for the night where a poor man is welcomed. These places are transfigured by the presence of Christ. But if all this is true and must not be forgotten, the place of worship in the fullest sense is the assembly of the Church gathered together to experience the fourfold sign of Christ's presence.

But the efficacy of the means appointed by Christ is not under the control of the Church. There is not an automatic connexion between the means of grace and the real presence of the Lord, for Jesus Christ did not simply institute such means as an assurance of His presence, He also promised to send the Holy Spirit. The means are efficacious only by virtue of the agency of the Spirit. They are the normal instruments for the impact of the Spirit, but they are not traps which close upon Him. For the Spirit is God, and God is sovereign. He is not at the beck and call of the Church. The latter can only pray that the Lord will come into her midst— the Maranatha—she can but implore the Holy Spirit to come to animate the Bible; the bread and wine; men, so that they may be born again to their true ministry as was born again, under the force of the Spirit, the great host of Ezekiel's vision (Ezek. 37: 1ff.). Once again, we see how true it is that there simply cannot be a Christian cult without the epiklesis.

But if the Spirit who gives life to the means of grace is sovereign, He is also faithful. When the Church becomes a place of worship by its assembly in the name of Jesus; when, in its midst, the Bible is opened, the bread and the wine distributed, the faithful blessed or absolved; when the sick and poor are relieved and brought before God in intercession —the Church need not ask itself if it is heard or not: it can know that God wishes to hear and answer its prayers, that He is not a sadistic and capricious tyrant who promises His presence but does not grant it—God is not a Godot! And if unhappily the Spirit does not answer the Church's appeal, in the fulness of His promised power, or if He answers by silence, it is not because He is thinking of something else, that He holds aloof, or is on a journey or is sleeping (cf. 1 Kings 18: 27); it is that the failure springs from the Church itself: lack of faith (Mark 6: 5), lack of obedience (1 Cor. 11: 30ff.), lack of purity (cf. Heb. 12: 14ff.; Josh. 7), which compromise the efficacy of the cult, and weary and vex the Lord.

Before continuing, it is important at this point to add two remarks, the first of which concerns the bread and the wine of the Lord's Supper.[1]

[1] If we were dealing with the whole of liturgy we should have to speak also of the water of baptism, and of the anointing oil which

(i) As regards the bread, we have two traditions: the Western Roman tradition, to which the Anglican Church and many Lutheran churches have usually remained faithful, uses unleavened bread in the form of hosts or wafers; and the Eastern tradition which firmly holds to the use of leavened bread, that is, ordinary bread. In the sixteenth century the Reformed Church hesitated: on the one hand, the *panis cibarius*, ordinary bread was preferred, but on the other hand the Bernese Church, for example, imposed the use of hosts in 1538, a measure which was not revoked for the Churches in obedience to it until 1605/6, but which has been maintained up to the present time by certain Churches of German Switzerland. Normally however the Reformed Churches have fallen in with the Eastern tradition by using ordinary bread. They have no reason to change.[1] Of course the use of unleavened bread does not invalidate a celebration. But the arguments that might be advanced to justify unleavened bread as opposed to ordinary bread are not convincing. Certainly unleavened bread facilitates reservation and avoids crumbling; but these concerns are less important than the usefulness of showing that the Supper is a meal, where bread is broken and shared among the communicants. They are also less important than the usefulness of bringing out the symbolic bearing of the rite: to take a host or a wafer, that is, something other than what is normally understood by bread, while saying that the Lord took "bread", is bewildering and—here is the most important argument—could easily lead to the misunderstanding that salvation distorts, changes, transubstantiates what it takes into its service; whereas in fact it makes choice of and transfigures precisely what the world gives us.[2] Hence, it is well to keep to the Reformed and Eastern tradition of using leavened bread.

As regards the wine, the Reformers, Luther, Calvin and

---

although it plays a part in the NT is usually completely neglected by Protestantism.

[1] Whether Jesus used unleavened bread is difficult to decide. If the institution took place at a Kiddush meal, He must have used leavened bread, but if it was a passover meal, the bread was unleavened.

[2] It is a process of emasculation: unleavened bread, non-alcoholic wine, celibates for the ministry.

their associates deviated from what had been the usual custom of the Church by ceasing to use wine mixed with water. The custom of mixing water with wine, explicitly attested for the first time by Justin Martyr and which perhaps goes back to Jesus Himself, has had in tradition different explanations: St. Cyprian saw in it a symbol of the mystical union between Christ and His Church; Ambrose saw it in an allusion to the wound in the side of Christ from which blood and water flowed; the Orthodox think it symbolizes either the two natures of Christ or the presence of the Spirit (the water used being hot). To try at this stage to return to this ancient and widespread tradition does not seem to me essential, seeing that it is not from monophysitism (like the Armenians) that we do not mix water with wine. It would also create the impression that these points are essential, whereas they are only marginal. We shall use pure wine then. But what sort of wine? Red wine or white wine? Non-alchoholic or fermented? Red wine seems preferable, although this does not condemn the use of white wine. It is preferable because it is most likely that the Jews used red wine for the Passover and especially because of its greater symbolic power as a sacrament of the blood of Christ. As a rule it is desirable that the symbolism of sacramental rites should be as exact as possible and this is certainly much more the case if we use red wine.[1]

On the other hand, fermented wine seems to me almost essential. First, because it may be taken for granted that Jesus used real wine and that such wine was used in the apostolic Church (as is clear from the fact that at Corinth it was drunk until the point of intoxication was reached). (1 Cor. 11:21). Secondly, because here again, as for the bread, it is important that the sacramental species should be chosen from among the things of this world, that divine grace should not give us the impression that it can reach only things that are emasculated, impoverished, deprived of their true nature. Certainly the use of non-alcoholic wine is not more improper than the use of unleavened bread; but I think that we wrong God to put at His disposal things we do not like, and which

[1] In the Roman Church white wine is normally used, whilst in the Orthodox Church, red wine is preferred.

do not give us the opportunity of tasting "that the Lord is *good*" (Ps. 34: 8; 1 Pet. 2: 3). And if indeed the argument which asserts that the use of fermented wine is to be avoided so as not to expose ex-alcoholics to temptation, did not spring from an almost blasphemous theological stupidity and a sentimental philanthropy, I should say let them in that case weaken wine with water, so as thus to follow the general tradition of the Church—which can very well take yet another interpretation! In any event we shall do well not to follow the fantastic ordinance of Julich and Berg of 1671: "Those who by nature find wine so nauseous that they cannot tolerate either its smell or taste, shall receive from the hands of the minister, along with the bread, some drink to which they are accustomed."[1] Tea, perhaps?[2]

Thus for the sacramental elements we should use what corresponds best to the institution of the Lord's Supper, following the sound advice of the Reformed Synod of Herborn (1586): *Ecclesia utatur iis ceremoniis tum quas praescripsit institutio Domini sine superstitione et quae ad aedificationem ecclesiae faciunt.*[3] In detail this implies that we shall use bread and wine (and if possible real bread and real wine) and not some other food or some other drink. Obviously one might ask whether, in countries where bread and wine are unknown, it would not be legitimate to find in the native foods and drink some substitute for the eucharistic bread and wine, and so use food and drink *qui panis et vini vicem sustinet et corpori roborando ac cordi exhilarando idoneus est.*[4] Must we deprive of the Lord's Supper those who have not bread and wine but only manioc and beer, fruit pulp and milk? I think that in principle it would be better to cultivate the growing of corn and the vine in such countries rather than adopt other elements as eucharistic species, or to import them (as wine for the Eucharist is imported into Scandinavia and England).

This also means that the whole Church will be allowed to

---

[1] Art. 126, cf. W. Niesel, *op. cit.*, p. 322.
[2] In the ancient Church some sects, such as the Encratites, the Ebionites and the Aquarians, used water instead of wine, against which the Church rightly protested.
[3] W. Niesel, *op. cit.*, p. 296.
[4] As is proposed by Hermannus Witsius.

communicate in two kinds. I do not suggest that communion in one kind only is therefore invalid. We cannot in fact preclude the possibility that the ancient Church was familiar with a type of communion which included only the breaking of bread. But the basic point is that all the communicants should take part in the whole communion and that there should not be introduced a distinction between the clergy and the laity which from every point of view is—as they would have said in the sixteenth century—superstitious.

Thus the conformity of the celebration to the dominical institution presupposes both that bread and wine will be used, and that all the communicants will communicate in the bread and the wine.

(ii) The second remark concerns the respect which the Church owes to what Christ has chosen as attestation of His presence. Here we have a subject as vast as it is delicate, and one which has immense ramifications. To take the problem at its most delicate point: what is to be done with the eucharistic species once the communion is ended?

The practice of the ancient Church, maintained in the Orthodox Church and revived by the Reformation, reflects the principle—expressed in extremely brutal form—that *extra usum a Christo institutum nihil habet rationem sacramenti*. This does not mean that there has not been a real consecration of the species according to the fine definition of Bullinger who says that to consecrate *est Deo et sacris usibus dedicare, hoc est a communi usu separare et juxta ordinationem Dei singulari et sacro usui destinare et addicere*. But it does mean that once the communion is finished, the bread and the wine cease to be the signs of the real presence of Christ. "Apart from the act in which the bread is distributed, the latter has no significance. It is no more than what it was before Christ took and offered it. It retains the possibility of being taken and used by the will of Christ. It is in His control, but it is not in the control of man in so far as it is the Body of Christ."[1] But supposing, after the celebration, there remains some bread and wine? We must not forget that "they have truly been bearers of the body and blood of

[1] Fr. J. Leenhardt, *Ceci est mon corps*, Neuchâtel and Paris, 1955, p. 59.

Christ" and that "the creature which has been assumed by Christ into sacramental union, is entitled to respect" (P. Brunner). This respect would be compromised if the species were treated with contempt, as also if they were used for magical acts. Hence we shall avoid both the profanation committed, I am told, by a pastor of Neuchâtel who "reserves" the species which remain in order to make with them a *fondue*, and also the Roman way of reservation, for "idolatry is so close to us that we may not let the threat of it become the price we pay for the very relative advantage of preserving in the bread a recollection of the permanent nature of Christ's self-donation".[1]

Hence we may either consume with the elders what remains of the consecrated bread and wine (but for this purpose it is necessary to know before the consecration how much bread and wine should be prepared, so that as little as possible remains over, and it is not always easy to ascertain this); or we may, as in the ancient Church, carry what remains to the sick so that they too may share in the parish communion. R. Paquier wonders whether the remaining species should not be burnt, just as the remnants of the Passover meal were burnt (Exod. 12: 10). If I may be allowed to say something in confidence here: when I was a pastor my custom was to pour out on the ground near to the church the wine which remained in the chalice, and as for the bread, I used to give a slice to each of my children to crumble up, and then one of them would give it to the wild birds—not to the hens I used to keep!—with a prayer for them.

I do not wish to dwell at length on these points; but I think that we have here a link with the question of Christian burial: the body of a Christian, because through baptism it has been a bearer of Christ and the Spirit, has a right to decent burial and a decent burial service. We have a link too with the question of the veneration which in the Church should surround the Virgin Mary. She was the bearer of Christ and therefore the mother of God. As is well known, the Reformation was much more conservative on this point than one might think in view of the character of modern Protantism. The Later Helvetic Confession speaks of *Maria semper virgo*; U. Zwingli published "a sermon on the eternally pure maid Maria, the Mother of Jesus Christ, our Redeemer", in which he is very close to the Mariology of the undivided Church of the first millennium. For my part I am not sure whether the *semper virgo* does not jeopardize the reality of Christ's birth and hence His humanity; but I think with the Reformers that Mary never had any other children than Jesus; that her motherhood of the divine Son of God marked her for ever, and consecrated her for ever to be the mother of Jesus only. She was blessed for all generations because she was chosen to give flesh and blood to the divine Son of God (cf. Luke 1: 48). It is in this climate of beatitude that we must think about the elements that are left over from the communion service.

(d) We have noted that the place where the presence of God is pre-eminently to be found is Jesus of Nazareth. We have also noted that at the Ascension He appointed certain signs of His presence, which the Holy Spirit quickens, and which, thus quickened, constitute the true Church, the Body of Christ. Before pointing out how Christian Churches are justified to the extent to which they exhibit these signs, we must briefly recall that the Body of Christ, the Church meeting to celebrate the liturgy, is not the only place of worship for there is also the heavenly temple (Rev. 14: 17) which will last as long as this world lasts before giving place, after the parousia, to the new Jerusalem in which there will no longer be any temple for "the Lord God Almighty and the Lamb is its temple" (Rev. 21: 22). This celestial temple—whatever be the origin of the term—reminds the Church that here below it is not an institution which ensnares and fetters God, that it is in short that we might call the "sacrament of the celestial temple". Thus in the Lord's Prayer, we do not say "Our Father which art on earth" but "Our Father which art in heaven"; the Creed too confesses that Our Lord, although present, is seated on the right hand of God the Father Almighty, since He has ascended into heaven; and for the same reason, from the very earliest times, we have in the Eucharist before the canon of the mass the exclamation: *Sursum corda*: "Lift up your hearts", to which the congregation replies: "We lift them up unto the Lord" (cf. Col. 3: 1-4). This certainly does not deny the reality of Christ's presence with His followers (and thus the reality of the Church on earth); it does not favour some sort of dualism; but it does show that everything we say about the Church on earth must be placed in the context of sacramental life and does not give us any coercive power over God. A Christian Church will not therefore be, like a pagan temple, a house made by the hands of men (Acts 17: 24; cf. 7: 48; Heb. 9: 11, 24), a theologically pretentious place, a cage for God or a coffin for God. It can only be, in humility and thanksgiving, a framework in which the Christian congregation may meet to invoke the name of its Lord and to rejoice in the signs of His real presence.

2. The place of worship as a witness to the presence of Christ

(a) A history of Christian churches would take us too far, hence we shall be content with a few brief remarks.

First, it is clear that the Church, which, by its very nature, must meet, has always had places for its assembly. I am not thinking of meeting places which have an essentially missionary purpose, such as Solomon's porch (Acts 5: 12, 15; 3: 11; cf. also 2: 46; 5: 42) or the synagogues of the Diaspora (Acts 13: 14, 44; 17: 1f., 10, 17; 18: 4, 19; 19: 8) or the school of Tyrannus where Paul argued at Ephesus (Acts 19: 9). But I am thinking rather of places where the early Church met for the breaking of bread (Acts 20: 7). Doubtless they were private houses[1] like that of Mary, mother of John Mark, at Jerusalem (Acts 12: 12) or that of Lydia at Philippi (Acts 16: 15). And in this connexion one cannot fail to be struck by the care with which St. Luke notes the names of the owners of the houses where Peter and Paul stayed. One might also ask whether among these private houses where the Church assembled for its worship in an upper room (HYPEROON: Acts 1: 13: 20: 8; cf. 9: 37, 39) there was not one which stood out from the rest, namely that of Mary, mother of John Mark, where

---

[1] They must have been numerous at Jerusalem since the Christians soon numbered 5,000 (Acts 4: 4; cf. 1: 15; 2: 41; 21: 20).

Jesus probably instituted the Supper, appeared to His disciples at Easter eventide (Luke 24: 33), and which was no doubt the scene of Pentecost. Finally, it might be asked whether the injunction to bishops that they should offer hospitality (1 Tim. 3: 2; Tit. 1: 8) does not seem to imply that the house of the bishop must have served as a place of meeting. This situation, in which the Church assembled mainly in private houses (sometimes in very large houses), remained general for a long time, although in 138 the emperor Hadrian permitted Christians to build. But even if we know or suppose that much ecclesiastical building then took place (such properties were confiscated and then restored to bishops twice in the course of the third century according to the ebb and flow of persecution), it was still not a question of churches proper but rather of house churches, which often had several storeys and which had to suffice for all the needs of the community (catechetic, charitable, clergy dwelling, etc.), not merely for meetings for worship and the Eucharist. Today such buildings would be called parochial halls. It was only later, from the fourth century onwards, that is, from the time when the alien character of the Church in relation to the world began to grow blurred in proportion as the world became Christianized, that church buildings were increasingly constructed for the sole purpose of worship. In the history of church architecture the style of these varies according to the theological emphasis of different elements in worship, according to secular aesthetic influences, to a strengthening or a slackening of the faith, in the course of the centuries between the building of the church of the Nativity at Bethlehem (first half of the fourth century) and Corbusier's church at Ronchamp.

(b) The place is important and we must now consider its component parts, their functional arrangement and their symbolic meaning.

In its chapter on "sacred meetings of the Church", the Later Helvetic Confession speaks of the subject in the following terms: "Choose then spacious houses or temples and let them be cleansed of whatever is inappropriate to the

Church; let them be furnished with all that is requisite to sacred dignity (Latin: *decoro*), necessity and decency; let nothing be lacking which is needed for the services and usages of the Church (Latin: *ad ritus et usus ecclesiae necessarios*)."

So as not to get lost in details, let us recall straightaway that liturgical tradition has made use, with every justification, of many types of ecclesiastical structure and arrangement, and that there is no imperative rule beyond the principle of decent furnishing just quoted from the Later Helvetic Confession; let us remember too that the Church is also a sphere where the principle of Christian liberty should be able to show itself, as also that "sociological" character of the community of which we spoke in Chapter VI.

In listing the furnishings required for a church and its services it is sufficient to remember the constituent features and the ministers of the cult: in a place of worship one must be able to read and preach the Word of God and to celebrate the sacraments. The faithful too must be able freely to fulfil the ministries which are proper to them. Hence certain things are necessary; certain places for the arrangement of those things; and a certain atmosphere to impart to these things and their arrangement a symbolic meaning.

The things "requisite to sacred dignity, necessity and decency" are, at the least, a lectern for the reading of the Word, a table for the celebration of the communion, a baptismal font,[1] seating accommodation, or at least places for the various ministers which will include a "chair"[2] for the preacher. In Western tradition—with an interruption at Zürich in the crisis of the Reformation—there is normally added, if possible, to these "requisite things" an organ to lead and accompany the singing of the officiating ministers and the congregation.

How shall we arrange these requisite things? What

[1] That is, if the parish church is chosen as the place for baptisms. Although this was not done in early Christianity, it is right and desirable.
[2] We ought rather to say a pulpit, for the chair (i.e. *cathedra*) has disappeared from the equipment for preaching since it has been customary for the preacher to stand when he proclaims the Word of God.

principles shall we adopt? For in this matter it is not possible to do without deliberate planning which—as we shall see in detail in a moment—will necessarily have a symbolic meaning.

It is often required that the major principle of arrangement should be of a confessional character. How shall we construct a church that is clearly Protestant, or Roman Catholic, etc.? It is, indeed, inevitable that the place of worship should betray the confessional character of the congregation that meets there, and in regard to liturgy, we have seen that uniformity is neither traditional nor desirable. However, I think it is absolutely wrong to build a church with the intention of justifying the divisions of Christians; it is sinning against truth as much as against hope. The controlling principle behind the arrangements in a place of worship will therefore be not the confessional character of the congregation but the doctrine of Christian worship, namely the principle that worship is a recapitulation of the history of salvation, a self-manifestation of the Church and an action which implies both the end and the future of the world. The recapitulation of the history of salvation will require precise arrangements, facilitating the kerygmatic and sacramental commemoration of this history; the self-manifestation of the Church will require a translation into architectural terms of the whole structure of the church; the eschatological character of the cult will demand the use of symbols.

Let us begin with the architectural expression of the structure of the Church. We have seen in Chapter VII that there are various participants in the cult, each with its own characteristic ministry: the pastor, the deacons, the laity, and, more marginally, the elders and, in some circumstances, the choir or the organist. This distribution of liturgical roles will bring about, in architectural terms, what is called the choir (the locus of the ministry of the pastor, the deacons and the elders), the nave (the locus for the ministry of the laity), and sometimes the gallery (locus for the ministry of the choir and the organist). Thus the church resembles a sort of boat.[1] I do not propose to enter into a detailed

---

[1] This "nautical" shape of the church was underlined by the *Apostolic Constitutions* of the fourth century.

justification of this scheme (which is the most traditional) but will confine myself to the following remarks:

It has often been thought desirable, especially among Reformed Christians, that a church should symbolize the truth that where two or three are gathered together in the name of Christ, He is there in the midst of them. Hence the faithful are grouped around what?—the pulpit? the holy table?—like scouts around a camp fire, or like an audience round a theatre stage, or like medical students around a dissecting table. This is, if need be, a possible arrangement: but I think it would eventually become intolerable for the following reasons: firstly because the dual nature of the means of grace, the major signs of Christ's presence, viz. the Word and the Lord's Supper, would tend to lose its balance; for this type of arrangement we should have to be content with the holy table only. Next, because such a disposition weakens the eschatological tension, persuades us that we have already arrived, or else, on the contrary, turns the congregation into a worldly social group, the members of which find themselves facing each other;[1] it is the Schleiermachian ecclesiology which dictates such an arrangement, and it is astonishing to see that it finds defenders even among Barthians. Finally, because this arrangement weakens the character of worship as an encounter between the Lord, present in the Word and the Eucharist, and His people, we risk regarding Jesus as no longer Lord, but as a good companion whom we gather around, much as we gather around a champion cyclist after his victory in a race.

If this semi-circular arrangement seems to me unfavourable to worship, it does not necessarily mean that the church building should be particularly narrow and long—seeing that the only liturgical gathering attested by the NT, that of the 5000 present at the miraculous feeding, consisted of rows of fifty (Luke 9: 14)[2]—but it does mean that the participants can face each other and hence that those who represent Christ can truly meet the assembled eschatological people. For this reason the existence of a choir and a nave

[1] Facing a lady with a new hat, or a fat gentleman yawning, or so many things which can distract the attention!
[2] Mark 6: 40 says some rows of 50, others of 100.

seems to me desirable, provided that we always remember that these are not two opposite things but are persons or groups of persons who signify the Body of Christ and manifest the face of the Church. By this means too we adopt the most ancient mode of constructing churches, in which the confrontation of minister and congregation seems to have played a more determinative part than the placing of the holy table.

In saying choir and nave, we are not saying "sanctuary" and nave. In spite of the liturgical tradition which in the course of centuries has fostered the unfortunate reduction of the Christian priesthood to the clergy alone, and has therefore favoured an unhappy secularization of the baptized, we must repudiate the idea that in church all the baptized may not freely approach the Lord's table, that the latter is reserved for the clergy alone. I am fully aware of the seductive symbolical interpretations by which it is attempted to justify the idea—one can find fine symbols for the worst abuses! It does not, however, alter the fact that ordination to the sacred ministry does not confer a privilege in connexion with salvation or nearness to the Lord. The sacred ministry certainly gives the right to act in church in the name of God (a right which must be respected, and can be for example by seating the ministers in the choir), but the ministry does not confer on the minister the right to appear before God in a privileged way. Ordination, which is indispensable for the exercise of the ministry, is a divine authorization of the minister in his relation to the people, but it does not promote him to a liturgical status which would bring him nearer to God than does the sacrament of baptism. In relation to the laity, the minister has no prerogative or higher status as far as the soul's salvation is concerned. Thus in a church there are no places more sacred than other places, no places from which are to be excluded men and women who have become members of the Body of Christ through baptism; there is only an arrangement which is required by the order and progression of the liturgy. It is the place of worship as a whole which is the "sanctuary" (otherwise the laity are degraded from the nobility of their baptismal status), and in this sanctuary there is a choir and a nave.[1]

[1] It is pleasing to see, in modern Roman Catholic church building,

256

Let us begin by the arrangement of the choir. It is thence that the Word of God resounds, it is where the Lord's table is placed, it is to that point that the confession, the offertory and the praises of the people are directed, and it is there that are seated the ministers who preside over the cult in the name of Christ. Let us point out the following:

Firstly, for the reading of the Word, a lectern will be used; for its preaching, an ambo, a small platform or a pulpit. From about the eleventh century, the tradition was established that the Gospel should be read from the right of the episcopal *cathedra* which was situated at the back of the choir, in the centre, and to the left of the people assembled in the nave. And there is no objection to putting the ambo or pulpit to the right of the holy table, just in front of the choir. In this case the lectern will be placed to the left of the holy table, parallel or almost so, to the ambo or pulpit which since the Middle Ages has been called the epistle side. It seems to me quite useless—just in order to continue or revive a very artificial symbolism—not to read the Gospel from the same side as the Epistle (and the OT). To raise the status of the Gospel reading, rather than move the reader, it is surely better to make the congregation stand up. Hence, as a rule the pulpit or ambo will be placed at the extreme right of the choir (seen from the holy table), and the lectern on the left. If, as is desirable—for reasons of seeing and hearing[1]—the choir is raised by a few steps, we should be careful not to raise the pulpit too much.[2]

But the choir is not only the place from which the proclamation of the Word rings out. It is also the place where Christ invites His followers to His table that He may give Himself to them and that they may offer themselves to Him

---

that the present situation, where the secularization of the western world permits a new emphasis on the priestly character of the Christian people, is clearly understood. But the same understanding has not yet liberated the iconostasis of the Eastern Orthodox Church from that function of being a sacred screen which it has fulfilled since the sixth or seventh centuries.

[1] It is well to mistrust too facile symbolic reasons.

[2] Here again facile symbolic reasons are easy to find: the Word must descend from heaven, but the preacher should not confuse himself with the ascended Lord!

as a holy and living sacrifice. Hence it is the spot where the holy table will be situated; and, to use the words of K. Barth, since the communion service is the peak point of the cult, the table will be placed in the centre of the choir, the place which forms the focus of the people's gaze. A large number of problems arise, among which we shall confine ourselves to essentials.

First of all, we should insist that the holy table should be surrounded by ample space; this was the general tradition until in the eleventh century in Western Europe, the altar was pushed to the back of the choir where the *cathedra* of the bishop had formerly been installed. This tradition was restored by the Reformers, and today the Romans are likewise trying to revive it and to make it more widespread. In effect, the minister who presides over the Lord's Supper and consecrates it must be able to face the people. But the holy table is not only the place where Christ gives Himself to His followers in the bread and the wine; it is also the place where the Christian people give themselves to their Lord in response to His self-giving; consequently it is not only the place where the offerings collected from the people are laid, but also the place from which the ministers conduct the prayers of the people (and to do so, it is right and proper that they should put themselves at the head of the people, just as officers march at the head of their troops, that is, the ministers will look in the same direction as the people and will turn their back to the latter).

It is at this juncture that we might ask whether it is legitimate to call the holy table an altar. As is well known, traditions on this point vary: the Romans normally speak of the altar, as do the Lutherans, and often the Anglicans. The Orthodox have no objection to the term but prefer to speak of "holy table". Reformed churchmen usually have a violent aversion from the term altar (which however is unhesitatingly used by some of them,) and prefer to it such terms as table of the Lord (which is Biblical, 1 Cor. 10:21), or holy table or communion table. I feel that there is no compelling reason to adopt the term altar; to succeed in doing so would not be a victory or an achievement in an oecumenical sense; but I think, on the other hand, that the

NT has a conception of Christian life and worship which is much more sacrificial than the traditional thought of Protestantism would wish to admit. The latter is in fact morbidly poised to attack whatever is sacrificial, because it never thinks of anything but propitiatory sacrifices which might imperil the uniqueness of the sacrificial death of Christ, or because it scents afar off the worst side of the Roman theology of the mass. We need not nurse either a superiority or an inferiority complex if we decide to renounce the use of the term altar, and remain faithful to the ancient term Table of the Lord; but I think, too, that we should not see in this terminological problem the basic and exclusive theological choice which we often insist on seeing in it; otherwise the Lutherans and Anglicans would have been sensitive to the implication. However, if we wish to use the term, we ought not to do so as if we were law-breakers. We should explain and justify the reasons for the change, though in my opinion they are needless even if valid.

Having spoken about the situation of the holy table and its name, it might be worth while to say a word about its material. For a long time, it was made of wood and in certain Orthodox churches it has remained so to the present time. The Reformed Church of the sixteenth century returned to this practice in general, but in many of our churches since that date the communion table has been of stone, and we have not felt conscious of committing any crime in using stone. Here again, as in the case of the term altar, freedom of choice should prevail, with perhaps (this is at least my personal feeling) a preference for the wooden table. Nothing should be placed on the holy table which has not its natural and legitimate place there: chalice, cups and paten for the Eucharist, the white linen, the altar cloth and frontal, sometimes the appropriate candlesticks, and the service books. Two things in particular have no place there: bouquets of flowers which transform the holy table into an occasional table proper to a drawing room, and a large open Bible which is out of place for three reasons: firstly, because it is useless on account of its out-of-date translation; secondly, because it appears to be a clumsy counterblast to the Roman tabernacle, adopted with the help of an interpretation of divine inspiration very much akin to that implied by the Roman doctrine of transubstantiation, and, finally, because it is put there simply to hide the absence of a regular weekly eucharistic celebration in the Reformed Church. So long as we do not return to the weekly communion service, the holy table will necessarily be embarrassing to us because it is so empty!

The choir is also the place where from the earliest times the ministers of the Church were seated: the pastor presiding over the cult, the presbyteral college around him, and the deacons who assist. Originally, the bishop's throne was, throughout the whole service, the true centre of the assembly, and it seemed in fact to be more important than the holy table, according to a rather Ignatian line of thought which suggested that it was the PROISTAMENOS who was the prime guarantor of Christ's presence and of the authenticity of the cult. I think that today, for reasons all of which are not perhaps valid, Christian feeling would no longer easily endure this clerical predominance. And if it is true that the architect who plans a sanctuary must envisage the celebrant in his presidential seat, and arrange this in a position which makes it not accessory and optional, but organic and permanent, this position must not, in my opinion, be at the centre of the back of the choir (where it has become customary, and rightly so, to place a cross), but at the side, and the choir should be large enough for all the ministers of the parish—pastor, assistants, elders and deacons—to be able to find, not simply a place, but their proper place.

It may be asked, lastly, whether the choir should not also be the place where baptisms are held. If church discipline provides—and this is the authentic Reformed tradition—for baptisms to be celebrated when the congregation is assembled for worship, and not at special services which could take place elsewhere (e.g. in a baptistry near to the church), then the baptism service should take place in the choir, where for the purpose there should be a baptismal font placed at the south end of the choir and opposite the pulpit. In any event, we shall avoid using *sauciers* (as Montaigne called our baptismal jugs in his *Journal de Voyage*), still far too widely used. We shall also avoid making the communion table the baptismal sphere of operations.

The nave is not a casual place for "public" assembly; it is also an integral part of the church, and the more the liturgical renascence teaches the congregation to realize afresh their own characteristic contribution to the service, the more this structural unity will become apparent. Perhaps then we shall renew the old tradition which segregates men and women in church (the women to the left as one enters and the men to the right, or the men in front and the women behind as has also been known), and this not only from propriety but also because it would permit antiphons between them as Zwingli wished to have. Perhaps also we shall establish once more, for reasons both disciplinary and liturgical, special seating for the catechumens (excommunicate and unbaptized too?). But the following points must also be noted:

Firstly, it is essential that the congregation, in order to share fully in the service, must be able to follow it completely both with their eyes and ears. Hence as far as possible it is strongly advisable not to have pillars separating the central nave from the side-aisles. Secondly, the nave, like the choir, must be so constructed as to make it possible for people to move easily, and the places of the congregation must be so arranged as to avoid bottle-necks, especially at the time of the communion; there should also be a central aisle wide enough to facilitate the processional entry and exit of the ministers. Thirdly, the size of the nave should be adapted to the number of the faithful. Nowadays, we must no longer build places of worship that are too large, but rather we should aim at the dispersal of churches in accordance with the demands of missionary work and the distribution of big towns, remembering that they will now house communities rather than crowds; it is preferable to hold two or three services on high festivals than to have churches which most of the time are disproportionately big. Moreover in places of worship that are too large it should be a matter of course to shut off by a rope the seats at the back while the front seats remain unfilled. Finally, it may be asked whether pews or chairs should be chosen for the seating of the laity. The

Reformation introduced almost everywhere fixed pews, a solution which seems now to be increasingly adopted by the Roman Church, since pews have the advantage of providing at least one extra seat in four and of eliminating clatter. If this solution is adopted, however, it should be our care to construct the pews in such a way that they do not make it uncomfortable either to kneel, or to stand, which is the best attitude for the worshipper.

In a church, we usually also try to find a place for organ and choir. There are many different views on this point: some think that the organ should be brought as near to the holy table as possible but our own tradition prefers to put it in a gallery which faces the chancel and to seat the choir in the gallery. This seems to me the best solution. It should be pointed out, however, that the presence of an organ and a special place for the choir is not a necessity to a church, but rather a luxury. To say, as some do, that among the main components of a church is undoubtedly the organ is going too far: a church does not need an organ to be a Christian church. In Christian antiquity a musical instrument for the accompaniment of the hymns and prayers was unknown, and the Eastern Church has continued to refuse to use one. Antiquity was familiar with the organ for worldly and profane uses, and it was from Byzantium that it was introduced to the West. The Eastern Emperor Constantine Copronymus V gave an organ to Pippin the Short in 757, and in 812 one of his successors gave one to Charlemagne, who placed it in the cathedral of Aix-la-Chapelle, and until the sixteenth century nearly all cathedrals, college chapels and large churches had organs built. At the Reformation, the Church of Zürich under the influence of Zwingli abolished organs in churches only to rebuild one at the Grossmunster in 1598; all the other churches had maintained them.

There is no reason, I think, to be as radical as Zwingli; nor are there any reasons of principle for objecting to a gallery provided it is not used, as nearly always happens, to split up the worshippers, that is, on condition that it is arranged for the choir and does not serve as a sort of refuge for those who do not wish to worship but only to be present as spectators—on this point we have every reason to be cautious and somewhat obstructive. In regard to the gallery for the choir "vicarious worshipping" should be avoided as much as possible. In regard to organs we are somewhat doubtful because of the arrogant demands of organists, and the foolish pretensions of parishioners, the result of which is that vast sums of money are swallowed up, out of all proportion to the real contribution made by the organ. In any case, the beauty or even the mere decency of the church, the liturgical furnishings and equipment, the ornaments, are infinitely more important than the claims and pretensions of a performer on the organ who imagines himself to be a John Sebastian Bach. And it is very likely that among us the exorbitant sacrifices made for the sake of the organ are nothing but an implicit confession of the poverty of the spiritual life of the parish: we compensate for this by having pretentiously magnificent organs, just as Roman parishes compensate for it by a baroque altar overloaded with gilt ornaments. All that may be a camouflage for a spiritual void.

Should there be annexes to a church? In any event, if the church is not in the immediate vicinity of the presbytery, one annexe is indispensable, viz. the sacristy. It is not to be made a store-room for everything; it is the place where the ministers prepare for the services, get things ready for the celebration of communion, put on their robes and return once the service is finished. It is also becoming more and more a place where people can be seen privately for pastoral guidance. As a rule it will be better to situate it so that it is entered from the nave rather than from the choir; not only to facilitate a processional entry of the clergy, but also to make clear that the latter are not actors coming on to the stage, nor holy persons who must be protected from any contamination by the laity.

It is also important that as far as possible the church should be so constructed as to make it easy to welcome the congregation: a narthex or entrance porch is desirable; the church should be set a little apart, both to isolate it from the roar of traffic and also to make it clearly visible to the world (this is the justification for the building of a tower or campanile).

In connexion with annexes, arises the question whether it is legitimate to have in a church side-chapels for special acts of worship. These were unknown in the ancient Church. They were introduced into the West, from the sixth century, on account of the authorization of private masses, and were later justified by the Roman system of discipline which encouraged each priest to celebrate his own mass daily. This deviation from the ancient law of one altar should be resisted, in spite of the distinct advantage it carries with it for very big churches. At least, if we accept the principle of side-chapels—for the saying of offices, and for acts of worship at which there will be a small attendance—it will be enough to put in them a lectern or ambo, seats and possibly a large candlestick. They should have no holy table for the celebration of communion, since we have seen that in principle, and it is a principle which must be defended, we should confine ourselves to one parish Eucharist per Sunday.

Coming now to the problem of the symbolism of churches, we arrive at something very delicate from the point of view of both systematic and pastoral theology. As for the systematic aspect, which concerns the place and function of the creature in Christian revelation, we shall only make such brief preliminary observations as will enable us to pursue our investigation. I think the following factors should be taken into account:

Although a purely etymological interpretation is insufficient, we must remember that SYMBOLOS is the opposite of DIABOLOS: as opposed to what separates and wrenches apart, it is what brings together and reconciles. This means that for the Christian every symbol will be basically allusive to the reconciliation effected by Jesus Christ and will have directly or indirectly a Christological reference. As Fr. Buchholz rightly remarks: "a symbol is only possible for us because Christ has overcome the devil, because the *symbolos* has defeated the *diabolos*". This does not preclude the possibility of symbols before the incarnation, but they were valid only by reference to Jesus Christ just as now, for a Christian, events or things may become symbolic which faith and not sight refers to Jesus Christ.

A doctrine of symbolism must also quite specially take into account the fact that the symbol, because of its Christological reference, is pregnant with the future. To be sure, as long as this world lasts, the fact of Good Friday will preserve many symbolic attestations; but theology in general and liturgy in particular need not try to express them in a special way because they appear automatically, as a shadow cast before, as soon as we seek to express paschal symbols. It is the latter which are properly speaking the object of the Church's enquiry and expression. If the Apostles' Creed relates—and how fully—the process of self-emptying under-gone by Christ (born, suffered, died, buried, descended into hell), it is as though to inflict on Christ alone the whole misery of this world, so as to be able to speak later not of sins but of the remission of sins, and not of eternal perdition but of eternal life. Hence it is normal—provided that we do not try to conceal these symbols of Good Friday which are self-evident—that the Church in its symbolism and especially its liturgical symbolism should express its protest against this world which slays the Christ and persecutes His followers, and should express it by what one might call a paschalization of symbols, a drawing out of their eschato-logical implications. Here again I would like to quote Fr. Buchholz: "The symbol is a function which can only be rightly understood in the light of eschatology, that is, as an anticipation of the basic meaning of the world, whereby the life of men is disclosed as a pilgrimage which proceeds from Creation and the Fall to Redemption." And if the Reformed Church shows itself, in its traditional form of worship, to be the least paschal of the Christian confessions, that is because its protest against liturgical symbolism in the sixteenth century exceeded all limits and impaired the paschal character of God's people. Again, symbols require serious examination and justification. This, having pointed out their necessarily Christological basis and their necessarily eschato-logical implications, is what we must now emphasize. They have in fact a tendency to get out of hand, to proliferate, and to become self-centred. We need only think of the accumula-tion of symbolism in the liturgy of the Eastern Orthodox Church or in that of the Western Middle Ages, and of the self-justification of the cult which stems from this tendency.

Now a symbol which becomes its own justification ceases to be useful. The usefulness of a symbol lies in its power of transmitting the love and victory of Christ, in revealing the reality of salvation in a manner comprehensible to us Christians; one might say that its function is to appeal to the eye just as the voice of the preacher appeals to the ear. Here again we must remind ourselves that Jesus did not cure only the deaf. It is not, as we might be tempted to believe by reason of our confessional prejudices, because of the relation between grace and nature that we must be cautious about symbols (otherwise we should run the risk of attacking the doctrine of the incarnation); it is in the first place because of the Christian doctrine of justification: self-justification has no right to exist in the Church, in which we can welcome only that which finds its justification in Christ. But there is a second reason for this need for caution; it is important to protect symbols against themselves by stylization, by pruning them of excrescences so that they are readily if not automatically understandable. That is why we must take care to reduce their number.

Necessary Christological reference, eschatological implication, firm control to prevent their self-justification, their proliferation and complexity: that is what in principle must be said about symbols. We may now consider what this implies concerning the Church and its worship.

I begin by the symbolic significance of the church in itself. We have already touched on this in showing that the relation between choir and nave must recall the structure of the Church, as composed of ministry and laity. But there are at least two things to be said about the symbolism of the building as such. First, its orientation. Many indications lead us to suppose that from apostolic times Christians in saying their prayers turned towards the East (not towards Jerusalem like the Jews). Because of such texts as Matt. 24: 27, Luke 1: 78ff., 2 Pet. 1: 19, Rom. 13: 12, 1 John 2: 8, and Rev. 1: 16, G. Delling thinks that this orientation is a kind of translation into a gesture of the meaning of the name Jesus, that it goes back to apostolic days and that it symbolizes two things. First, that all Christian prayer is uttered in the name of the "dayspring which has visited us from on high" (Luke 1: 78), and, second, that all Christian prayer is truly eschatological; it is an expectation and a hope of the time when, like the sun, the day of Christ's return will dawn. And if there are ancient churches, and even famous churches, whose choirs point towards the West, they are exceptions which prove the right rule.

Secondly, I think it is useful to say a word about the symbolic meaning of the relation between the interior and the exterior of a church. It is very noteworthy—it may still be seen, for example, at Ravenna—that in ancient times beauty was expressed within rather than without. Just as the adornment which Christian women should seek does not consist in externals such as plaiting their hair, wearing gold jewels or sumptuous dresses, but is an inner adornment hidden within the heart, the incorruptible purity of a gentle and quiet spirit (1 Pet. 3: 3f.), so it is symbolically meaningful if the beauty of a church is more marked within than without, for then the interior is likely to be really beautiful. A consuming quest for exterior beauty risks giving to the whole edifice—both exterior and interior— pretentious appearance, or else fostering the tragic confusion, which so easily arises, between beauty and richness.

A point to which perhaps insufficient attention is paid is the symbolical significance of the genuineness of the materials used in church building and equipment. What is artificial and "pseudo" in character has also a symbolic bearing, but it symbolizes precisely what the Church has no right to be; it spells that love of the false from which the Church has been freed. Therefore we must choose material that is not simulated or impure: natural rather than artificial stones, plain wood rather than the products of synthetic resin, real leather for the binding of books used in worship, wool, silk, and linen for the vestments and altar cloths, wax candles rather than those electric bulbs shaped so as to look like candles, pipe organs rather than electronic organs, just as we take for communion real bread and real wine. It is true that we cannot always provide absolutely genuine materials, but we must insist that it is done as much as possible, for symbolic reasons; since the Church abhors falsehood of every kind, it must oppose it in every way. We must try to show, perhaps more so than ever today, that salvation does not distort or adulterate what it touches, that on the contrary it draws out and justifies the true nature of all that it touches. The nobleness, the simplicity and the solidity of a full leather binding inspires more confidence in the contents of Holy Scripture than an imitation leather binding. The Gospel is opposed to what is false, and the same applies to everything connected with the Church.

If the Church abhors falsehood of every kind, so also it abhors darkness since its members, having passed from darkness to light (Acts 26: 18; Eph. 5:8; 1 Pet. 2: 9), having been united with Him who is the light of the world (John 8: 15; 9: 5, etc.), have become children of light (Luke 16: 8; Eph. 5: 8; 1 Thess. 5: 5; cf. Matt. 5: 14, etc.). This luminosity of the Church which is one of the most frequent themes in the NT, has been symbolized from the earliest times; consequently the Church must be a place of light, or rather a building which shows that darkness is being resisted and overcome by light. This means in practice that we shall take care to see that the light of the sun can pierce the church in resplendent shafts or—as in the upper room at Troas (Acts 20: 8)—that, if worship takes place at night time, the light will exceed what is merely necessary to show clearly that the Gospel dispels the darkness of this world, and creates a focus of light which draws the attention.

But the symbolism of light is not exhausted by this demand that churches should be well lit and luminous. We know from the Book of Revelation (which doubtless transfers to the heavenly cult characteristic traits of the earthly cult) that each Church had to have a lampstand[1] which must have symbolized its life before the Lord, since the extinction of this light signified the extinction and death of a Church (2: 5; cf. 1: 12–13, 20). Later tradition is familiar with the use of wax candles, into the history of which we need not enter now. Let us merely observe that St. Jerome, writing in 378, reports that as a sign of joy candles are lit at the moment of the reading of the Gospel—which doubtless does not yet refer to the procession with candles preceding the Gospel reader but to the fact that the faithful themselves carried candles. We might note also that before the eleventh

---

[1] LYCHNIA: had it seven lamps like that of Exod. 25: 31–39 and Zech. 4: 1ff.?

or twelfth centuries, it would not have occurred to anyone to place candlesticks on the holy table: they were placed around it or above; whereas now this is an almost universal custom. Personally I think we have no reason to be proud of the fact that we have no candles on the holy table, for this is not because of the faithfulness to early Christian practice, but because the abolition of altar lights in the sixteenth century suppressed all the symbolism of light which was so characteristic of the early Church. Hence, I think it would be very desirable for us to restore this symbolism. We could do it by placing a large candle-holder behind the holy table which would be lit for every service. It would symbolize at once the light of the world, the Pentecostal flames, the life of the assembled Church (this, too, may only use itself up in shining: *in serviendo consumor*) and the expectation of the eternal day. If the acquisition of such a candle-holder was too costly, I see no absolute reason forbidding us to place a small candlestick on the holy table. Perhaps in this case we should need two, for the sake of parallelism, but then we are in danger of introducing worldly associations such as the festal joy of a candlelight supper. But why should we not dare also to rejoice quite simply in the Lord's Supper, as did the Palestinian Christians of the fourth century: *ad signum laetitiae demonstrandum*?

Close to the symbolism of light is that of colour, since white is the basic obligatory liturgical colour. The history of liturgical colours is full of surprises and contradictions: the East—perhaps because the liturgical year was there never so rigid as in the West—never fixed a precise order concerning the number and the season of colours, and in the West it was not until the twelfth century that precise directions were given; but there have always been exceptions to the rule, since Milan has maintained up to the present rules that are peculiar to its diocese and in which red plays a much greater part than elsewhere. Moreover, the current rule is hardly more than a convention, for quite recently the Roman *ordo* has changed the colour for Palm Sunday to that of red. Thus it is not surprising that divergent suggestions are made with regard to liturgical colours, and especially in Churches which, like our own, are seeking to reintroduce them. The symbolism of colours—which is obvious but full of contradictions—does not seem to me the important point about liturgical colours, or at least it is not the search for this symbolism which should be a guiding motive in the choice of colours. These were used in worship above all for reasons of the beauty and joy they seemed to radiate, and it is this beauty and joy that they primarily symbolize. But to avoid excesses, to avoid the bad taste which so often threatens Christians especially when they become wealthy, it seems to me that the decision taken by Innocent III in the twelfth century is absolutely right and wise: that liturgical colours be reduced to four and distributed over the Church year so that henceforth they may symbolize the liturgical season and remind worshippers of it. I see then no reason to change the colours that are traditional in the West, or the mode of their distribution.

Thus we shall have white (or perhaps the yellowish gold which is its equivalent, and which stands out better) for the great festivals of Christ—from Christmas to Epiphany and from Easter to the eve of Pentecost; violet for the penitential seasons which prepare us for the great feasts, i.e. the four Sundays of Advent and the Sundays in Lent;[1] red for Pentecost; and green for the time between Epiphany and Lent, and that between Trinity and Advent. I see no reason either not to have red for some other occasions, e.g. baptism Sundays,[2] Confirmation Sunday, Reformation Sunday, and the Sunday when, among us, the pastor's sermon is replaced by the witness of a layman. Nevertheless, we must always bear in mind the distrust with which we should regard any baroque overloading of the Christian year. We might choose violet for the day of the "Federal Fast". To see in the use of liturgical colours something permissive, rather than a rigid law that must be obeyed, is a sign of the legitimate joy that we may feel about them. Let us remind ourselves, however, that the best games have their rules.

When we move on to the question of vestments, we are still within the sphere of legitimate joy, something "added unto us" when we know how in this world to rejoice in the

[1] Rather than from Septuagesima.
[2] Not on a day fixed by the parents.

world of the resurrection: we must not be like Judas Iscariot, who thought that it was a waste of time and money to consecrate to Jesus a thing as futile and unnecessary as perfume (cf. John 12: 5). But we must realize that this permissive joy only becomes legitimate (as in the case of liturgical colours) when the Church is faithful in the essentials of its worship, when it respects every aspect of the cult; the delight in vestments would become not only ridiculous but false and out of place if it were used to conceal liturgical poverty, if it were not simply a way of exulting in the light and gladness of the Easter mystery. But as an expression of liturgical AGALLIASIS we may well be concerned about vestments.

It is difficult to reach well-established conclusions about the history of Christian liturgical vestments. Firstly, because the NT does not say much on the subject. If indeed it is aware of a symbolism of vestments (especially those worn by Christ: cf. John 19: 33; Rev. 1: 13), if it declares that the redeemed in the Kingdom will be dressed in white robes (cf. Rev. 3: 4ff.; 4: 4; 6: 11; 7: 9, 13, 14; cf. 3: 18, etc.), it gives no hint that the ministers of the primitive Church wore any special dress when celebrating worship. It is difficult also because if the ministers of the pre-Nicene Church wore in any event their lay clothes, they were certainly their best clothes, and it is further clear that antiquity had ideas about dress quite different from ours. Therefore, we are not saying quite the same thing if we say that the liturgical vestments of the ancient Church consisted of lay dress (of fine quality), and then go on to infer that the liturgical vestments of today ought to consist of ordinary lay dress. According to ancient sentiment, which lasted until the eighteenth century, garments do not cloak their wearers in anonymity; on the contrary they serve to reveal the personality of him who wears them, as is suggested by that wise dictum of Georges Louis Leclerc, Count of Buffon: "A sensible man should regard his dress as part of himself, since in the eyes of others it is an essential element of his personality, and contributes to the total idea that is formed of him."

Thus, for example, if the Reformed Protestants (unlike the

Lutherans, who on this point were for a long time very conservative) abolished Roman liturgical vestments, it was not in order to dress their pastors like everybody else (for nobody dressed just like other people) but in order to require them always to wear the dress distinctive of their status and profession, namely the robes proper to academics. Hence, the Reformed churchmen did not abolish clerical dress, they abolished liturgical dress. None the less, traditional liturgical vestments before the sixteenth century were former lay dress, at times slightly modified, but retained for the celebration of the Christian cult long after they had gone out of fashion in ordinary life. It was once a cleavage had arisen between liturgical vestments and the dress of the laity that mediaeval churchmen began to discover in these garments which had once been lay garments all sorts of symbolic virtues, sometimes complementary, sometimes contradictory. We cannot enter into details.

But until a deeper study is forthcoming (which needs to be done) we can notice the following points of principle:

Firstly, it must be admitted that in the Christian Church there have been three fresh starts in celebrating worship in lay garments but as fine as possible. Twice at least and perhaps each time this was done to make a break with liturgical vestments: in the apostolic period (perhaps as a protest against Jewish and pagan sacerdotal vestments), in the sixteenth century (as a protest against the vestments worn by the Roman priesthood), and in the nineteenth century (as a pietistic and revivalistic protest against the dress of the Reformed clergy). Each time this dress which was originally lay was maintained, once it had gone out of fashion, as an ecclesiastical dress, and thus became "clerical" and acquired certain symbolic virtues. This repeated process leads us to suppose that if today it was desired to abolish ecclesiastical dress in favour of lay dress, in seventy years' time our conventional modern dress (black jacket and striped trousers) retained for ecclesiastical purposes would have become solely liturgical. That is why I think it would be wise, firstly, to accept the fact of ecclesiastical dress, which incidentally has the advantage of sinking the individual in his function, and then to choose it to express a precise and simple symbolism, without worrying too much about confessional traditions in the matter.

I would provide then the following types of dress:

For the pastor, a black cassock (all Biblical dress consists of robes, and those raised from the dead are never pictured in trousers!), over which will be worn a white surplice, not covering it entirely, and with the addition of a stole in the appropriate liturgical colour. The symbolism is clear: the black cassock represents the old Adam; the white surplice represents the robe of righteousness and pardon which awaits him, but does not entirely conceal the cassock since the Kingdom is not yet manifested. The double vestment signifies the tension between the two ages which marks the life of the Church here below. The coloured stole signifies the yoke of Christ who comes, suffers and dies, who becomes incarnate and rises from the dead, who sends the Holy Spirit, who reigns in glory and who guides His Church. To show that the celebration of the Eucharist is not a means of conveying more grace than is done by the proclamation of the Word, this pastoral dress will not be added to at the Lord's Supper.

As for the elders or deacons, who take up the offertory, read the scriptures, share in the distribution of the eucharistic species, their dress is debatable: they may be dressed like the clergy (though perhaps reserving to the latter the stole). This simplifies matters, since then the Church will have only one type of liturgical vestment, it will militate against a proud clericalism, and will be very appropriate symbolically since those who are not pastors have just as much need of the promise of purity to efface the blackness of the first Adam. But another dress for the elders might be devised, and this too would have its symbolism, at least in Switzerland where each parish has its coat-of-arms. The elders (or deacons) might wear an ample tippet of the colour which predominates in the parish coat-of-arms with, embroidered on the left side, the heraldic emblem which ornaments the parish escutcheon. This suggestion which I have made elsewhere usually meets with a scarcely concealed smile of pity from Protestants (though not so much from Roman Catholics). None the less, I maintain the suggestion, not only because of the beauty which it would impart to synodal processions, but also because of its symbolic meaning: the pastor by his dress would symbolize the hope of the Church, while the elders would wear a dress symbolizing the truth that the Church has deep local roots in this world.

As for the laity, while recommending for Sunday worship their best dress, there are certain special moments in their life as Christians when they have a right to wear special liturgical garments: when they are baptized, when they are confirmed,[1] and when they are laid to rest in the tomb. On those occasions they should be dressed entirely in a white robe to symbolize that for the moment the continuance of the present aeon is forgotten. For symbolical reasons, too, it is useful that this entirely white robe should be reserved to the laity.[2]

Finally, also to be considered are the ornaments for the holy table, the pulpit and the lectern. Different solutions are possible. In order that the holy table may look as much like a table as possible, it is best to use a large white cloth which hangs well down, and over it can be laid, hanging down in front and at the back, a cloth of suitable dimensions and in the colour appropriate to the liturgical seasons.[3] A similar coloured cloth, perhaps symbolically embroidered, may be hung from the desk of the ambo or pulpit and from the lectern. In Switzerland we Protestants have not yet any workshop for the making of ecclesiastical ornaments, but would not the community of Grandchamp find a further work in this field? It is certain that the supply would be matched by quick demand.

A word must also be said about the symbolism of various

[1] For these occasions albs are to be preferred to "communion dress", and even to the veils of girls who are about to be confirmed, because they hide social distinctions. The white dress of brides, the symbol of virginity, is not really liturgical dress.

[2] A warning—no modification in the liturgical dress of the pastor before the elders and deacons have rediscovered their proper liturgical function and a dress appropriate to it. Otherwise what should be an outward sign of liberty and joy will look like an insufferable action by the clergy.

[3] It is possible to use table-runners in the liturgical colours, which should be arranged in the form of a cross over the front and sides of the table. Or, instead of using the liturgical colours on the table, we could place a curtain in the appropriate liturgical colour behind the choir.

postures. We have already touched on this point, and here will make only the following remarks. Firstly, that it is good to stand for the reading of the Gospel, since we should not remain seated when the Lord is speaking. Next, it is a useful symbolism to follow the ancient tradition of not kneeling between Easter and Pentecost; it is especially desirable to mark the great Paschal Week in this way. Lastly, I think it would be good symbolically to encourage the minister to change his position in the service: let him take the basilical position when addressing the assembly in the name of the Lord (absolution, preaching, invitation to communion, blessing), or when, as shepherd of the flock, he makes the announcements and gives liturgical directions. When he is leading the prayers of the people he should face in the same direction as the congregation, i.e. towards the East. It is anomalous to lead the prayers facing the people, and it would be possible to explain why it is better to do the opposite, especially in these days when confessional reactions are weakening. Otherwise the congregation will continue to declare that the past or has addressed *to them* a very fine prayer!

Ought we to add an observation about the symbolic significance of incense? In view of the NT, which clearly sees in it a symbol of prayer, as is suggested by Ps. 141: 2,[1] we may be right to do so, especially as it is possible that the first century Church—above all the Judaeo-Christians who were familiar with its use—used incense liturgically. In any event, the liturgical use of incense had completely disappeared by the second and third centuries when the *turificati* (the censers) were apostates who burnt incense before Caesar and his emblems. However, its use had been restored by the end of the fourth century, doubtless rather with the intention of counteracting noxious smells in places of worship than from liturgical motives. It is also used at this period in processions (by analogy with secular processions where incense was swung before the principal personage of the group); but it was only from the tenth or eleventh centuries onward (the East was accustomed to it earlier) that the use of incense for

[1] Cf. Rev. 5: 8; 8: 3, 4; Luke 1: 10, possibly sacerdotal reference in Phil. 4: 18; Matt. 2: 11. Cf. also Mal. 1: 11.

the eucharistic celebration became widespread in the West. If Reformed churches of the sixteenth century completely rejected it, this was not so among the Lutherans or the Anglicans.

Generally speaking, the symbolism of incense has played a less important part in traditions of worship than the symbolism of light and there is no reason to complain of this, for the sense of smell is the least of the senses. If, in order fully to practise the NT suggestions about liturgical symbols as a spiritual aid, we wished to re-introduce incense, I think it would be best to restrict its use, following the Book of Revelation, to the symbolization of prayer, and not to cense persons or things with the idea of exalting them as was done in profane antiquity.

In this section, there is a last point to be mentioned briefly, namely the legitimacy or otherwise of images.

First, it must be recognized that in spite of the Reformed Protestants—the other Reformers, here again, were far less radical—we now have images in an increasing number of churches; stained glass almost always, crosses,[1] and often frescoes. This practice is now generally accepted, but without our having developed any doctrine on the subject, or officially modifying the iconoclastic teaching of our fathers. There is thus a divergence between what we claim theologically and what we tolerate or even favour in practice. This is dangerous and I would here like to make an appeal for courage to reconsider the problem, after the therapy of violent purgation and fasting which our Church has had to endure. Calvin said: "As soon as there are images in a church, it is like

---

[1] If crucifixes date from the fifth century (though they suggested triumph, as do Orthodox crucifixes still) it was only from the eleventh century that they were placed on the holy table, a custom which has been maintained by the Lutherans. In Reformed churches we increasingly find an unadorned cross in monumental form. Luther defended the rightness of the crucifix: "If it is not sinful to bear the image of Christ in the heart, why should it be sinful to have it before one's eyes?" (W.A. 18, p. 83. But let it be the Christ who promises the resurrection (cf. Mark 8: 31; 9: 31; 10: 34, etc.) like the crucifixes of the first millennium or those of the Orthodox Church, and not the morbidly sensual crucifixes which became widespread in the West from the thirteenth century, of which the reredos of Isenheim, Grunewald, is the worst example. Personally I prefer the big plain cross.

raising a banner to attract men into idolatry".[1] If he was right, then we must resume the iconoclastic struggle in our churches: if he was mistaken or unduly generalizing, then we must say why. There is a sort of spiritual dishonesty in allowing images to be used in our churches while our official doctrine excludes their use. The reasons for a fresh and calm reconsideration of the question of images seem to be as follows:

Firstly, because our traditional position has isolated us confessionally. We can, of course, without difficulty quote many iconoclastic fathers, and recall also that the Early Church had no images: the Reformed Christians were not the sole iconoclastic voices raised in the history of the Church. In principle, then, our position may be perfectly right. But it may also be a judaizing and archaizing position. Because of the very isolation into which it has thrust us, it requires a fresh examination. When, in the communion of the Church we find ourselves isolated, it is not automatically a sign of either obedience or disobedience; but it certainly prompts us to consider the matter very closely, and to listen carefully to the questions or criticisms of those from whom we are isolated. Hence we cannot, without proud obstinacy, remain content with Calvin's attack of bad temper in order to condemn the 7th Oecumenical Council, the 2nd of Nicæa (787) which justified the use of images.[2] But we must again review the history of iconoclasm in the Church of the first millennium. We must also examine the underlying reasons for differences among the sixteenth-century Reformers on this point; and lastly the problem must be looked at in the light of contemporary theological debate.

The second reason is that it is not merely a question of the need that man has always felt to express artistically his interpretation of the world and its happenings: nor is it a question of helping the illiterate, since at least in western Europe there are no more of them.[3] It is rather a question of what is implied in the doctrine of the incarnation and of

[1] *Inst.* I. XI, 13.   [2] Cf. *Inst.* I, XI, 14–16.
[3] Today this means nothing more than repeating with Gregory the Great: "Pictura in ecclesiis adhibetur, ut hi qui litteras nesciunt, saltem in parietibus vivendo legant quae legere in codicibus non valent" (*Ep.* 105, *P.L.* 77, col. 1027).

eschatology. I think that in the approach to this problem the most interesting point of impact would be an attempt to unfold the meaning of the very profound difference—at least in practice—which separates the Orthodox East in this matter from the Roman West, and thus to bring out the divergent significance of icons and statues. One cannot avoid the impression that the West—perhaps with pedagogical intent—has deprived the icon of its eschatological meaning, and in consequence has sensualized almost all its imagery; but the icon is not only in the tradition of the incarnation, it is also, through the power of the Spirit, in the tradition of Christian hope,[1] since it is an incredible attempt to cause what the Spirit seeks to transfigure to "show through" here and now.[2] Fortunately we are beginning to possess, in the West, a literature which enables us to study directly the problem of the icon; and we should do well to pay attention to it, were it only because iconographs are perfectly in agreement with Calvin (contrary to Western imagery) as to the impossibility of representing God the Father. In consequence of such research it should be possible to say whether our theological iconoclasm is not decisively leading us towards a certain docetism, or whether it is not the involuntary testimony to a certain docetism, of which we find it so difficult to rid ourselves, and which has a bearing not only on the true implications of the incarnation for nature, but also, and as a consequence, on the hope of resurrection, which is in danger of being reduced to a somewhat dualist expectation of the immortality of the soul.

But our isolation in this matter, with its grave implications for Christology and eschatology, is not the only reason why we should not be afraid to face the problem afresh. There are, further, certain pastoral reasons.[3]

[1] It is interesting to note that images entered liturgical life to express the protest of faith against death: baptistries and cemeteries were decorated before churches.

[2] Is not the icon, like the preaching of the gospel (cf. K. Barth), an impossibility overcome?

[3] I leave out of account one aspect, namely that which concerns artists. In Chapter IV we noted that worship invited and justified the arts. Artists should understand their talent as a vocation and their work as a liturgy (in the East iconography has the character of prayer and this again differentiates it from the West: the East

Modern western man is overwhelmed with images which reach him, particularly from the world of advertising. He is also beset with abstractions and analyses. He needs decontamination and rest, he needs to find a sovereign principle which justifies and forgives. And the question which we Reformed Christians must ask ourselves is this: might it not be the case that liturgical images would contribute to bring about this catharsis, would free us from the eroticizing and sensualizing processes of the contemporary world, would gather us up in Him who justifies and sums up all things (Eph. 1:10), and would thus consolidate and integrate us? It is clear that here too it is indisputably the Orthodox icon rather than the Roman image, so pedagogic and empty of eschatological significance, that might conduce to the healing of our souls, for it witnesses to something other than ourselves, something which is not the offspring of our eager desires but the illustration of a promise.

For these three reasons I think we should do well to examine afresh this question, and to examine it with all the simplicity and trustfulness which flow from Christian liberty.

(c) The Later Helvetic Confession, speaking of churches, makes the following remark: "Now as (*sicut autem*) we believe that God does not dwell in temples made with hands, also we know that places dedicated to God and His service (*loca Deo cultuique eius dedicata*) are not profane, but sacred, on account of the word of God and the use of holy things in the service of which they are employed: and those who frequent them must converse in all modesty and reverence, remembering that they are in a holy place, in the presence of God and His holy angels (*utpote qui sint in loco sacro, coram Dei conspectus et sanctorum angelorum eius*)."[1] It is this question of dedication and sacredness in regard to holy places which must occupy our attention for a moment. Places of worship

---

would not dream of ordering frescoes for a church from a Jean Cocteau!). Or does it really suffice to say to them with Calvin (*Inst.* I, XI, 12) that art is very fine and useful, but essentially non-liturgical as soon as it ceases to be prayerful, poetic, musical, architectural and becomes plastic?

[1] Ch. 22.

are holy places, set apart for a specific office: namely to become the setting for the presence of Christ, the place of encounter between the Lord and His people. As a rule their site is not appointed by God Himself[1]—this is quite a different matter from the water of baptism or the bread and wine of the Eucharist—but is a decision of the Church which plans them, determines on them, builds and sanctifies them for the divine service, and "dedicates them to God and holy uses, in other terms, separates them from ordinary use to consecrate them, according to the will of God, to a special and sacred use", to use the terms employed by H. Bullinger, the successor of Zwingli.

Such dedications are inevitable so long as we are in this world. Not only does the OT bear witness to them (e.g. the dedication of the Temple at Jerusalem) (1 Kings 5ff.), but there is testimony to their use by the Church as soon as it was free to build its places of worship; and the fact that there was then no lively opposition probably shows that they were in use earlier. How could it have been otherwise, since baptism demonstrates that there is indeed a difference between the Church and the world? The very liturgy of baptism postulated, on a lower level of course and with different consequences, the consecration of churches. Hence we must not be surprised if later liturgies of dedication took on a richness and a profusion of symbolical meanings which today may appear empty or archaic, but a deep examination of which would assuredly enable us to deduce a very valid theology of the place of the cult.

Of course, we must avoid all superstition in the matter, as would have been said in the sixteenth century. Of course the dedication of a church does not magically transform it into a place that is taboo. A dedication is less an ecclesiastical claim than the offering of that spot to the Lord of all the earth, and the invocation of the Spirit to deign to come freely and set apart this place that is offered to God (which

[1] We must not confuse a church with places which God chooses to sanctify in His sovereign liberty; I am not thinking merely of the places of epiphany mentioned in the OT, or of the Holy Land as a whole, but of places where there has been a special theological radiation (e.g. Geneva in the sixteenth century) or eschatological radiation (e.g. Bad Boll in the second half of the nineteenth century).

means that the Holy Spirit, if the worst comes to the worst, may refuse to do so). But with these reservations, it must also be said that it would be intolerable to do whatever we please in a place of worship so long as it retains this character, so long as it has not been solemnly deconsecrated. For the same reason the custom of using Protestant churches for concerts ought to be resisted. Sometimes Protestantism manifests a kind of anti-sacral fury which borders on blasphemy; to show clearly that God is free, the spot He has deigned to choose for a revelation of His presence is "profaned" or degraded. The impulse is sometimes intended as a provocation: if there is a God, it is thought, let Him prevent us from provoking and scoffing at Him! But as a rule God does not react as He did after the return of the ark to Beth-Shemesh (1 Sam. 6: 19ff.). He reacts rather as He did when Christ was spat upon and beaten with rods, or as when He was told to come down from the cross. He is content to suffer, so slow is He to anger. Hence, rather than playing the free-thinker and the "tough" (cf. Rom. 14) in places of worship we should give heed to the valid recommendation of the Later Helvetic Confession, which is particularly applicable to us Reformed churchmen: "Those who frequent churches should converse there with all modesty and reverence, remembering that they are in a holy place, in the presence of God and His holy angels."

3. The sanctification of space

We have seen that Sunday and the Christian year sanctify time, i.e. claim it for Christ and devote it to Him (always in the setting of the Mass-Eucharist of which we have so often spoken). Similarly, a Christian church sanctifies space: it claims for Christ the spot where one can see Him (hence the church towers) and hear Him (hence the church bells) and this it consecrates and attaches to Christ. It therefore in this world runs up a signal which is both a challenge and a promise to other buildings and to space in general. For this reason we should not fear wherever possible to make churches plainly visible. Assuredly it is no longer permissible to indulge in mediaevalist romanticism and to rhapsodize about a church spire indicating the presence of a village and being, in relation to the surrounding houses, like a hen surrounded by her chicks. All that for the moment is a thing of the past. On the contrary, we must expect that in future we may have to camouflage churches once more. This, however, does not affect our argument, because if it is no longer possible for a church to make its mark on a neighbourhood (as Sunday already has ceased to impart a spiritual character to the week), the church will none the less remain the place where Christians will learn to conquer and occupy space, even if only the space of their private room. Hence because of this implication, both missionary and sacerdotal, of places of worship, because of the importance of the latter for the world, it is right to devote to them the theological and devotional concern to which they are entitled, as we have tried to do in this chapter: just as a Christian is for all men a summons and an opportunity (ought we to say: promise?) to share in the resurrection life, just as a Sunday is for the week a promise of eternity, so a church is for this world a promise of the new heavens and the new earth. Hence it is good that the church should be built facing East.

CHAPTER TEN

THE ORDER OF WORSHIP

In THIS second part, in which we have listed the elements of the cult, studied the roles of its participants, gone into details about the day and the place where it is normally celebrated, there now remains for us to consider the order of worship. This question is not peripheral, for the order of worship also forms part of the *lex orandi* which governs the *lex credendi*, or at least influences and enriches the latter. But in order to accomplish this task successfully, it would be necessary to insert at this point an extensive parenthesis on the history of the cult and the rules of comparative liturgiology. We cannot undertake this here, and so shall directly approach the teachings of this history, and examine later some of the major problems raised by the order of worship.

1. Teachings which result from the history of worship

(a) In drawing up a summary list of these teachings, we shall have to note the following points:

There is no church without its cult. Worship is one of the two essential elements in the life of the Church (the other being the evangelization of the world). Hence, just as it is possible to say: the Church spells missionary activity, so it is possible to say: the Church spells worship. For the Church has an inevitable twofold orientation—towards God in its worship, and towards the world in its apostolate. In studying the history of worship, it is the history of the Church that we are unfolding, or at least one half of the history of the Church. Before being an object of interest to historians and liturgiologists, or to masters of ceremonies and chiefs of religious protocol, worship is an expression of the very life of the Church.

The information that we have about worship in the early Church is rather meagre, not because worship did not play an important part but because "the cultic assembly is a focus that is taken for granted, it is the presupposition on the basis of which the whole Christian life is lived, and just for that reason there is no need to expound and describe it" (K. Barth, *Dogmatics*).[1] But in spite of its meagreness and vagueness such information as we have shows that the life of the Church, centred in worship, is governed by a rhythm with two phases: apostolic witness and communion in the body and blood of Christ. The history of worship suggests that this rhythm was maintained for the first fifteen centuries of the Church's life. It certainly suffered injury, and grave distortions. But in spite of these ill effects, in spite of certain atrophies and hypertrophies, the alternate pulse-beat of liturgical life, the Word—the Eucharist continued until the Reformation.

Worship is a way of life and this life has a rhythm. The third lesson we learn from the history of worship is that the form which the latter takes can vary according to time and place. Thus the worship of the third century is different from that of the seventh at many points, while again the worship of the Churches of Egypt differs in various ways from that of the Churches of Gaul. These variations do not compromise the basic unity of the cult and of the Church, even if the points of difference are often not inconsiderable. Through these variations the characteristics of different ages and countries are expressed in worship, and this expression is not merely legitimate, it is necessary, since the cult is not only the expression of the Church in itself, but also the expression of such and such a Church situated in time and space. Certainly it becomes quickly apparent that two great liturgical families emerge, to produce towards the end of the first millennium the Eastern liturgy shaped by that of St. John Chrysostom (which absorbed the other Eastern liturgical traditions) and in the West that of the Roman

---

[1] Note that if the Corinthian church had properly celebrated the Eucharist, and if St. Paul had not had to intervene in the matter, serious scholars would be affirming that in the time of St. Paul, the Church—at least the Gentile Church—had no Eucharist!

mass which arose from the fusion of certain Western liturgical traditions. This duality, which in effect put an end to the previous diversity, has certainly been more harmful to Christian unity than would have been the maintenance of the liturgies proper to Egypt (liturgy of St. Mark), Syria (liturgy of St. James), Gaul (the Gallican mass), Spain (the Mozarabic mass), co-existing with the liturgies of the East and the Roman mass.

Perhaps even the practical continuance of these various liturgical traditions—theologically liturgical diversity was normally accepted—would have prevented, or at least lessened, the distortions and adulterations which intruded into liturgical celebration in the East and more particularly in the West. In fact, if the history of worship shows the legitimacy of liturgical divergences which authentically reveal different "sacrificial" responses to the Gospel in different places and at different times, it also shows that the cult has no immunity from lopsidedness, parasitism, nervous tensions, hypertrophies. Its history is not the history of a continuous and deepening obedience. Thus, if it is not to fall a victim to the deviations induced by self-centredness, it needs a norm by which it can be tested. In its "sacrificial" aspect the cult, being subject to the wiles of Satan, must be open to reform.

Such a reformation, however, must be carried out in accordance with the norms and conditions of liturgical formulation which we have noted. We cannot go into the details of changes which took place at the time of the Reformation. Luther on the whole was very conservative, but Lutheran worship, in Germany at least, became very decadent before the modern liturgical revival; Reformed worship in its Germanic expression is rooted not in the traditional liturgy of the mass, but rather in the sermon, which became widespread from the end of the Middle Ages in the regions of south Germany; French Reformed worship, on the other hand, was much more influenced by the traditional pattern of the mass although as a rule it had no regular celebration of the Eucharist. It was as if Calvin found here another way of protesting against the deprivation of the Eucharist which the civil authorities forced the Church to endure, and left "blank" the place of the Eucharist. But the characteristic of all these liturgies is that they changed the emphasis in liturgical tradition by giving up the weekly Eucharist. It is true that the Lutherans at first maintained the weekly Eucharist whether there were communicants or not;[1] the Anglicans provided for it also, but insisted on five or six communicants, with the result that in most country parishes, right up to the nineteenth century, sacramental life was as impoverished as much as it was among the Reformed, where in general no Eucharist was provided for except at the great festivals. But this, and it must be under-lined, meant that the faithful communicated three or four times more often than the Roman Catholics, among whom, from the thirteenth century, only an annual communion was insisted on.

We may sum up these results as follows: (i) The breaking of the rhythm, Word-sacraments, even though not based on theological reasons (for the Reformers would never have imagined that they might be accused of wishing to suppress the sacraments), even though marked in the life of the Church only for a short period—none the less brought into existence a new type of church, namely, the "Protestant" church, which was quite unknown to the previous tradition. (ii) We can, however, recover from this "Protestant" type without denying the basic intention of the Reformers (since the latter wished to do nothing but reform the one Christian Church). The proof of this lies in the liturgical renewal of the recent decades which has vitally affected Lutheranism, Anglicanism, and the Reformed Churches. But it must be realized that this new attempt to give expression to the liturgical ideas of the Reformation is as serious a challenge to the "Protestant" traditions of worship as was the challenge made in the sixteenth century to the Roman mass.

(b) Thus a basic question arises with regard to liturgical order: will this order be "Protestant" or traditional? In other words, will this order steadily respect the rhythm,

---

[1] As far as I am aware, only the Danish Church has maintained this practice up to the present; it is the only Church where children can communicate if accompanied by adults.

Word—sacrament, which is both that of the NT and of the first fifteen centuries?

All that we have seen so far suggests a clear reply: we must give up the order typical of "Protestant" worship in order to restore the order typical of traditional worship. We have no right—that is, if we wish to remain a Church that is reformed *according to the word of God*—to confirm our confessional liturgical peculiarities in their most notorious features, that is, in their breaking of the normal rhythm of Christian worship. We have no right to remain attached to a mode of worship which precludes the people of the baptized from assembling to obey the command: "Do this in remembrance of Me." We have no right to continue to celebrate our worship without re-integrating the Lord's Supper into it, or it into the Lord's Supper.

We have many liturgical rights, since liturgical diversity is fully legitimate; we have the right to replace the *confiteor* by congregational prayers of penitence and absolution; we have the right to give up the graduals; we have the right to draw up a list of scriptural readings special to ourselves, or the right not to draw up any list at all; we have the right to abolish singing in church (although it is perhaps hymnology that has been our most valuable contribution to Christian worship); we have the right to put the Lord's Prayer in a position which it occupies in no other tradition; we have the right to prefer the Apostles' to the Nicene Creed (since the former is the *credo* used in catechism); we have the right to give up set prayers, to suggest to the ministers simply a plan for prayer, or even not to fix at all the place in the service and the content of prayers; we have the right to dress our ministers just as we please, or even to give up the idea of any special liturgical dress; we have the right to require the faithful to kneel between Easter and Pentecost, or to suggest that they never kneel at all; we have even the right to cease to observe the ecclesiastical year in order to try to give to each service the character of a full recapitulation of the process of salvation. We should doubtless be stupid to exercise most of these rights, but we have them, and to exercise them in liberty rather than in obstinate pride would in no way imperil our communion in the great Catholic Church. But we have not the right, unless we wish to injure the catholicity of our confession, to regard the Eucharist as an optional rather than an essential element in the cult.

These preliminary remarks will determine what we have to say about the order of worship. We should be wasting our time on aesthetics or archaeology, and the deeper the exercise seemed to be, the more stupid it would be, if we were now to try to present a pattern of worship which lacked its peak point, viz. the Eucharist. What we must aim at in our Church is the healing of our liturgical troubles by the restoration of the primitive and normal rhythm—namely, the Word and the Sacrament—and all other things will follow. Not that we should despise principles or the finer points of order, but they must come within the framework of permitted diversity. The fidelity of the Church is not at stake in such matters, but it is at stake in so far as that basic rhythm is concerned.

2. *The order of worship*

(a) Let us begin by recalling a few points of principle. The whole history of Christian worship—whether it be the most traditionally catholic type or the most revivalistic—shows that we cannot do without an order. Otherwise we should have not liberty but chaos. But if it is clear that some order is necessary, if only out of respect for the God whom we serve (cf. I Cor. 14: 40), history shows that there are several schemes. Some are better adapted to the liturgical event than others; some are more intelligent than others; some are more fervent than others. But all are legitimate, in so far as they respect the constituent features and the normal officiants in the cult.

With regard to the scheme of worship, the following points should be noted: It is absolutely essential that the act of worship should be open towards God, that God may intervene in His saving power. It must not be self-justifying, in other words, the element of *epiklesis* is of vital necessity. We must must be free from prejudices or enviousness. Certainly we have every right to borrow as we please from various traditions and to integrate such borrowings into our own tradition. But such borrowings should be made with a view to the increasing of our fervour, and not out of fear of being conspicuous, or from personal likes and dislikes. It is not because a liturgical practice is Orthodox, Roman, Anglican, or Reformed, that it is valid. And if we wish to borrow from other liturgies let it be in the spirit of that fraternity which is the offspring of liberty, let it be because we hold fast to that which is good (1 Thess. 5: 21) and not because we are being drawn as satellites into some impressive tradition. There is one point on which we as Reformed churchmen should be ashamed of our cult, viz. what K. Barth calls "the senseless divorce between preaching and the sacrament" which makes the Eucharist not a regular feature of worship, but "a solemn exception" (K. Barth, *Dogmatics*). But we need not be ashamed of having a pattern of worship which is really our own.

Each time that the Christian cult is celebrated, the Lord's death is proclaimed against the background of the expectation of His return (1 Cor. 11: 26). This has various repercussions on the order of worship:

Firstly, the past of which the cult is a memorial is not a matter of Christian archaeology but the historic fact of Christ's death. While we must not despise liturgical tradition (and what we have said so far shows that we do not despise it) neither must we base the validity of a cult mainly on the fact that it is in line with the *Apostolic Tradition* of Hippolytus or the *Euchologion* of St. Serapion of Thmuis.

Secondly, the future which the cult awaits and foreshadows is not the institutional confirmation of the reigning ideology, whether it be the *Aufklärung*, or socialism, or Marxism, or existentialism, but the Return of Christ. We must not despise the location of the cult in a given time and place, but neither must we judge its validity by whether or not it is "up-to-date". Moreover, and the same is true of preaching, the more it sets out to be up-to-date, the less likely is it to speak with a really relevant message to its age.

Lastly, the proclamation should be readily understandable, stylized, self-evident, free from all baroque excrescences (the latter being a requirement connected with its necessary immersion in the contemporary world). We must distrust

T   289 whatever complicates the pattern of worship. And in this connexion I will allow myself a brief remark about the so-called "spontaneous" chants, i.e. the sung responses. We must not complain of them, but we must not suppose that they are the only way in which the laity can take their due part in the service. In our Church, this impression is sometimes given, and when we wish to increase the participation of the congregation we think it necessary to offer them or impose on them extra "spontaneous chants", whereas it would be much better to suggest that they recite the Lord's Prayer, and the Creed, and utter the Amens to express their association with the prayers made in their name.

Seeing that this study is not a prelude to the work of a liturgical commission, we do not intend in what follows to put forward an *optimum* order of worship and to justify it. Once again, the legitimate diversity of patterns of worship is something we learn from the history of worship, and it must be respected. Again, although we must place our cult in an oecumenical and traditional context, and although we have many reasons to be influenced by other traditions, our own tradition, at least as it has been reinvigorated in recent decades, is a valid point of departure. And even this confessional datum is still very varied, as is shown for example by the place of the Lord's Prayer in some of the official French Reformed liturgies of today: that of Geneva (1945) places it at the end of the "mass of the catechumens", as does that of the Reformed Church of France (1955), whereas the liturgy of the Bernese Jura (1955) places it in the "mass of the faithful". Hence our point of departure will be the schemes of worship that are current, and we shall consider some of the more important problems arising from the division of the cult into its two main sections.

(b) *Some problems arising from the "Galilean" phase of the cult*

Let us recall that the kernel of this first part is the saving event of the proclamation of God's word (whether anagnostic or prophetic). Hence in this part we have the reading of scripture and preaching. There are three problems that I wish briefly to discuss.

First, the moment of humiliation. Without going into

details, let us simply note that for the first millennium the confession of sins had no place in the cult itself, but took place beforehand. The faithful came to worship cleansed by forgiveness, and this lent a truly eucharistic character to worship, after the pattern of the return of the Seventy (Luke 10: 17ff.). From the beginning of the eleventh century, a *confiteor*, a mutual intercession that God's pardon might cover the sin confessed with a contrite heart, made its entry into western liturgy. Lastly, Calvin replaced the *confiteor* by the mystery of penance itself, with a declaration of absolution given to the whole congregation. I think that in principle this moment of humiliation is quite right. Were it not there, as in ancient and Orthodox tradition, I think we should have to have it before worship. However, I will make the following three remarks: Firstly, in order to make manifest the exultant character of that week of weeks which goes from Easter to Pentecost, to show that it would be taking our sins far too tragically to dwell on them in this time when victory over Satan is specially celebrated, I think it would be right during this period to give up the moment of humiliation.

Secondly, it must be pointed out that of all the characteristically Reformed features of worship, this is the one which least bears repetition, and where a certain automatism becomes most threatening (the same criticism is rightly directed to the way in which many Roman Catholics practise the sacrament of penance): every Sunday, sins are confessed over again and, what is more, receive absolution, with no trouble at all! And it is no sufficient cure for the trouble to vary the texts of the commandments on the basis of which repentance is made, or to vary the prayers, or to use at some times precatory formulae of absolution in the first person plural, and at other times indicative formulae in the second person plural.

That is why I should be glad to see the pure Calvinistic system maintained (i.e., indicative absolution in the second person plural) for Christmas Day and Easter Day (after which there would be no moment of humiliation until Pentecost),[1] and on the other Sundays the *confiteor* used.

[1] If this cannot be accepted for the whole paschal season, it should

The *confiteor* seems to me very remarkable both from the general ecclesiological point of view and the special liturgical point of view, from the former because it is a very effective weapon against clericalism, seeing that the leader of the congregation confesses before it that he is a sinner, that he repents of his sins, that he needs God's forgiveness and his brothers' intercession, thus placing himself exactly on the same level as the laity who will follow his example. This of course demands the *confiteor* in its dialogue form, as expressed in the traditional formula, and in my opinion it also demands that the minister at this point should kneel facing the congregation. Liturgically it seems to me remarkable, because it not only shows the form of mutual spiritual aid which the Christian liturgy assumes, but also attests that for the celebration of the cult forgiveness of sins is first necessary—which, however, is equally well shown by the traditional Reformed practice.

There is no objection to the Reformed tradition which brings this confession of sin into connexion with a reminder of the Law, and it seems to me logically preferable to follow what has become the traditional order (found also in the Anglican Prayer Book), namely recalling the Law first (the Law revealing to me my sin), rather than adopting the purely Calvinist system in which the tables of the Law are chanted by the people after the absolution (the Law teaching me to walk in the way of salvation).

The current Reformed liturgies, at least the French ones, are accustomed to place in the "Galilean" part of the cult the *credo*, the intercession, and sometimes the Lord's Prayer. This no doubt springs from that Calvinistic astuteness which protested against the political ban on a weekly eucharistic celebration by transferring to the "mass of the catechumens" elements which normally form part of the "mass of the faithful". We must ask ourselves whether a return to the regular celebration of the two phases of the cult should not liberate the "Galilean" phase from these elements which are traditionally "Jerusalemite". I think we should answer the question affirmatively for the following three reasons.

---

at least be done on Easter Day when, if need be, a moment of humiliation might precede the service to free the faithful for paschal jubilation.

Firstly, and this seems to me of great importance, it is not only the communion, it is the whole eucharistic celebration which is reserved to the baptized alone (i.e. those who have committed themselves to the life of faith). In order to be able to confess the faith, repeat the Lord's Prayer, intercede in the name of Christ, one must be in Christ, just as one should when approaching the holy table. This is my main reason.

Next, it is desirable that the first part of the cult should be as welcoming as possible to those outside, i.e. as missionary as possible. It should not commit, by a compromising liturgical participation, those who have not yet committed themselves. Otherwise these liturgical elements will cease to be liturgical acts requiring full self-giving and become mere formulae which can be repeated without the heart being in it, without the life being staked. Hence the "Galilean" phase should not be liturgical.

Finally, it is desirable to restore to the Jerusalemite phase these elements which are proper to it, so as not to denude or curtail it. It is with the eucharistic event to which they belong that they can most harmoniously be integrated, and in it that they can find their full meaning. The Lord's Prayer is much more itself when the first foretaste of its answer is the Eucharist; the *credo* is much more itself when it is not a doctrinal recitation, but is integrated in the fraternal self-offering of the Church at the moment of communion; the intercession is more appropriately placed when, before the communion, the congregation gathers into itself the whole Church and the whole world to present them to God's forgiveness and grace. Also, if the Jerusalemite phase is denuded of these elements which are proper to it, the void will probably be filled by instruction and exhortation which would threaten to rationalize and moralize the communion service, weighing it down and depriving it of its true character.

Among all these problems I note a third, minor one: have the notices their place in the first or the second part of the service? In our present rather ambiguous church situation, it is practical rather than theological reasons which count here. Theologically it would be desirable to put them as close as possible to the intercession, to address them to those who are truly committed, and hence to reserve them to the second part. In practice, however, it is important that they should reach as many people as possible and hence they may be placed in the first part.

But just when? One solution in any case seems to be absolutely wrong: that so frequently found of reading them at the very beginning of the service, before the invocation. It is wrong in the first place because it gives the impression that these notices which reflect the sorrows and joys, the projects and duties of the parish, are unworthy of forming part of the service proper. If so, we should also have to exclude from it the intercessions! It is wrong also for reasons of simple decency: at the moment when the Church is assembled for its worship, we begin with announcements, and this tactlessness is usually carried to the point of heading them with a notice of the object of the collection. The place which I feel is the least unsuitable is after the sermon, when an invitation to communion is given. Moreover to put the notices not on the edge but in the service will doubtless have as its consequence that they will be sifted a bit, and a leaflet in the porch will give information about the price of a ticket for the choir's recreational evening, a detail which need not be obtruded in the service.

(c) *Some problems raised by the "Jerusalemite" phase of the cult*

Let us remember that the heart of this is the celebration itself with its memorial of the unique sacrifice of Jesus Christ, with its nuptial note of communion, of mutual self-dedication, the Lord to the Church (Eph. 5: 25), and the Church to her Lord (Rom. 12: 1; 1 Cor. 6: 13, etc.), and with its further note of eschatological joy in the real presence of the Risen Saviour.

Let us recall also that this moment is also the most appropriate one for the liturgical confession of the Church's faith, for the intercession, and for the boldness of saying to God "Our Father . . .". And because the whole Church is thus, as it were, concentrated in the cult of such and such a congregation, the eucharistic moment is rightly the point at which the Church takes stock of itself, realizing that the particular congregation is but the manifestation, at a given place and time, of something infinitely vaster: namely, the Holy Catholic Church. That is why we are justified here in making a *memento* of the living and the dead, in proclaiming our oneness with angels and thrones and dominations, in their heavenly worship.

We shall now be concerned with only two problems, somewhat technical: that of the offertory and that of the way of making one's communion.

"None of you shall appear before me empty-handed", says the Lord in the paschal laws of the old covenant (Ex. 23: 15), and despite the romantic abuse of the concept of man's destitution before God, the recommendation remains valid when we come before God, not for the first time, or when returning to Him in repentance (like the prodigal son), but when we come before Him in worship. It is not perhaps very "Protestant" to express the matter thus; but if we object, then we ought to abolish the offertory, which we never think of doing! Let us then make our offerings with a good conscience and in the realization of what we are doing. What we are doing is what the Magi did (Matt. 2: 11), or the first two servants in the parable of the Talents (Matt. 25: 14ff.), or the woman who anointed Jesus (Matt. 26: 6ff.; John 12: 1ff.), or Joseph of Arimathea who offered the tomb (Matt. 27: 57ff.), or the kings who bring their glory to the new Jerusalem (Rev. 21: 24); that is, an act of thanksgiving, such as the third servant in the parable of the wicked husbandmen were unwilling to perform, a sort of material return to match the giving of spiritual gifts (cf. 1 Cor. 9: 11). It is with regard to such offerings that the Apostle likes to use the language of sacrifice (cf. 1 Cor. 16: 2; 2 Cor. 8–9; Phil. 4: 18, etc.), and the point is not unimportant. Such offerings, however made, form part of the normal Christian cult. Originally they consisted essentially of offerings in kind (especially bread and wine which were to be in part used for the communion) and it was from the eleventh century that they began to consist more and more of money gifts. This is still generally the case today. Without going into the theological side of the matter, nor into an examination of the Church's finances nor of the best way of receiving the offerings, we shall confine ourselves to the following remarks:

Although—as the history of the Church proves—the gifts of the faithful at communion cannot supply the Church with the financial resources it needs for the maintenance of its ministers, its work of evangelization, the services it renders, and the rates on its properties, nevertheless the Eucharist is the point from which all the income and expenditure of the Church should be controlled. Hence it is important to give to this aspect of the cult an exemplary significance in regard to the upkeep of the Church. In practice, I think the simplest and most dignified procedure is for the elders or deacons to take round collection bags and then to bring them up to the minister who will receive them and, with a prayer of dedication, consecrate them to their new purpose. He will then return the whole to one of the elders who will place it where it will not be in the way during the rest of the service. Placing it on the holy table does not seem to me essential. The collection can quite well be made during the singing of a hymn.

It will be said that by this method those who participate only in the "Galilean" phase of the cult will be deprived of joining in the liturgical act of the offertory (or rather, shall we say, the church treasury will be deprived of their gifts). But why not? Ancient liturgical tradition confirms that this act primarily concerns those who have the right to take part. In any event, when the weekly Eucharist is restored, the collection of the offerings must take place in the eucharistic part of the service, and this may mean that even before this restoration of the Eucharist we shall have to abandon the dreadful habit of the "retiring collection" and integrate the offertory into the act of worship. As for those who are present only at the first part of the service, they may, if they wish, place their gifts in a box as they leave the church.

We now come to a certain number of presuppositions.

Firstly, that there will be no celebration of the Eucharist without an invitation to communicate and a real communion of the people. The whole ancient Church understood the Eucharist in this way, and the Calvinistic and Anglican Reformation were perfectly right to give up celebrations which were not in effect communion services.

Further, that those who remain for the communion are

those church members who have the intention of communicating rather than those who have the right but not the intention of so doing. All this in order to avoid—despite the Reformers' affection for the Augustinian idea of the *"Verbum visibile"*—a resumption of the movement which resulted in the notion of a purely spiritual participation and which overemphasized the sacrificial character of the service or reduced it to the status of a spectacle: hence it is presupposed that all present at the service do in fact communicate and do so in both kinds, bread and wine (in that order), taken separately and not by intinction of the wafer (a custom which from the fourth century became prevalent in the East for the communion of the laity), and which is still found among the Baltic Lutherans.[1]

Lastly, that the Eucharist will include the words of institution, the fraction of the bread, the act of thanksgiving over the chalice, but that the liturgy will not try to express its fidelity by a servile and archaizing reproduction of Christ's own Last Supper, at which the guests reclined in the eastern manner, for "we are not in a position to copy this meal as it is described in the gospels" (H. Asmussen).

Bearing these points in mind, let us approach some practical problems.

(i) In what order will the communion take place? As a rule the celebrant communicates first, then those who assist him in the administration and the other clergy present, and last, the people. In the communion of the people there can also be an order. Chapter VIII of the Apostolic Constitutions, after speaking of the communion of the bishop, the presbyters, the deacons and the subdeacons, enumerates that of the readers, the precentors, the ascetics, the deaconesses, the virgins, the widows, the children, and then the rest of the people. The same rule was current in the Churches of the Reformation: the first to communicate was the celebrant, then came his assistants and the other ministers, and only afterwards the people, the men communicating before the women. At the time of the Reformation there was also

[1] It might be adopted in time of epidemics, so as not to replace the common cup by individual cups.

practised, for what seems to have been a brief period, the system according to which the celebrant communicated or could communicate last, doubtless in order that he might consume, if not all the wafers or bread, at least all the wine which had been consecrated. I think that on this point there is no reason to find fault with the normal custom, and that it is the duty of the celebrant to communicate first. Humility could here only be misplaced or false; the pastor is not the lackey of his congregation, but the minister of Christ, and he will serve the people best not by making polite gestures to them but by leading them.

(ii) Who will distribute the species? In the ancient Church, in addition to the presiding minister, i.e. the bishop or the presbyter who represented him, there were normally the deacons (or even deaconesses?) who shared in the distribution of the species to the communicants and if the custom fell into disuse in the East because a separate distribution of the bread and wine was abandoned, and in the West because the people were deprived of communion in the blood of Christ, it was restored at the Reformation when normally a deacon administered the chalice while the pastor administered the bread.

Wherever the celebrant takes part in the administration, he seems to have a prior right to be the distributor of the bread; it is this and not the chalice which he administers. This does not mean that the deacons or elders have not the right to administer anything but the chalice (it is the celebration and the consecration which are more important than the administration); but tradition suggests that the distribution of the bread is part of the "liturgy" of the pastor, and there is no reason to object to this. Hence as a rule the celebrant will not only preside over the service, but will distribute the bread, whereas an elder or a deacon will administer the chalice.

But seeing that communion is not taken but received, once the consecration is performed, will the celebrant communicate himself or will he ask a deacon to give him the bread and the cup? Generally, the minister communicates himself; yet, among the most ancient Roman customs, there is a tradition which requires that the Bishop of Rome, while taking the bread himself, shall receive the cup from the hands of the archdeacon. This tradition seems to me worthy of imitation—and why not also for the bread? Thus it might be desirable that, after the consecration, a deacon should first give the bread and the wine to the pastor, before the latter begins the administration.

(iii) What procedure shall we adopt for the administration? The first question is: will the laity go up to receive the communion, or will the bread and wine be brought round to the congregation which remains seated? In all probability, the most ancient tradition suggests that the congregation should not move, but should wait in their seats until the deacons come and bring them the species. This custom, for which a symbolic explanation can easily be found, was already being abandoned in the fourth century, but was restored particularly by Zwingli and has been retained by some Anglo-Saxon Nonconformist Churches. But there is nothing to prevent our preferring the procedure which has been adopted now almost everywhere, and which requires that the congregation should move in order to go and make their communion, moving up (through the central aisle) towards the table where the Lord invites and awaits them.

At the holy table, what are they to do? Are they to pass from the minister who administers the bread to the one who administers the chalice? Are they to sit around the table as is the custom in most of the Reformed Churches beyond the Rhine; or are they to form a semi-circle around the table (or a row in front of the table), each being served in turn by the minister distributing the bread and the one distributing the wine? This last method, recommended, among others, by the Liturgy of the Reformed Church of France (1955) and by that of the Bernese Jura (1955), seems to me the best for the following reasons: it does not (like the first method) oblige the communicant, on account of the press of those following, to consume the species *ambulando*, and it thus conduces to quiet and meditation; it does not isolate the communicant (like the first method) but reminds him— and this is pastorally of great importance—that if he holds communion with his Lord, it is in so far as he is a member of a people and communicates alongside his brothers; it does not overemphasize the character of the rite as a meal; and obviates the embarrassment of the celebrant who may feel uncertain, liturgically and theologically, whether he should consecrate afresh for each "table" elements already consecrated; it does not suggest, like the second method, that a meal is in question, and thus the communicants are more likely to be content with a little bread and a sip of wine.

What is to be the attitude of the communicant, standing or kneeling (dismissing the idea of communion with the congregation seated)? In some Churches (the Roman, the Anglican, very often the Lutheran) the communicants kneel. The custom was known to the early Reformers, although they did not impose it on the communicants, who could also make their communion standing. It did not become widespread in the Western Church until the eleventh century (in the Eastern Church communion is received standing): thus it is clearly bound up with the doctrine of transubstantiation. The early Reformed, Anglican and Lutheran traditions show that its theological origin is not a decisive reason for rejecting it, for kneeling is the attitude most conducive to prayer and meditation. But perhaps here too the origin of the attitude should make us cautious; hence it will be preferable to communicate standing, in the paschal attitude, though one might recommend kneeling during Advent and Lent.

Should one take the elements, or receive them? We have seen that archaizing tendencies must be resisted. I think, however, that here it is right to insist on a symbolic expression calculated to show that we do not take communion but that it is given us (*edoken*, Mark 14: 22, 23 par.). We shall therefore receive the species with the necessary reverence. The manner in which this is done may vary: the simplest method—and the one which corresponds to the tradition prior to the habit, which spread in the West from the ninth century, of placing the host directly in the mouth of the communicant— is that the communicant should put his hands in the form of a cross, e.g. the left hand above, receiving in it the bread which he will place in his mouth with his right hand. As for the chalice, the communicant will take it with both hands (the deacon also carrying it in both hands), drink of it and then return it. Here again we shall avoid anything which might lead to the belief that the clerical function authorizes a eucharistic manipulation forbidden to the laity: it is the consecration, not the distribution, which is reserved to the pastorate. Hence the communicant has the right to use both hands for both the bread and wine, on condition that he does so reverently.

Need we remind the reader that to the one loaf should correspond the one cup (cf. 1 Cor. 10: 16ff.) and that therefore the acquisition or use of individual cups is inadvisable as especially injurious to the communal character of the communion?[1] Fortunately, it is hardly necessary, because of the evident renewed awareness of the corporate aspect of eucharistic life.

(iv) Should the administration be accompanied by spoken words? In view of the words accompanying the consecration this might seem superfluous, and in fact certain Protestant forms of worship either refrain from such words, or advise against their use, or recommend that one sentence be spoken to the whole row of communicants, which seems a very acceptable solution. During the administration the congregation may sing some hymns (Easter hymns rather than Good Friday ones!) or read Biblical passages, e.g. John 6 or Isaiah 55 or else, going back to an old tradition, Psalm 34 (because of v. 9).

There is no reason why we should not say to each communicant a sentence to accompany the distribution. Oecumenical liturgical tradition is very rich in this respect: some of these phrases are confessions of faith (rather than words of catechesis), e.g. SOMA CHRISTOU and HAIMA CHRISTOU POTERION ZOES in the apostolic constitutions

[1] As also to its sacred character: individual cups are too reminiscent of cocktail glasses, and their use is especially odious when the communicants have to wait until all the glasses are filled before drinking. Mediaeval tradition had little tubes (*fistula*) which were not any more favourable to reverence. Were they introduced for the same deplorable reasons as individual cups, i.e. the fear of microbes, or perhaps the fear of putting to one's lips the cup from which a social inferior had drunk? Or was it to guarantee that no drop of wine should be spilt?

or the beautiful formula of Calvin's liturgy: "Take, eat, the body of Jesus who was delivered up to death for you"; "This is the cup of the New Covenant in the blood of Jesus which was shed for you." Other phrases are prayers such as that found in the Roman mass: "Corpus Domini Nostri Jesu Christi custodiat animam tuam in vitam aeternam." Some, e.g. Asmussen, think that "never perhaps can one speak to a person as frankly as at that moment" and consequently suggests that the words spoken should be words of spiritual guidance. This is also one reason for the spread among us of the practice of quoting a verse of the Bible when we administer the bread. Two other likely reasons for this custom are to be found in what tends to weaken modern Protestantism: a sort of magic surrounding the Word, by which we think we can escape more dangerous types of superstition (an attitude which results in devaluing both the Word and the Sacrament), and a fear lest what is repeated may become mechanical and cease to be aincere. The habit should be avoided not only because we often pick an unsuitable verse, thus causing quite unnecessary spiritual difficulties, but also because we thereby distract the attention of the communicant from the body and blood given to him that he may rise again on the last day (John 6: 54). If I may be allowed to be somewhat impertinent, I would say that this intinction of the bread in the Word is as harmful to the bread as is the putting of a lump of sugar in a *kirsch*; it is not the sugar one wants to taste but the drink, the *kirsch*. Just so, at this solemn moment, it is not the Word which is central, it is the bread. Hence if we wish to use a sentence, it will be one confessing the eucharistic faith, or a precatory word, and we shall not fear to repeat it, or to use alternately three formulae at most. Moreover it is by recovering the use of formulae of this sort that we shall teach our communicants to reply *Amen* rather than "Thank you" when they receive the bread and the chalice is offered them.

(v) One word about the immediate sequel to the communion. After the communicants have gone back to their place, they normally collect their thoughts in a silent and personal prayer. And here and there the habit has been maintained of saying this prayer kneeling. This is the only point in our worship where the pious use of gestures has not been entirely eroded by rationalism or liberal Protestantism in its various forms. The trouble is that the pews of our churches no longer provide for kneeling, so that for this prayer the communicants have to crouch with their backs turned to the holy table where the communion is still being administered. This is symbolically (and aesthetically) deplorable. I do not think therefore that this last liturgical act of kneeling should lead to its more widespread practice. Its only use is to show that we can still kneel; but it does not show how. Hence it can hardly be a basis on which we may try to recover the practice.

(d) *The transition from the "Galilean" to the "Jerusalemite" phase*

Should there be a break between the two parts of our service? Such a break (at least according to Synoptic testimony) evidently existed in the ministry of Jesus: the same ministry continues, but in quite a different atmosphere. And according to the unanimous testimony of the NT, a similar break will occur at the parousia: there will first be the judgment, when those who do not love the Lord will be anathematized (cf. 1 Cor. 16: 22), and, once the door is shut (cf. Matt. 25: 10), there will take place the marriage feast of the Lamb. Again, the whole of ancient church tradition reveals a division between the "mass of the catechumens" and the "mass of the faithful", between that aspect of the cult which is dominated by the proclamation of the Gospel and its teaching, and that aspect which is focused on the fruition of the Gospel blessings; for as long as possible the Church's worship offered the widest possible welcome, but, from a certain moment in the unfolding of the liturgy, the Church, "because of the very ordinance of Christ, must mark a limit, which renders visible the exclusive character of the anamnesis performed by the Lord's Supper" (P. Brunner). This might be described by saying that the "eschatological density" changes: in the first part of the cult, the world to come pierces the present world, seeking to persuade it, to appeal to it anew, to conquer it afresh: but in the second part, there remains only the thanksgiving for the advent of that other world, for the salvation accomplished by the Passion and Resurrection of Christ, and, by the Holy Spirit, a sort of drinking in of eternal fulness of life as far as is possible within the limits of the present transient world (cf. I Cor. 7: 31). Scripture and ancient tradition therefore fully justify a cæsura between the "Galilean" and the "Jerusalemite" phases, between the "judicial" and the "nuptial" aspects of worship.

This would raise no difficulty if our baptismal practice corresponded with that of the apostolic and ancient Church, that is, if we had not fallen into the sad mistake, whether explicit or not, of confusing baptism with the missionary Word, and thus of seeing in baptism, not the seal of grace received by faith, but the symbol of prevenient grace. Hence our situation is no longer that of the ancient Church, for nowadays those who refrain from communicating are practically all qualified to do so: they are not catechumens, but baptized members, they are not penitents (seeing that there is no longer any real discipline), they are not demoniacs (for rationalism has dispelled this conception), nor are they outsiders (in practice these no longer attend, cf. I Cor. 14: 23). They are the faithful who have no desire to join in the "mass of the faithful". Thus the impatience of pastors is quite understandable when they frown on this break in the service and ask those who wish to leave to do so as quietly and discreetly as possible, letting them go without a blessing. Theologically, this solution is the right one: its intention is fully to respect the rights of the baptized, and to remind them both to enjoy those rights and to do their duty. Again, it is an excellent inducement to the Church to re-examine its practice of baptism. But if theologically this solution is faultless, it would not be tenable in circumstances where in each parish the weekly communion service had been restored.

But what solution can we hit upon that is not too false? I think we must set aside the Orthodox practice which has maintained (to some extent, as a memorial only), a dismissal of the catechumens, demoniacs, etc., with a suitable blessing (which no longer expels or dismisses any one). We must equally set aside the Roman practice which omits the dismissal and hence the cæsura, but at the cost, almost invariably, of a falsification of the Eucharist (because it no longer necessarily includes the communion of the people, and because it is sufficient to be present at the moment of transubstantiation to qualify for valid attendance at mass).

In order to avoid the overshadowing of the communion and eschatological joy by the sacrificial element, we must safeguard the principle, undisputed in the ancient Church, that those who are present at the communion service are also those who take part in it by making their communion; or at least, we must be very vigilant about this. Hence I feel that a dismissal of some members of the congregation before the Eucharist begins is less serious than a mass celebrated as a spectacle in the presence of faithful, most of whom, have no intention of communicating. So long as the problem of baptismal practice has found no theologically valid solution,[1] and so long as we have no effective ecclesiastical discipline, I think that the question which concerns us here can have no solution that is satisfactory both theologically and pastorally. We must have the break in the service; but until the two problems mentioned have been solved at least in principle, this break cannot be the act of church discipline which it ought to be; it can only be an invitation, theologically odious, urging the faithful to exercise a self-discipline enabling them to decide whether they wish to communicate or to excommunicate themselves.

In these unsatisfactory circumstances, how shall we arrange this break? Various solutions seem possible, *a limine*. First, there is the one favoured by the Protestantism of the last century and which in many parishes is taking a long time to die out. In this, the service is terminated before the communion begins: the normal order of worship is maintained, without communion, from the invocation to the

[1] What is wrong is not paedobaptism, but its generalization in the modern world where the Church has no longer any control over the masses, which it still welcomes without being able to be responsible for them.

blessing. Then, for the sake of the few who are still devotees of magic and superstition, or for the sake of the few pure Christians who intend graciously to favour the Lord with their presence in His kingdom (according to one's point of view), a eucharistic appendix is added which again has an invocation, confession, etc. This solution which makes of the communion a solemn exception is happily condemned and is fast disappearing. This procedure, in which the break is marked by a solemn benediction, is rather more tolerable if the communion service is conceived as the climax of the first part rather than as an appendix.

Another solution is to invite the non-communicants to slip out quietly, without a blessing, during the singing of a hymn or immediately afterwards. This solution, theologically correct where one can be fairly certain that all those who come to church are baptized and hence could communicate, seems to me unacceptable from the pastoral point of view. Firstly, because it condemns all those who leave to appear as intruders, whereas in fact, for the first part of the service at least, they are certainly not such; secondly, because among those who leave there are usually some children who are not authorized, by our rules, to communicate, and who ought not to be "punished" by being deprived of the benediction; lastly, because among our church people there are so many who have suffered from an unbalanced or even false instruction that we ought not to punish these victims when we are unable or unwilling to lay the blame on those who are really guilty. Hence, the division between the two parts of the service should be marked by a blessing.

What form should it take? Certainly not the generalized solemn form which has just been rejected. But there are two forms which I think acceptable. For example one might —after telling the congregation that access to the holy table is free—simply say, without extending the hands in the normal gesture of benediction, something like this: "May Almighty God, Father, Son, and Holy Ghost, be with those who leave and those who stay". But might it not be possible, in line with old disciplinary traditions of the Church, to pronounce the blessing only on those who leave? In this case we should ask them and them alone to stand up and should then use the traditional gesture of the outstretched hands to bless firstly the catechumens and commend them to the illumination of the Holy Spirit, and secondly to bless those who cannot or who do not wish to communicate, commending their faith and their life to the Holy Spirit who strengthens and purifies.[1]

(e) *The Ordinary and the Proper*

The terms *ordinarium* (*missae*) and *proprium* (*de tempore* or *de sanctis*) became current in the history of Christian worship in the West during the Middle Ages. But what they denote—namely that the cult normally includes elements that are fixed and elements that are variable—goes back to the very origins of the Church, to the unity and the distinction between the Word and the Lord's Supper. Thus the sermon and the sacrament lie at the root of the fact that in the Christian cult we have elements that are invariable and others which are always changing. In this connexion, the sacrament is the principle of that which endures, at the heart of all change, while the proclamation of the Word is the source of change in the midst of persistence. This distinction between the ordinary and the proper was confirmed and justified by the adoption of the ecclesiastical year (*proprium de tempore*) and the memorials made of the great witnesses to the Gospel (*proprium de sanctis*).

We do not here propose to go into the history of this interplay between the ordinary and the proper. Let us simply recall, very broadly, that in ancient tradition, the Churches of the East were much more reserved with regard to the *propria* than those of the West (as they still are). In particular, the Gallican and Mozarabic Churches allowed the *propria* to predominate while the Church of Rome, whose tradition was finally victorious, adopted in this respect a balanced position. At the Reformation, the Lutherans and the Anglicans remained, *grosso modo*, under the influence of Rome, while the Reformed churchmen, as is shown for

[1] Always provided it is well understood that the pastors will adopt more severe measures if the greater part of the congregation form the habit of avoiding the communion and so, the grace of God: how can we bless those who openly despise grace?

example by their return to the *lectio continua* or their distrust of too great an importance being attached to the liturgical year, reduced the proper as much as possible to the advantage of the strict ordinary. This is probably one of the reasons why, with the triumph of individualism at the end of the eighteenth century, the Reformed tradition of worship found it more difficult than the Lutheran or the Anglican to maintain a real ordinary, and why today we still suffer from the accumulation not of authentic *propria*, but of variants of one sort or another, neither *de tempore* nor *de sanctis*, but *de psychologia, de theologia*, in place of the *ordinarium*.

These considerations show that there is no absolute rule to determine what is part of the ordinary and what is part of the proper. They show, however, that it is wise for the tension between the Eucharist and the sermon to be accompanied and made explicit by a tension between the liturgical *ordinarium* and *proprium*: in fact it is conceivable that if, in practice though not in principle, the Churches of the East seem to be withdrawn into their liturgy without being concerned with the world, and if, in practice though not in principle, the Reformed Church seems entirely absorbed by its concern for the world, it is at least partly because the former neglect the *proprium* in favour of the *ordinarium*, while the latter, after beginning in the same way, have finally become so wearied of the *ordinarium* that it has been split into a thousand variants which have not essentially much to do with a *proprium de tempore*. On the one side, a Church which seems rigid, on the other a Church which seems splintered and crumbling into fragments, because neither, maybe, has based its worship on respect for the *ordinarium* properly balanced by the *proprium*. As K. F. Müller rightly observes: "Just as what is fixed in the cult secures what is variable from arbitrariness and excrescences, so what is variable secures what is fixed from paralysis."

But the *proprium* must not be there to obviate what we Reformed churchmen wish to eschew at all costs: namely, monotony. This morbid fear is nothing less than proof that we have very little idea what worship is, and that we reduce it to what we hear in church. It is certainly not in order to avoid wearying God who is listening, but in order to avoid wearying the congregation who are also listening, instead of praying, that our Reformed liturgies are nearly always not so much liturgies in the true sense, i.e. prayer books which the laity also can use and know, but rather anthologies of liturgical texts for the use of pastors . . . and this does not specially confirm our claim to be (as opposed to the Church of Rome which is priestly, but in which none the less every lay member has his missal) the Church marked by the priesthood of all believers! A certain monotony, or rather a certain liturgical repetitiveness, is not at all harmful to the cult, quite the contrary. "The Lord's Prayer is the most decisive proof—both in view of its origin as also in view of its use in Christianity—that the repetition of the same formula in praying is in no way opposed to the spiritual vitality of the prayer. In fact one might even say the exact opposite" (P. Brunner). Thus it is quite normal that there should be a difference and a tension between the ordinary and the proper. But we must give to the proper a different purpose and meaning from that of overcoming the boredom of a congregation who seem to come to a service only to listen. This meaning will be conferred on it, during the peak points of the Christian year (Advent, Christmas, Epiphany, Lent, Passiontide, and the period from Easter to Pentecost) by allowing it to be a true *proprium de tempore*, and, during the periods characterized by the liturgical green colour, either by allowing it to be again a *proprium de tempore* (if we follow the Christian year with a strictness which I deem dangerous) or else by allowing it to be a *proprium de predicatione* (but in this case reserved to the first part of the cult, and affecting the introit psalm, the scriptural lessons, the collect and the hymns).

But the interplay between the ordinary and the proper should not prevent the use of free spontaneous prayers. The earliest traditions of Christian worship clearly had a place for them, although it is certain that the constant use of improvised prayers, which a Protestant romanticism would so much like to establish as a feature of the apostolic and subapostolic periods, did not in fact exist. We must not make of such prayers a fetich; they are not better than other types of prayer. Nor should we have a phobia about them: they may be as valuable as other types of prayer. The best course perhaps is to leave a blank space for them, both in the litany which will give us the opportunity of freely interceding) and in the preface to the eucharistic prayer (which will give us freedom in rendering thanks). And if these opportunities are not used either by the minister or the faithful,[1] we should not carry away with us the guilty impression that we have not worshipped in spirit and in truth.

(f) *The opening and the closing of the service*

When does the act of worship begin? when the assembled congregation invokes the presence of the Lord (as if He were not already there) or when the minister, in the name of the Lord, greets the congregation (for whom He was waiting)? When does the act of worship end? with the final blessing or (as in the Roman tradition) with the reading of the Prologue to the Fourth Gospel which follows the blessing? On these points, liturgical traditions vary, and this variety shows how impossible it is to fix with precision and incontestably the points which mark the beginning and the end of the cult. We may, however, give advice, so that the beginning and the end are conducted with dignity.

On arriving in church, there should be an act of quiet recollection, made kneeling, and the same on leaving the church. I feel that it is not indispensable that this act should be cloaked by organ voluntaries. It is desirable that the first and the last act of the congregation should consist of songs of praise: an introductory one, sung by the congregation standing, at the entrance of the clergy (who would themselves join in it) before the invocation or the salutation, and a final hymn, also sung standing, after the benediction, when the clergy leave the church (and here again the clergy should join in). This would certainly contribute to make

[1] Here too the rights of the laity must be respected. There is no reason at all why only the pastor should have the right to give a public exhibition of his spiritual moods, his spiritual outpourings, or his personal preoccupations, by means of improvised prayers. If the pastor has this right, so have the laity, who are equally qualified for acts of worship. Perhaps the best way to bridle the free and arbitrary prayers of the pastors is to invite the laity to use the same right; in which case people would soon be convinced that it is better to adhere to the ordinary and the proper.

better understood and better loved that joy of heaven on earth which is the worship of the baptized, when they are gathered together in the name and for the glory of the Father, Son and Holy Ghost.

CONCLUSION

WE HAVE spoken of the nature of Christian worship (which embraces the story of salvation, the manifestation of the Church, the end and the future of the world), of the inescapable duty of its formal expression, and of its necessity. Then we examined these data from the standpoint of liturgical practice, considering in turn the elements of the cult, its participants, the day and the place of its celebration, and its pattern. How shall we conclude, when there is still so much to be said, when we realize only too well that what we have achieved is but a sketch which should now be made more precise and above all amplified?

Ought we to show the repercussions of the life of Christian worship on the Church's mission to the world, or on Christian unity, or on daily spiritual life both communal and individual? Ought we to underline the need for people to be educated in the Christian liturgy so that our Church will soon rediscover the unsuspected, inexhaustible riches of an education *through* the liturgy?

Perhaps the most important thing now is to see what can be done, so that what we have learnt to feel and hope should not make of us frustrated dreamers or ungrateful and surly defeatists. The cult, whose pattern we have now learnt to understand, is badly reflected in the cult which we practise. And that for three reasons: First, because it is blunted, without its edge, because it does not find its culmination and completion in the Eucharist; next, because it does not allow the various participants, and especially the laity, to play their part in it; and, thirdly, because it shows distrust of the liberty, the exuberance, and the beauty of the life of the world to come. Hence we must place a new emphasis on the sacraments, we must make the service less clerical, and we must impart to it a note of paschal joy.

We cannot do everything at once and the important thing is to know where to begin. The answer to this is clear: we must begin where it is most faulty, and where the fault has the gravest implications. We must begin by emphasizing the sacraments. For four hundred years the best minds among us have been demanding a weekly communion service and protesting against the amputation of our worship. For four hundred years, or nearly, it has become more and more glaringly obvious how greatly this deprivation of sacramental life not only impairs our cult, but falsifies our Church. Hence it is there that we must begin: we must restore to our cult what will fully justify it, namely the Lord's Supper.

Let all those who do not wish our Church, reformed according to God's word, to die (unless it were to be reborn along with other Christian churches in a new-found Christian unity), let all such passionately demand, as starving men clamour for relief, the restoration of the Eucharist. Let them apply to the authorities of the Church, demanding the re-introduction of the weekly communion service, by a measure that will be concerted and deliberate, and the stages of which would take no more than sixteen years.[1] In doing this, they would only be reminding the authorities of the duty of obedience to Jesus Christ. It will not be easy, because obedience at this point will show clearly how divided and confused is our obedience at so many other points, and hence it will provoke very strong opposition from church members. But this is no reason to grow disheartened, and a good educator does not easily submit to the limits of progress imposed by those whom he wishes to educate.

Here then is where we must begin. If we do so, the other factors, a fuller participation of the laity and the introduction of a paschal character to the services, cannot fail to follow, probably more quickly than we think. In fact, if the Church has resisted attempts that have been made in these latter points by various liturgical movements, the reason is that

[1] For example: four years to introduce a monthly Eucharist in addition to the celebrations at festivals: four years to grow accustomed spiritually and catechetically to this first stage: four years for leading parishes in town and country to make experiments in the weekly Eucharist: four years to give to all the parishes the benefits of these experiments.

313

we have not decisively begun with the sacraments. If we begin there, it will not seem like a demand of the laity (or like a desire on the part of the clergy to involve the laity, who are quite happy to see the clergy alone assume responsibilities for which they are paid), nor will it look like a pursuit of aesthetic-catholic aims. It will be manifest as a matter of simple obedience to Jesus Christ, from which the rest will follow. But these other factors, as much as the new emphasis on the sacraments, will give to our Church a new look: it will again become, not Roman, certainly, but catholic. This we must know; and it is perhaps because we know it, or at least because we have a presentiment of it, that we are content to listen to our great doctors, from Calvin to Barth, demanding the weekly Eucharist, without giving effect to their demands.

But if, in order not to become once more catholic (in the fullest sense), we are unwilling to obey Jesus Christ through the restoration of the weekly Eucharist (with all its consequences, liturgically and ecclesiologically), then the day will soon come when even what we have will be taken from us (cf. Mark 4: 25 par.).

Select Bibliography

This is confined to certain works which the author considers important, and which in their turn indicate a wide range of publications essential to anyone who wishes to specialize in liturgiology. The present study also contains references to other works than those noted below.

1. Worship from the standpoint of Biblical theology

CHIRAT, H., *L'assemblée chrétienne à l'âge apostolique* (Lex Orandi, No. 10), Paris, 1949.

CULLMANN, O., *La foi et le culte de l'Eglise primitive*, Neuchâtel et Paris, 1963).

DELLING, G., *Der Gottesdienst in Neuen Testament*, Göttingen, 1952.

KRAUS, H. J., *Gottesdienst in Israël*, Grundnis einer alttestamentlichen Kultgeschichte, Munich, 1962.

2. History of worship

BAUMSTARK, A., *Liturgie comparée: principes et méthodes pour l'étude historique des liturgies chrétiennes*. 3rd ed. rev. Dom B. Botte, O.S.B., Editions de Chevetogne, 1953.

DIX, G., *The Shape of the Liturgy*, London [1943]. (Anglican.)

FENDT, L., *Einführung in die Liturgiewissenschaft*, Berlin, 1958. (Lutheran.)

HAGEMANN, H. G., *Pulpit and Table*, some chapters in the History of worship in the reformed churches (London, 1962). (Reformed.)

JUNGMANN, J. A., S.J., *La liturgie des premiers siècles jusqu'à l'époque de Grégoire le Grand* (Lex Orandi, No. 33), Paris, 1962.

JUNGMANN, J. A., S.J., *Missarum solemnia, eine genetische Erklärung der römischen Messe*, Vienna, 1958. (Roman Catholic.)

MAXWELL, W. D., *An Outline of Christian worship, its develop-
ments and forms*, London, 1936; new ed. with bibliog.,
1958. (Reformed Churches.)

MAXWELL, W. D., *The liturgical portions of the Genevan Service
Book*, London, 2nd ed. 1965 (Reformed).

STÄHLIN, R., *Die Geschichte des christlichen Gottesdienstes von
der Urkirche bis zur Gegenwart*, Leiturgia I, Kassel, 1954,
pp. 1–80. (Lutheran.)

3. Theology of worship

ASMUSSEN, H., *Die Lehre vom Gottesdienst*, Munich, 1937.

BARTH, K., *Gotteserkenntnis und Gottesdienst nach reforma-
torischer Lehre*, Zollikon, Zürich, 1938. Eng. trans.
Knowledge of God and Service of God, Hodder & Stoughton,
London, 1938.

BOUYER, L., *Le rite et l'homme* (Lex Orandi, No. 32), Paris,
1962.

BRUNNER, P., *Zur Lehre vom Gottesdienst der im Namen
Jesu versammelten Gemeinde*, Leiturgia I, Kassel, 1954,
(pp. 83–364). (With bibliog.)

HAHN, W., *Worship and Congregation* (Ecumenical Studies in
Worship, No 12). Lutterworth Press, London, 1963.

PAQUIER, R., *Traité de liturgique, essai sur le fondement et la
structure du culte*, Neuchâtel et Paris, 1954.

RAMSEYER, J.-PH., *La Parole et l'Image*, Neuchâtel et Paris,
1963.

4. Manuals

MARTIMORT, A. G., ed., *L'Eglise en prières, Introduction à la
Liturgie*, Paris-Tournai, 1961.

MÜLLER, A. D., *Grundriss der praktischen Theologie*, Gütersloh,
1950 (pp. 123–158).

RADO, POLYCARPUS, *Enchiridion Liturgicum*, complectens
theologiae sacramentalis et dogmata et leges, iuxta
novum codicem rubricarum, 2 vols., Rome, 1961.

RIETSCHEL, G., *Lehrbuch der Liturgik*, 2nd ed. rev. P. Graff,
Göttingen, 2 vols., in 1, 1951–1952.

Leiturgia, Handbücherei des evangelischen Gottesdienstes, ed.
K. F. Müller and W. Blankenburg, 5 vols., Kassel,
1954ff.

5. Periodicals

Jahrbuch für Liturgik und Hymnologie, ed. K. Ameln,
C. Mahrenholz and K. F. Müller, 1955ff. [Annual
classified and annotated bibliography of outstanding
works (700–800 titles p.a.) on liturgics.]
La Maison-Dieu, Revue de Pastorale liturgique, Paris,
1945ff. (Quarterly review of the Roman Catholic
Liturgical Movement in France.)
MILLER, JOHN H., *Yearbook of Liturgical Studies,* 1960ff.,
Notre-Dame, U.S.A.
Studia Liturgica, an international ecumenical quarterly for
liturgical research and renewal, Rotterdam, 1962ff.
Studies in pastoral liturgy, 1961ff., Dublin.
The Constitution of the Liturgy, adopted at the end of the
second session of Vaticanum II is also an indispensable
text for liturgical study. Excellent introduction, tables
and comments have been published (with the Latin
text and a French translation), by *La Maison-Dieu,*
Nos. 76 (4th quarter 1963) and 77 (first quarter 1964).
The comments have been translated into English in *The
Constitution of the Sacred Liturgy* by the Rev. C. Howell,
S.J., Cirencester, 1964. See also J. D. Crichton, *The
Church's Worship, considerations on the liturgical constitution of the Second Vatican Council,* London, 1964.